Fundamentals of Public Economics

Fundamentals of Public Economics

Revised English-language edition

Jean-Jacques Laffont

translated by

John P. Bonin and Hélène Bonin

The MIT Press
Cambridge, Massachusetts
London, England

Fifth printing, 1996

Printed and bound in the United States of America by Maple-Vail, Inc.

Library of Congress Cataloging-in-Publication Data

Laffont, Jean-Jacques, 1947–
    [Fondements de l'économie publique. English]
    Fundamentals of public economics/Jean-Jacques Laffont; translated by
John P. Bonin and Hélène Bonin.—Rev. English language ed.

    p. cm.
    Translation of: Fondements de l'économie publique.
    Bibliography: p.
    Includes index.
    ISBN 0-262-12127-1
    1. Microeconomics. I. Title.
HB173.L23713 1987   338.5—dc19   87-21895

Contents

Preface

This book is the first of a series of volumes intended to be used in a year-long course in economic theory designed for advanced undergraduate or graduate students. Each volume can be read independently from the others. In the introduction to the present book, I will review the background that I assume of the reader.

Avoiding whenever possible complicated mathematics, I have sought to make available to the student a treatise in microeconomic theory that takes into account the latest developments. The chapters end with optional (starred) sections that may be skipped in an initial reading and with lists of references and recommended readings that will allow the student to delve more deeply into the topics that have been discussed. These readings will fill in some of the gaps in my presentation and encourage the student to do further research. The volume ends with a series of exercises, which are preceded by a series of worked problems. These problems and exercises will help the student evaluate his or her understanding of the course.

The students of l'Ecole Nationale de la Statistique et de l'Administration Economique (ENSAE) and of the Master's Program in Econometrics at the Université des Sciences Sociales de Toulouse have greatly contributed to this work. I am also grateful to B. Belloc, M. Boyer, S. Barbera, C. Crampes, X. Freixas, L. A. Gérard-Varet, R. Guesnerie, A. Grimaud, F. Laisney, M. Moreaux, S. Moresi, P. Picard, and M. Salles for their helpful remarks on certain chapters. Finally, I wish to thank P. Champsaur ad G. Laroque for allowing me to use certain exercises they devised while teaching at ENSAE.

Mathematical Notation, Definitions, and Results

Notation

∃   there exist(s)

∀   for any

∈   belongs to

⊂   is a subset of

⇔   if and only if

⇒   implies

A function is said to be C^n if it is n times continuously differentiable. Let $x \in \mathbf{R}^n$, $y \in \mathbf{R}^n$. Then

$$x \cdot y = \sum_{l=1}^{n} x_l y_l$$

denotes the inner (dot) product.

$|A|$ number of elements in the set A

$\propto$ proportional to, with a positive multiplicative constant

Definitions

1. A binary relation R^i defined on X^i is

reflexive ⇔ $\forall x^i \in X^i$, $x^i R^i x^i$.

transitive ⇔ $\forall x^{i1}, x^{i2}, x^{i3} \in X^i$,

$$x^{i1} R^i x^{i2} \text{ and } x^{i2} R^i x^{i3} \Rightarrow x^{i1} R^i x^{i3}.$$

complete ⇔ $\forall x^{i1}, x^{i2} \in X^i$, $x^{i1} R^i x^{i2}$ or $x^{i2} R^i x^{i1}$.

A preordering is a reflexive and transitive binary relation. Since we always consider a preordering to be complete, we say that a preordering is a complete, reflexive, and transitive binary relation.

2. A set $Y \subset \mathbf{R}^L$ is convex ⇔ $\forall x \in Y, \forall y \in Y, \forall \lambda \in [0, 1]$,

$$\lambda x + (1 - \lambda)y \in Y.$$

A function $f(.)$ defined on $\mathbf{R}^L$ is quasi-concave $\Leftrightarrow \forall \lambda \in \mathbf{R}$, $\{x : x \in \mathbf{R}^L, f(x) \geqslant \lambda\}$ is convex.

3. A preference relation R^i is convex $\Leftrightarrow \forall x^{i1} \in X^i$, $\forall x^{i2} \in X^i$, $\forall \lambda \in [0, 1]$,

$x^{i1} R^i x^{i2} \Rightarrow (\lambda x^{i1} + (1 - \lambda)x^{i2}) R^i x^{i2}$.

4. A function $f(.)$ defined on $\mathbf{R}^L$ is concave $\Leftrightarrow \forall \lambda \in [0, 1]$, $\forall x \in \mathbf{R}^L$, $\forall y \in \mathbf{R}^L$,

$f(\lambda x + (1 - \lambda)y) \geqslant \lambda f(x) + (1 - \lambda)f(y)$.

5. An $n \times n$ bistochastic matrix is a matrix for which the sum of the ith row or the jth column is 1 for all $i = 1, \ldots, n$ and $j = 1, \ldots, n$.

    A permutation matrix is a bistochastic matrix for which only one element of row i or column j is nonzero for all $i = 1, \ldots, n$ and $j = 1, \ldots, n$.

Results

AN EXAMPLE OF A SEPARATION THEOREM   A set $A \subset \mathbf{R}^n$ is *closed* $\Leftrightarrow$ for any convergent sequence x_n in $\mathbf{R}^n$,

$$\lim_{n \to \infty} x_n = x, \quad x \in \mathbf{R}^n, \ x_n \in A, \ \forall n \Rightarrow x \in A.$$

Then the theorem is: If A and B are two closed convex sets in $\mathbf{R}^n$ such that $A \cap B = \hat{x}$, there exists a $p \in \mathbf{R}^n$ such that

$\forall x \in A, \quad p \cdot x \leqslant p \cdot \hat{x}$,

$\forall x \in B, \quad p \cdot x \geqslant p \cdot \hat{x}$.

A set $A \subset \mathbf{R}^n$ is *compact* if it is closed and bounded.

THE MAXIMUM THEOREM (simplified version)   Let $f(x, y)$ be a continuous function on the compact set $X \times Y$ that is strictly concave in x. Then the unique solution to the problem of maximizing $f(x, y)$ with respect to x is a continuous function of y.

Fundamentals of Public Economics

Introduction

Before beginning this book, the reader should have a complete understanding of the two fundamental theorems of welfare economics derived from the "basic microeconomic model." These theorems are developed, for example, in the first five chapters of Edmond Malinvaud's *Lectures in Microeconomic Theory*. In this introduction, I review briefly their significance after presenting the notation of the basic model that will be used throughout the book. This volume is devoted to some fundamental problems of public economics, with the problems themselves presented in terms of welfare economics.

I.1   Notation

The economy consists of L economic goods indexed by $l = 1, \ldots, L$, I consumers indexed by $i = 1, \ldots, I$, and J firms indexed by $j = 1, \ldots, J$. The indices corresponding to economic agents will always be superscripts and those corresponding to goods will be subscripts.

Let X^i be the consumption set for consumer i; this set is often taken to be the positive orthant $\mathbf{R}_+^L$.[1] The quantity consumed of good 1 by consumer i is represented by x_l^i, and $x^i = (x_1^i, \ldots, x_L^i) \in X^i$ characterizes the consumption bundle of consumer i. Consumer i's preferences are represented either by a preordering (that is, by a complete, reflexive, transitive binary relation)[2] denoted by R^i, or by a utility function denoted by $U^i(.)$. Then $x^{i1} R^i x^{i2}$ means: consumer i either prefers the bundle of goods x^{i1} to the bundle of goods x^{i2} or is indifferent between them. Substituting P^i for R^i indicates strict preference. The preordering R^i is represented by a utility function $U^i(.)$ if and only if

$$x^{i1} R^i x^{i2} \Leftrightarrow U^i(x^{i1}) \geqslant U^i(x^{i2})$$

$$x^{i1} P^i x^{i2} \Leftrightarrow U^i(x^{i1}) > U^i(x^{i2}).$$

Consumer i's initial endowment is denoted by $w^i \in \mathbf{R}_+^L$. Let $y^j = (y_1^j, \ldots, y_L^j)$ be the production vector for producer j. We usually follow the convention that outputs (products) have a positive sign and inputs (factors) a negative sign. Essentially, this convention permits us to write the profit of firm j as the inner (dot) product

---

1. $\mathbf{R}_+^L = \{x : x \in \mathbf{R}^L,\ x_l \geqslant 0,\ l = 1, \ldots, L\}$.
2. See the mathematical definitions, p. ix.

$$p \cdot y^j = \sum_{l=1}^{L} p_l y_l^j$$

where $p \in \mathbf{R}_+^L$ specifies the price vector.[3] The technology of firm j is represented either by the production set $Y^j \subset \mathbf{R}^L$, or by the production function $f^j(y^j) = 0$. When the firms are privately owned, θ^{ij} indicates the share of firm j owned by consumer i, $j = 1, \ldots, J$, $i = 1, \ldots, I$.

I.2   The Fundamental Theorems of Welfare Economics

A *private property competitive equilibrium* is characterized by a price vector $p^* \in \mathbf{R}_+^L$ and an allocation $(x^{*1}, \ldots, x^{*I}; y^{*1}, \ldots, y^{*J})$ such that

(i) y^{*j} maximizes profit $p^* \cdot y^j$ in the production set Y^j, that is,

$$p^* \cdot y^{*j} \geqslant p^* \cdot y^j \quad \text{for any } y^j \text{ in } Y^j \qquad j = 1, \ldots, J;$$

(ii) x^{*i} maximizes utility $U^i(x^i)$ in the budget set given by

$$B^i = \left\{ x^i : x^i \in X^i \text{ and } p^* \cdot x^i \leqslant p^* \cdot w^i + \sum_{j=1}^{J} \theta^{ij} p^* \cdot y^{*j} \right\} \qquad i = 1, \ldots, I;$$

(iii)   supply equals demand on all markets:

$$\sum_{i=1}^{I} x^{*i} = \sum_{j=1}^{J} y^{*j} + \sum_{i=1}^{I} w^i.$$

The assumption of competitive behavior indicates that each agent takes prices as given; we say that he exhibits parametric behavior with respect to prices. We justify this assumption by modeling the economy with a large number of economic agents so that each agent is "negligible."

An allocation $(x^1, \ldots, x^I; y^1, \ldots, y^J)$ is said to be *feasible* if and only if

(i) $x^i \in X^i$ for $i = 1, \ldots, I,$

(ii) $y^j \in Y^j$ for $j = 1, \ldots, J,$

(iii) $\sum_{i=1}^{I} x^i \leqslant \sum_{j=1}^{J} y^j + \sum_{i=1}^{I} w^i.$

---

3. When the consumer supplies labor, the labor component of his consumption bundle also has a negative sign. Then the consumption set cannot be characterized by $\mathbf{R}_+^L$.

A *Pareto optimum* is a feasible allocation $(x^{*1}, \ldots, x^{*I}; y^{*1}, \ldots, y^{*J})$ such that there exists no other feasible allocation $(\tilde{x}^1, \ldots, \tilde{x}^I; \tilde{y}^1, \ldots, \tilde{y}^J)$ that would give at least as much utility to all consumers and more utility to at least one consumer, such that

$$U^i(\tilde{x}^i) \geqslant U^i(x^{*i}) \qquad i = 1, \ldots, I,$$

and there exist i' such that

$$U^{i'}(\tilde{x}^{i'}) > U^{i'}(x^{*i'}).$$

In this book, we will make strong assumptions on the preferences and on technology in order to facilitate the presentation of specific problems fundamental to public economics. In this spirit, the two fundamental theorems of welfare economics are presented with convenient assumptions.

THEOREM 1   If $U^i(.)$ is strictly increasing with respect to each of its arguments for $i = 1, \ldots, I$, a private property competitive equilibrium (if it exists) is a Pareto optimum.

To be able to prove the existence of a private property competitive equilibrium, we must make much stronger assumptions. However, the Pareto optimality property of the competitive equilibrium (if it exists) is quite general and can be grasped intuitively. Theorem 1 indicates that equilibrium price signals are sufficient to coordinate decentralized economic activities in a satisfactory way according to the Pareto criterion. By his individual maximization behavior, each economic agent responds to prices by equating his marginal rates of substitution (for consumers) and transformation (for firms) to these prices. Since all agents face the same prices, all the marginal rates are equated to each other in the equilibrium. Combined with market equilibria, these equalities characterize Pareto optima in a convex environment.[4]

Although this intuition is useful in interpreting the role of prices, it does not help us understand the optimality of the competitive equilibrium (when it exists) in nonconvex environments. For this purpose, a very simple argument by contradiction will suffice. If the competitive equilibrium is dominated by a feasible allocation (refer to the definition of a Pareto optimum), then the value of the consumption bundle for consumer i' in this

---

4. By a convex environment, I mean nonincreasing returns for firms and convex preferences for consumers.

new allocation, at the competitive equilibrium prices, is greater than the value of his endowment (otherwise he would have chosen this allocation in the competitive equilibrium). For every other consumer, the value of his consumption bundle in the new allocation, at the competitive equilibrium prices, must be at least as large as the value of his endowment. Consequently the new allocation cannot be a feasible allocation.

The second theorem, although just as fundamental, is more difficult to understand intuitively.

THEOREM 2   If $U^i(.)$ is continuous, quasi-concave[5] and strictly increasing on the consumption set $X^i = \mathbf{R}^L_+$ with $w^i_l > 0, l = 1, \ldots, L, i = 1, \ldots, I$, and if Y^j is convex, $j = 1, \ldots, J$, for any given Pareto-optimal allocation $(x^{*1}, \ldots, x^{*I}; y^{*1}, \ldots, y^{*J})$, there exists a price vector $p^* \in \mathbf{R}^L_+$ such that

(i) x^{*i} maximizes $U^i(x^i)$ in the set

$$\{x^i : x^i \in \mathbf{R}^L_+, \; p^* \cdot x^i \leqslant p^* \cdot x^{*i}\} \qquad i = 1, \ldots, I,$$

(ii) y^{*j} maximizes $p^* \cdot y^j$ in $Y^j, j = 1, \ldots, J$.

Thus, under the convexity assumptions, Pareto-optimal allocations may be decentralized in the following sense. If we give each consumer an income[6] of $R^{*i} = p^* \cdot x^{*i}$ and if we announce to all economic agents the price vector p^*, profit maximization by firm $j, j = 1, \ldots, J$, and utility maximization by consumer i subject to the budget constraint $p^* \cdot x^i \leqslant R^{*i}$, $i = 1, \ldots, I$, lead to consumption and production plans that are compatible and that coincide with the chosen Pareto-optimal allocation. This result is fundamental to understanding decentralized planning and can be interpreted in a private property economy as follows. Pareto optimality of the private property competitive equilibrium is satisfactory with respect to the efficiency criterion but it may lead to undesirable income distributions. The second theorem states: whichever Pareto optimum we wish to decentralize (therefore, whichever Pareto optimum corresponds to the justice criterion taken), it is possible to decentralize this allocation as a competitive equilibrium so long as the income of the agents is chosen appropriately, that is, in a private property economy so long as the appropriate lump-sum transfers are made.

---

5. See the mathematical definitions, p. ix.
6. R is used to denote an income as well as a preordering.

I.3   The Purpose of This Volume

Taken together, the two theorems make up the theoretical foundation of liberal thought; we therefore need to examine the range of application and the robustness of these results. This volume considers the following particular problems.

(1) The basic model ignores very important issues such as externalities (for example, pollution), the multitude of public goods that are not exchanged in market transactions, and fundamental nonconvexities, in particular production under increasing returns. We study the degree to which these complexities invalidate the fundamental theorems of welfare economics in a private property economy. Then, we look at instruments of public intervention designed to restore the Pareto efficiency of the competitive mechanism or to achieve Pareto optimality through planning.

(2) Our search for criteria to evaluate public intervention having allocational or distributional goals will lead us to reflect on the theory of the government as an aggregator of individual preferences as well as on the difficulties faced by any collective decision-maker in obtaining information in a world where information is decentralized.

(3) For most of this book, we adopt a dichotomous approach in the spirit of theorems 1 and 2. We treat allocational and distributional problems separately by invoking the feasibility of lump-sum transfers, which are very powerful instruments of political economics. However, the need to treat both problems simultaneously in many situations emerges as a major conclusion to this volume, one which is analyzed in detail in chapter 7.

Since they require a more complex benchmark than the basic microeconomic model provides, many problems of public economics are not considered in this book. Public economics problems that arise from an absence of future markets (for example, the choice of a social discount rate) would be topics for a book that concerned itself with the extension of the basic microeconomic model to an intertemporal framework. Problems that arise from an absence of contingent claims markets (for example, consumer quality protection) would be treated in a book on the economics of uncertainty and information. Finally, the main part of our analysis is undertaken in a Walrasian world; the theory of public economics in a disequilibrium situation remains for future work. (Refer, however, to sections 7.6*–7.8*.)

1 Externalities

The theory of external effects or externalities is basic to environmental economics. In this chapter, we present the essential results necessary for addressing questions such as: In what respect is pollution an economic problem? Should it be eliminated completely, or, on the contrary, is there an optimal level of pollution? What should we understand by the slogan, "polluters should pay"? What are the advantages and disadvantages of various economic policy solutions such as taxes, subsidies, the creation of markets in pollution rights, or awarding quotas of rights to pollute?

1.1 The Nature of Externalities

We start from a classic definition of externality, namely, any indirect effect that either a production or a consumption activity has on a utility function, a consumption set, or a production set. By "indirect," we mean both that the effect is created by an economic agent other that the one who is affected and that the effect is not transmitted through prices.[1] This definition indicates that the basic notion of externality depends on the definition of economic agents and the existence of markets that coordinate transactions among these agents.

For example, consider two firms that pollute each other's environment; each one imposes a negative external effect on the other. If both firms merge, the external effects simply become technical relationships within one firm: hence, the externalities are internalized. If a market in pollution rights is created between the firms, firm j must buy from firm j' a pollution right just as it would buy any other product from it: hence, the externalities are incorporated into market transactions.

In a barter economy, that is to say, an economy without markets, any exchange may be decomposed into two externalities. Quantity q_l^j of good l accepted by agent j in exchange for agent i's quantity q_k^i of good k creates an externality for agent i. Agent i's utility depends on his own trade offer q_k^i but also on that of the other agent, q_l^j. Alternatively, a market could be created for each component of each agent's activity vector as it relates to each of the other agents. In that case, no externalities would exist. If all economic agents are grouped into a single unit, no externalities can exist. However, the problem of organizing economic activity within this unit

---

1. External effects of this sort are categorized as technological (or nonpecuniary). For a discussion of pecuniary externalities, the reader is referred to section 1.8*.

would be quite complex.[2] The more the economic agents are subdivided into groups, the more externalities are generated in the economy.

Starting with an economic system, that is, given a set of economic agents and existing markets, externalities may or may not come into play. The existence, and eventually the justification, of these external effects may be understood only after an explanation of the size of economic units and a determination of the number of markets is given. Unfortunately, the conventional wisdom about these two problems is quite limited. The impossibility of excluding users of a public good, technological nonconvexities and fixed entry costs on markets, transaction costs, the availability of information, and the cost of transmitting and acquiring information appear to be fundamental determinants of the size of economic units and of the number of markets. There is no general equilibrium analysis that, starting from an elementary definition of agents and their objectives, yields endogenously the definition of an observed economic system (in the sense mentioned above).

The Arrow-Debreu general equilibrium model does not attempt to treat as variable the size of agents and the number of markets, just as it does not attempt to explain the agents' tastes. Rather, given agents and markets, the model analyzes the functioning of the economy.[3] In this chapter, we remain constrained by this model although we try to keep these general considerations in mind, especially when we derive public policy prescriptions.

We illustrate externalities formally with the help of three examples.

A firm's polluting of a river and thus decreasing the possibilities for swimming is an example of the first type of externality, namely the external effect of a production activity on a consumption set. Without pollution, the consumption set allows any swimming consumption up to 24 hours on a daily basis and any vitamin consumption (see figure 1.1). On the other hand, the presence of pollution, y, decreases the physiologically feasible daily consumption of swimming to a level $\alpha(y)$ less than 24 hours. However, this level increases with the consumption of vitamins.

More generally, if $X^i \subset \mathbf{R}^L$ is the consumption set in the absence of externalities, the consumption set with externalities becomes a correspondence that associates to each economic environment of consumer i

2. From this problem stems the eventual need for planning methods adapted to technological interdependencies when information is decentralized (the reader is referred to Aoki 1971 and chapter 6 of Laffont 1977).
3. However, the reader is referred to the last paragraph of section 1.5.

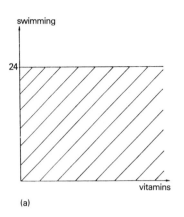
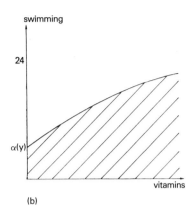

Figure 1.1
Consumption sets: (a) Without externalities; (b) with externalities.

(that is to say, the production levels of the firms and the consumption levels of the other consumers $(y^1, \ldots, y^J, x^1, \ldots, x^{i-1}, x^{i+1}, \ldots, x^I))$, a set of physiologically feasible consumption vectors

$$X^i(y^1, \ldots, y^J, x^1, \ldots, x^{i-1}, x^{i+1}, \ldots, x^I).$$

The noise emanating from the stereo system of one's neighbor is a typical example of a second type of externality, namely, a consumption externality that is formalized by considering that the utility function of a concerned consumer i depends on agent j's music consumption x_m^j, that is,

$$U^i(x^i, x_m^j).$$

More generally, all the environmental variables may affect $U^i(.)$.

Meade's famous example (1952) of the beekeeper and the orchard is a good illustration of the third type of externality, namely a mutual production externality. Since his bees pollinate the flowers, the beekeeper (firm 1) affects the production possibilities of the orchard in a positive way. Conversely, by providing flowers from which honey can be gathered, the orchard (firm 2) promotes the production of honey (see figure 1.2). More generally, the technology of firm j represented by a production set or by a production function depends on its entire environment $(y^1, \ldots, y^{j-1}, y^{j+1}, \ldots, y^J, x^1, \ldots, x^I)$, that is,

$$Y^j(y^1, \ldots, y^{j-1}, y^{j+1}, \ldots, y^J, x^1, \ldots, x^I),$$

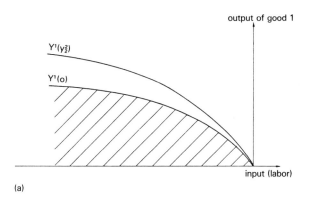

(a)

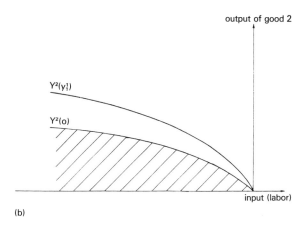

(b)

Figure 1.2
Production sets with and without externalities: (a) of the beekeeper; (b) of the orchard.

so that

$$f^j(y^1, \ldots, y^{j-1}, y^j, y^{j+1}, \ldots, y^J, x^1, \ldots, x^I) = 0.$$

1.2   Optimal Allocation of Resources

Consider an economy with two goods, two firms, and a single consumer. There are two externalities affecting firm 2, one generated by the consumer's consumption of good 1, x_1, and the other by the production of good 1 by firm 1, y_1^1. We can think of the example of the pollution of a river by a city and a firm that affects a water-using firm located downstream. The technologies are characterized by

$$y_1^1 = f^1(y_2^1) \qquad f^1 \text{ is differentiable and concave}^4$$

$$y_2^2 = f^2(y_1^2, y_1^1, x_1) \quad f^2 \text{ is differentiable and concave}^5.$$

The consumer has a utility function $U(x_1, x_2)$ that is differentiable, increasing, and strictly quasi-concave, and an initial endowment (w_1, w_2). The Pareto optimum for this economy is obtained by solving the problem

Max $U(x_1, x_2)$

subject to $y_1^1 + y_1^2 + w_1 - x_1 \geqslant 0 \qquad \lambda_1$

$\quad y_2^1 + y_2^2 + w_2 - x_2 \geqslant 0 \qquad \lambda_2$

$\quad -y_1^1 + f^1(y_2^1) \geqslant 0 \qquad\qquad \mu_1$

$\quad -y_2^2 + f^2(y_1^2, y_1^1, x_1) \geqslant 0 \quad \mu_2,$

where $(\lambda_1, \lambda_2, \mu_1, \mu_2)$ are the Kuhn-Tucker multipliers associated with the constraints. In much of this book (with some exceptions), we will simplify the optimization problems by making assumptions that lead to interior optima; in particular, we will frequently ignore inequalities and boundary solutions.

The first-order conditions for the above optimization problem (which, given our assumptions of concavity, are also sufficient) can be written as:

---

4. See the mathematical definitions, p. ix.
5. $df^1/dy_2^1 \leqslant 0$, $\partial f^2/\partial y_1^2 \leqslant 0$ because inputs are of negative sign.

$$\frac{\partial U}{\partial x_1} - \lambda_1 + \mu_2 \frac{\partial f^2}{\partial x_1} = 0$$

$$\frac{\partial U}{\partial x_2} - \lambda_2 = 0$$

$$\lambda_1 - \mu_1 + \mu_2 \frac{\partial f^2}{\partial y_1^1} = 0$$

$$\lambda_2 + \mu_1 \frac{df^1}{dy_2^1} = 0$$

$$\lambda_2 - \mu_2 = 0$$

$$\lambda_1 + \mu_2 \frac{\partial f^2}{\partial y_1^2} = 0.$$

Eliminating the multipliers yields the marginal equalities

$$\frac{\dfrac{\partial U}{\partial x_1} + \dfrac{\partial U}{\partial x_2} \cdot \dfrac{\partial f^2}{\partial x_1}}{\partial U/\partial x_2} = -\frac{\partial f^2}{\partial y_1^2} = -\frac{1 + \dfrac{\partial f^2}{\partial y_1^1} \cdot \dfrac{df^1}{dy_2^1}}{df^1/dy_2^1}, \tag{1}$$

which express the equality of the social marginal rate of substitution and the social marginal rates of transformation.

From Pigou (writing in the 1920s), we know that, in order to evaluate the relevant marginal rates of substitution and transformation for the optimality conditions, we must take into account both the direct and indirect effects of economic activities. Thus, the consumer's marginal rate of substitution must take into account the fact that, by substituting one unit of good 1 for one unit of good 2, the production of good 2 is affected by $\frac{\partial f^2}{\partial x_1}$ and therefore his utility level is changed by $\frac{\partial U}{\partial x_2} \cdot \frac{\partial f^2}{\partial x_1}$. Therefore, the social marginal rate of substitution is

$$\frac{\dfrac{\partial U}{\partial x_1} + \dfrac{\partial U}{\partial x_2} \cdot \dfrac{\partial f^2}{\partial x_1}}{\partial U/\partial x_2}.$$

Since the activity of firm 2 creates no externality, its social marginal rate of transformation is equal to its private rate, $-\partial f^2/\partial y_1^2$. On the other hand, firm 1 must consider that by using one additional unit of good 2 as an input, it produces df^1/dy_2^1 and consequently affects the production of good 2 by $\dfrac{\partial f^2}{\partial y_1^1} \cdot \dfrac{df^1}{dy_2^1}$ from which it follows that the social marginal rate of transformation is given by

$$-\frac{1 + \dfrac{\partial f^2}{\partial y_1^1} \cdot \dfrac{df^1}{dy_2^1}}{df^1/dy_2^1}.$$

The first lesson to be drawn from this example is that the optimal organization of production does not necessarily require a total elimination of externalities even when they are negative. If consuming and producing good 1 affect the production of good 2 negatively, this does not mean that good 1 should no longer be produced at all. Rather, in evaluating the social cost of good 1, external costs must be internalized.

1.3   Private Property Competitive Equilibrium

The definition of a competitive equilibrium for a private property economy with externalities is quite similar to the usual definition of a competitive equilibrium. The only difference is that, in solving his individual maximization problem, each agent considers as parameters not only prices but also the other variables that characterize his decision set. In equilibrium, these variables must be equal to the choices of the other agents.

Let $(p_1, p_2) \in \mathbf{R}_+^2$ be the vector of prices. Since firm 1 is not affected by externalities, its maximization problem is simply

$$\text{Max}\{p_1 y_1^1 + p_2 y_2^1\}$$

subject to $y_1^1 = f^1(y_2^1),$

from which we derive the marginal condition

$$-\frac{1}{df^1/dy_2^1(y_2^1)} = \frac{p_1}{p_2}. \tag{2}$$

The consumer's income R consists of the value of his initial endowment and the profits made by the firms. His maximization problem is written as

$$\text{Max } U(x_1, x_2)$$

subject to $p_1 x_1 + p_2 x_2 = R,$

from which we derive the marginal condition

$$\frac{\partial U/\partial x_1(x_1, x_2)}{\partial U/\partial x_2(x_1, x_2)} = \frac{p_1}{p_2}. \tag{3}$$

Firm 2 is affected by the environmental variables x_1 and y_1^1 chosen by the other agents. Taking the value of these variables $\bar{x}_1, \bar{y}_1$, as given, firm 2 solves the problem

$$\text{Max}\{p_2 y_2^2 + p_1 y_1^2\}$$

subject to $y_2^2 = f^2(y_1^2, \bar{y}_1^1, \bar{x}_1),$

from which it follows that

$$-\frac{\partial f^2}{\partial y_1^2}(y_1^2, \bar{y}_1^1, \bar{x}_1) = \frac{p_1}{p_2}. \tag{4}$$

A competitive equilibrium with externalities is a vector of prices $(\bar{p}_1, \bar{p}_2)$ and an allocation $(\bar{x}_1, \bar{x}_2, \bar{y}_1^1, \bar{y}_2^1, \bar{y}_1^2, \bar{y}_2^2)$ such that

(a) $(\bar{y}_1^1, \bar{y}_2^1)$ maximizes $\bar{p}_1 y_1^1 + \bar{p}_2 y_2^1$ subject to the constraint $y_1^1 = f^1(y_2^1);$

(b) $(\bar{y}_1^2, \bar{y}_2^2)$ maximizes $\bar{p}_1 y_1^2 + \bar{p}_2 y_2^2$ subject to the constraint $y_2^2 = f^2(y_1^2, \bar{y}_1^1, \bar{x}_1);$

(c) $(\bar{x}_1, \bar{x}_2)$ maximizes $U(x_1, x_2)$ subject to the constraint

$$\bar{p}_1 x_1 + \bar{p}_2 x_2 = \bar{p}_1 w_1 + \bar{p}_2 w_2 + \Pi(\bar{p}) = \bar{R},$$

where

$$\Pi(\bar{p}) = (\bar{p}_1 \bar{y}_1^1 + \bar{p}_2 \bar{y}_2^1) + (\bar{p}_1 \bar{y}_1^2 + \bar{p}_2 \bar{y}_2^2);$$

(d) $\bar{x}_1 = w_1 + \bar{y}_1^1 + \bar{y}_1^2,$

$$\bar{x}_2 = w_2 + \bar{y}_2^1 + \bar{y}_2^2.$$

Here (a), (b), and (c) express the maximization behavior of the economic agents and (d) expresses equality of supply and demand in both markets.

Self-interest maximization leads each agent to equate his private marginal rate (of substitution or transformation) to the price ratio and results in the equalization of private rates (that is, the simultaneous equalization of (2), (3), and (4)), whereas Pareto optimality requires the equalization of social rates. In general, a competitive equilibrium with externalities is not Pareto optimal. However, we must point out that the optimality of

competitive equilibrium is not synonymous with the absence of externalities since we might very well have

$$\frac{\partial f^2}{\partial x_1}(\bar{y}_1^2, \bar{y}_1^1, \bar{x}_1) = \frac{\partial f^2}{\partial y_1^1}(\bar{y}_1^2, \bar{y}_1^1, \bar{x}_1) = 0,$$

in which case, conditions (1) and (2) = (3) = (4) coincide.

In general, economic decisions appear to be too decentralized at a
competitive equilibrium. Often a firm generating negative externalities
will produce too much and a firm generating positive externalities will
produce too little. However, the general equilibrium effects, namely the
changes in price and income variables, may countervail these intuitive
results of partial equilibrium analysis. For example, if the good produced
by the firm generating negative externalities is an inferior good for the
consumers who own this firm, a competitive equilibrium may correspond
to an output from this firm that is too small (with respect to the Pareto
optima that treat all consumers in a similar manner). Indeed, a larger
output yielding higher profits cannot elicit a sufficiently high enough
demand. Finally, we note that, in a competitive equilibrium, agents maximize their objective functions with respect to their own activity variables.
Therefore to prove the existence of an equilibrium, it is sufficient to assume
that the utility functions and the production functions are concave
with respect to only these activity variables and not with respect to the
externalities. In the above example, it is sufficient that $f^2(.)$ be concave
in y_1^2.

1.4   Types of Public Intervention

In the framework of the Arrow-Debreu model in which agents and markets
are well defined but externalities exist, we study government intervention
to restore Pareto efficiency assuming that the cost of intervention is zero
and without examining the ultimate justification for public intervention.

1.4.1   Creation of Markets by Specifying Property Rights

This economic policy consists of establishing a complete system of competitive markets that incorporate externalities. It corresponds to a fundamental
idea found in many areas, such as intertemporal economics and economics
of uncertainty: creating the appropriate number of markets so that the

assumptions of the basic model presented in the introduction are satisfied. The main question is the viability of these markets.

We return to the above example and assume that two pollution rights markets are created. Firm 1 must buy from firm 2 the right to pollute. Let q_1^{12} be the price of this right. Firm 1's problem becomes

$$\text{Max}\{p_1 y_1^1 + p_2 y_2^1 - q_1^{12} y_1^{12}\}$$

subject to $y_1^1 = f^1(y_2^1)$

$$y_1^{12} = y_1^1,$$

where y_1^{12} is the quantity of pollution rights demanded by firm 1. Institutionally, the firm is constrained to buy as many rights as it creates units of pollution ($y_1^{12} = y_1^1$). The first-order condition is written as

$$(p_1 - q_1^{12})\frac{df^1}{dy_2^1} + p_2 = 0. \tag{5}$$

Similarly, the consumer must buy from firm 2 the right to pollute. Let p_1^{12} the price of this right. The consumer's problem becomes

$$\text{Max } U(x_1, x_2)$$

subject to $p_1 x_1 + p_2 x_2 + p_1^{12} x_1^{12} = R$

$$x_1^{12} = x_1,$$

where x_1^{12} is the quantity of pollution rights demanded by the consumer. Institutionally, the consumer has to buy as many rights as he creates units of pollution ($x_1^{12} = x_1$). The first-order condition is written as

$$\frac{\partial U/\partial x_1}{\partial U/\partial x_2} = \frac{p_1 + p_1^{12}}{p_2} \tag{6}$$

Firm 2 will supply quantities of pollution rights equal to $(\mathring{y}_1^{12}, \mathring{x}_1^{12})$ at prices q_1^{12} and p_1^{12} according to the solution of the profit maximization problem

$$\text{Max}\{p_2 y_2^2 + p_1 y_1^2 + q_1^{12} \mathring{y}_1^{12} + p_1^{12} \mathring{x}_1^{12}\}$$

subject to $y_2^2 = f^2(y_1^2, \mathring{y}_1^{12}, \mathring{x}_1^{12}),$

from which we derive the first-order conditions

$$p_2 \frac{\partial f^2}{\partial y_1^2} + p_1 = 0$$

$$p_2 \frac{\partial f^2}{\partial y_1^1} + q_1^{12} = 0 \qquad\qquad\qquad (7)$$

$$p_2 \frac{\partial f^2}{\partial x_1} + p_1^{12} = 0.$$

In addition to the usual conditions, the definition of a competitive equilibrium requires equality between supply and demand on the two markets for pollution rights:

$$\mathring{y}_1^{12} = y_1^{12} \qquad \mathring{x}_1^{12} = x_1^{12}.$$

Combining equations (5), (6), and (7) for competitive equilibrium values yields condition (1) immediately. The competitive equilibrium of the economy in which the space of goods has been enlarged by adding markets for pollution rights is a Pareto optimum. Several remarks must be appended to this result.

On the pollution rights market between agent i and agent j, there is only one buyer and only one seller. Consequently, competitive behavior in this market is unlikely and any strategic behavior may lead to an allocation that is less desirable than the laissez-faire equilibrium defined in section 1.3 (see also problem 1). Nonetheless, the policy of creating pollution rights markets may be appropriate in certain cases as is demonstrated in the following example.

Consider a lake that is used as a swimming spot by the inhabitants of a large city. Many producers located at the edge of the lake generate pollution; the externality is impersonal in the sense that the effect of pollution depends only on the sum of garbage produced and not on the individual polluter. There is a level of pollution $\bar{A}$ that is naturally cleaned up so that it is compatible with swimming. The nature of the goods produced by the firms and the possibility for cleaning up the pollution lead one to the common sense conclusion that $\bar{A}$ is the socially optimal level of pollution. Then, the supply of pollution rights is determined inelastically by these physical considerations which do not generate any incentive for strategic behavior. A pollution rights market may be created in which a price is determined by the laws of supply and demand at a quantity of pollution rights equal to $\bar{A}$.[6] The large number of producers leads us to presume competitive behavior on the demand side. Then the pollution rights market yields an efficient allocation of the restricted possibilities to pollute because the agents who have the greatest need for the rights will buy them.

The existence of a competitive equilibrium in an economy with pollution rights markets requires the usual convexity assumptions in the enlarged space of goods.[7] Starrett (1970) showed that negative externalities lead to fundamental nonconvexities as diagrammed in figure 1.3. Indeed, a negative externality contracts the production set of the affected firm. However, there is a limit to this contraction since the worst-case scenario is one in which the firm will be incapable of producing anything.

Assume that point O (figure 1.3) represents the Pareto-optimal production vector. The externality price that supports this allocation is positive; therefore optimal behavior for the firm consists in demanding an infinite amount of externality and producing nothing, so as to be assured of an infinite profit. Consequently, the point O may not be realized as a *competitive* equilibrium with property rights markets. A quantitative constraint that limits to $\bar{e}$ the level of the externality a firm may demand would allow the problem created by the nonconvexity to be solved. However, the simultaneous calculation of the externality price and the quantity constraint $\bar{e}$ is difficult in the absence of perfect information about the technology.

Until Coase's contribution (1960), it seemed natural from the Pigouvian perspective to consider the no-externality situation as the appropriate benchmark. Thus it was implicitly assumed that every agent had the right to a clean environment so that the polluter was taxed, justifying the slogan: "polluters must pay." Above, we have embraced this viewpoint by requiring firm 1 to buy from firm 2 the right to pollute. Alternatively, why not ask firm 2 to buy from firm 1 a reduction in its level of pollution? Firm 1 could be allocated the right to pollute at a level $\bar{Q}$ and firm 2 would have to buy any reduction of pollution from this level. Similarly, the consumer could have been allocated a quantity of pollution rights $\bar{x}$ that is greater than or equal to his desired level.

The consumer's optimization problem would then be characterized by

---

6. The impersonality of externalities yields an identical externality price for all polluters. Verify that in equation (7) $q_1^{12} = p_1^{12}$ if $y_2^2 = f^1(y_1^2, \mathring{y}_1^{12} + \mathring{x}_1^{12})$.
7. These assumptions are implied by the assumptions made in section 1.2.

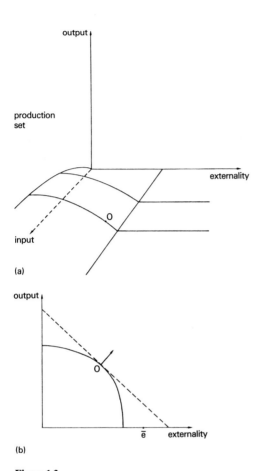

Figure 1.3

Max $U(x_1, x_2)$

subject to $p_1 x_1 + p_2 x_2 = R + p_1^{12}(\bar{x} - x_1^{12})$

$$x_1^{12} = x_1,$$

where $(\bar{x} - x_1^{12})$ is the amount of pollution reduction that he supplies. The consumer's budget constraint may be rewritten as

$$p_1 x_1 + p_2 x_2 + p_1^{12} x_1^{12} = R + p_1^{12}\bar{x}.$$

Therefore the marginal conditions that characterize the consumer's optimum are equivalent to those that apply when producer 2 is granted the right to a clean environment. The new allocation of rights changes only the composition of the consumer's income.[8]

Thus the allocation of rights appears to be a political or distributional issue because it does not affect Pareto optimality but has only distributive consequences. Altering the initial allocation of property rights among firms may appear to leave the equilibrium unchanged because it only changes the entrepreneurs' objective functions up to a constant. However, to the extent that it influences consumers' incomes through the distribution of profits, it may affect the equilibrium. Similarly, altering the initial allocation of property rights among consumers changes the equilibrium.

Are there cases in which the appropriate benchmark would be an allocation with externalities? Before referring the reader to Coase (1960), I shall provide two examples of these. A city dweller who moves to the countryside hardly seems justified in asking for indemnities because a peasant's rooster causes him to wake up early. Here justice seems to imply that the former city dweller should purchase the property right by buying the rooster. Similarly, a multinational corporation settling on a river in the Pyrénées that is slightly polluted by the inhabitants of a village upstream is not in a position to demand a pollution-free environment.

1.4.2 Optimal Taxation

Normalize prices so that $p_2 = 1$ and let t be the tax paid by consumer per unit of good 1 consumed. Let τ be the tax paid by firm 1 per unit of good

---

8. Since here we have a single consumer, the increase of income due to the sale of property rights is exactly compensated for by a decrease in income due to the decrease in profits. In general, consumers' incomes are affected by a change in the allocation of rights and therefore the equilibrium is modified.

1 produced. The amount of taxes collected is redistributed to the consumer as a *lump-sum transfer T*. The lump-sum transfer T added to the consumer's income is considered by him to be independent of his own choices. To be sure, the latter assumption would be justified only in an economy having a large number of consumers; therefore our example is a stylized one.

   A competitive equilibrium with externalities and taxes t and τ is a vector of prices $(\bar{p}_1, 1)$ and an allocation $(\bar{x}_1, \bar{x}_2, \bar{y}_1^1, \bar{y}_2^1, \bar{y}_1^2, \bar{y}_2^2)$ such that

(a) $(\bar{y}_1^1, \bar{y}_2^1)$ maximizes $(\bar{p}_1 - \tau)y_1^1 + y_2^1$ subject to the constraint $y_1^1 = f^1(y_2^1)$;

(b) $(\bar{y}_1^2, \bar{y}_2^2)$ maximizes $\bar{p}_1 y_1^2 + y_2^2$ subject to the constraint $y_2^2 = f^2(y_1^2, \bar{y}_1^1, \bar{x}_1)$;

(c) $(\bar{x}_1, \bar{x}_2)$ maximizes $U(x_1, x_2)$ subject to the constraint

$$(\bar{p}_1 + t)x_1 + x_2 = \bar{p}_1 w_1 + w_2 + \bar{T} + \Pi(\bar{p}),$$

where

$$\bar{T} = \tau \bar{y}_1^1 + t\bar{x}_1$$

$$\Pi(\bar{p}) = (\bar{p}_1 - \tau)\bar{y}_1^1 + \bar{y}_2^1 + (\bar{p}_1 \bar{y}_1^2 + \bar{y}_2^2);$$

(d) $\bar{x}_1 = w_1 + \bar{y}_1^1 + \bar{y}_1^2$

   $\bar{x}_2 = w_2 + \bar{y}_2^1 + \bar{y}_2^2.$

Conditions (a) and (b) represent profit maximization by firms taking as parameters all prices, taxes and the actions of others agents; (c) expresses utility maximization by the consumer taking prices, taxes, the lump-sum transfer and the profits he receives as given. Finally, (d) characterizes the equality between supply and demand on both markets.

   Taxes will be chosen to insure that the optimizing behavior of the agents (here characterized by their first-order conditions) leads to a Pareto optimum. We impose as taxes the marginal effects of activities x_1 and y_1^1 on the output of good 2 evaluated at the optimum (*) obtained in section 1.2:

$$t^* = -\frac{\partial f^2}{\partial x_1}(*) \qquad \tau^* = -\frac{\partial f^2}{\partial y_1^1}(*)$$

The first-order condition for the consumer is now written using the prices $(\bar{\bar{p}}_1, 1)$ of the competitive equilibrium with externalities associated with taxes t^* and τ^*, that is,

$$\frac{\partial U/\partial x_1}{\partial U/\partial x_2} = \bar{\bar{p}}_1 + t^*.$$

Similarly for producers 1 and 2, we have respectively

$$-\frac{1}{df^1/dy_2^1} = \bar{\bar{p}}_1 - \tau^* \qquad -\frac{\partial f^2}{\partial y_1^2} = \bar{\bar{p}}_1$$

The Pareto-optimal allocation is indeed a competitive equilibrium for prices $(\bar{\bar{p}}_1, 1)$ proportional to the Kuhn-Tucker multipliers (λ_1, λ_2) of the problem in section 1.2. In fact, we have

$$\frac{\lambda_1}{\lambda_2} = \bar{\bar{p}}_1 = \frac{\frac{\partial U}{\partial x_1}(*) + \frac{\partial U}{\partial x_2}(*) \cdot \frac{\partial f^2}{\partial x_1}(*)}{\partial U/\partial x_2(*)} = -\frac{\partial f^2}{\partial y_1^2}(*) = -\frac{1 + \frac{df^2}{dy_1^1}(*) \cdot \frac{df^1}{dy_2^1}(*)}{df^1/dy_2^1(*)}.$$

If firm 2's production function is (strictly) concave in y_1^2 and if x_1^* and y^{*1}_1 are considered parametrically, the firm chooses (necessarily) (y^{*2}_1, y^{*2}_2) since its marginal condition is

$$\bar{\bar{p}}_1 = -\frac{\partial f^2}{\partial y_1^2}(y^{*2}_1).$$

If firm 1's production function is (strictly) concave in y_2^1, it chooses (necessarily) y^{*1}_1 and y^{*1}_2 since its marginal condition is

$$\bar{\bar{p}}_1 = -\frac{1}{\partial f^1/\partial y_2^1(*)} - \frac{\partial f^2}{\partial y_1^1}(*).$$

Finally, if we distribute to the consumer the profits $(\bar{\bar{p}}_1 - \tau^*)y^{*1}_1 + y^{*1}_2 + \bar{\bar{p}}_1 y^{*2}_1 + y^{*2}_2$ and the lump-sum transfer $\tau^* y^{*1}_1 + t^* x_1^*$, by (strict) quasi-concavity of $U(x_1, x_2)$, he will choose (necessarily) x_1^* and x_2^* since his marginal condition is

$$\bar{\bar{p}}_1 = \frac{\partial U/\partial x_1(*)}{\partial U/\partial x_2(*)} + \frac{\partial f^2}{\partial x_1}(*)$$

and since he can buy x_1^* and x_2^* at prices $(\bar{\bar{p}}_1, 1)$.

With market prices given by $(\bar{\bar{p}}_1, 1)$ and taxes by t^* and τ^*, the allocation corresponding to the (unique) competitive equilibrium coincides with the Pareto optimum. Notice again that market prices are proportional to the multipliers of the scarcity constraints of the problem characterizing the Pareto optimum. However, there is a difficulty with this policy prescription.

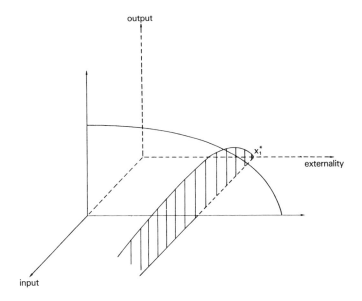

Figure 1.4

For taxes given by t^* and τ^*, other equilibria that are not Pareto optimal may exist. Decentralization of the Pareto optimum requires the announcement of the correct prices as well.

First of all, we note that the convexity assumptions necessary to insure that we have an equilibrium are weaker than the assumptions necessary for decentralization by property rights markets. It is sufficient that f^2 be concave in y_1^2 only. Since firm 2 maximizes its profit by considering x_1^* and y_1^* as parameters, firm 2 maximizes its profit on a section of the enlarged production set considered in figure 1.4.[9] The section is convex if we have a production function with nonincreasing returns for each value of the environmental parameters.

The second observation is that, with this taxation policy, the agents who suffer from pollution are not necessarily compensated for the damages accruing to them (depending on the tax burden) whereas they were to some extent compensated with the property-rights markets policy. In general, the amount of taxes collected is not equal to the damages incurred. We have assumed in the above example that the government's budgetary

9. Here we assume that y_1^1 does not influence f^2.

surplus is redistributed by lump-sum transfers.[10] Finally, we note that this tax payment implicitly assumes that the units of pollution can be observed. If such information is costly, it may be optimal to add to the pollution tax a penalty associated with a rate of control that discourages any tendency to conceal the externality.

1.4.3   Integration of Firms

Consider a simplified version of our example in which only firm 1 pollutes firm 2, that is,

$$\frac{\partial f^2}{\partial x_1} \equiv 0.$$

Integrating both firms yields a joint profit maximization problem:

$$\text{Max}\{p_1 y_1^1 + p_2 y_2^1 + p_2 y_2^2 + p_1 y_1^2\}$$

subject to $y_1^1 = f^1(y_2^1)$

$$y_2^2 = f^2(y_1^2, y_1^1),$$

from which we derive the first-order conditions

$$p_1 \frac{\partial f^1}{\partial y_2^1} + p_2 \frac{\partial f^2}{\partial y_1^1} \cdot \frac{df^1}{dy_2^1} + p_2 = 0$$

$$p_2 \frac{\partial f^2}{\partial y_1^2} + p_1 = 0$$

or

$$\frac{p_1}{p_2} = -\frac{\partial f^2}{\partial y_1^2} = -\frac{1 + \dfrac{\partial f^2}{\partial y_1^1} \cdot \dfrac{\partial f^1}{\partial y_2^1}}{df^1/dy_2^1},$$

which are the conditions of productive efficiency.

The competitive equilibrium is therefore a Pareto optimum. Both firms are interested in merging because their profits increase, taking prices as fixed parameters. However, unless the firms are infinitely small with respect to the industry (perfect competition), equilibrium prices will be altered by the merger with the possibility that total profit will be less than the sum of

10. See problem 2, where this assumption is relaxed.

the individual profits obtained before the merger. Only oligopolistic behavior can help them understand this result.

1.4.4   Pollution Abatement

By identifying a level of the externality with a level of an input or an output, we have so far assumed implicitly that there was a nonseparable
relationship between these quantities. However, pollution abatement techniques are aimed precisely at eliminating or decreasing the level of pollution while maintaining at the same level the activity initially generating the
externality. To introduce these into our analysis, we must therefore define
some new notation.

Return to the example in section 1.2 and consider only firm 1 generating
an externality for firm 2. We denote as z the amount of pollution. In the
absence of pollution abatement technology $z = y_1^1$. From now on, firm 1
may modify this relationship by an expenditure of good 1, d. Let

$$z = \phi(y_1^1, d) \quad \text{with} \quad \phi(y_1^1, 0) \equiv y_1^1.$$

The optimum is characterized by the solution to the problem

Max $U(x_1, x_2)$

subject to $y_1^1 + y_1^2 + w_1 - x_1 - d \geqslant 0$

$\qquad\qquad\quad y_2^1 + y_2^2 + w_2 - x_2 \geqslant 0$

$\qquad\qquad\quad -y_1^1 + f^1(y_2^1) \geqslant 0$

$\qquad\qquad\quad -y_2^2 + f^2(y_1^2, \phi(y_1^1, d)) \geqslant 0.$

After simplification, the first-order conditions are given by

$$\frac{\dfrac{\partial U}{\partial x_1}}{\dfrac{\partial U}{\partial x_2}} = -\frac{\partial f^2}{\partial y_1^2} = \frac{\partial f^2}{\partial z} \cdot \frac{\partial \phi}{\partial d} = -\frac{1 + \dfrac{\partial f^2}{\partial z} \cdot \dfrac{df^1}{dy_2^1} \cdot \dfrac{\partial \phi}{\partial y_1^1}}{\dfrac{df^1}{dy_2^1}}.$$

The new wrinkle in this problem is that pollution abatement techniques
should be employed to equate the marginal productivity of a unit of
good 1 spent for pollution abatement $\dfrac{\partial f^2}{\partial z} \cdot \dfrac{\partial \phi}{\partial d}$, to the marginal productivity
of a unit of good 1 used directly in the production of good 2, $-\dfrac{\partial f^2}{\partial y_1^2}$. Notice

that d seems to be a positive externality accruing to firm 2 activity as a result of firm 1's. The optimum may be decentralized by subsidizing this activity at the rate p_1^* up to the amount $p_1^* d^*$ (which induces firm 1 to choose the optimal level of pollution abatement) and by taxing the output of good 1 at a rate equal to

$$-p_2^* \frac{\partial f^2}{\partial z}(*) \frac{\partial \phi}{\partial y_1^1}(y^{*1}_1, d^*).$$

More directly, pollution can be taxed at the rate

$$\tau^* = -p_2^* \cdot \frac{\partial f^2}{\partial z}(*)$$

and the firm may be left to choose freely its level of pollution abatement and its level of activity. Then the firm solves the problem

$$\text{Max}\{p_1^* y_1^1 + p_2^* y_2^1 - \tau^* z + p_1^* d\}$$

$$\text{subject to} \quad -y_1^1 + f^1(y_2^1) \geq 0$$

$$z - \phi(y_1^1, d) \geq 0,$$

from which we obtain the first-order conditions of the Pareto optimum.

The policies of the Financial Agencies of Bassin in France may be considered to be a combination of these two policy prescriptions. These agencies tax the polluters and directly subsidize pollution abatement, subject to a balanced-budget constraint. Let $\bar{d}$ be the amount of pollution abatement that is subsidized. By an argument similar to that above, we see that for any $\bar{d}$,

$$\tau^* = -p_2^* \cdot \frac{\partial f^2}{\partial z}(*)$$

insures that the first-order conditions of the Pareto optimum are met. To balance the agency's budget, it is sufficient to choose $\bar{d}$ such that

$$p_1^* \bar{d} = \tau^* z^* \qquad \bar{d} = z^* \frac{\partial f^2 / \partial z(*)}{\partial f^2 / \partial y_1^2(*)},$$

which will be possible if $\bar{d} \leq d^*$ (see Kolm 1975).

In this section, we have neglected both the fact that pollution abatement techniques often involve fixed costs that would invalidate the marginal approach (see Bohm 1970, and note the nonconcavity of the function $f^2(y_1^2, \phi(y_1^1, d))$). However, we note that the first type of policy solution developed above requires only concavity in y_1^2 as in section 1.4.2 above.

1.5   Conclusion

To summarize, we can associate a property rights market to each externality and thus include it as a transaction in the market economy. However, the creation of such markets may be impeded by a nonconvexity that would lead to the nonexistence of an equilibrium (justifying the absence of this market in the initial economy). Furthermore, the thinness of this market in general makes the assumption of competitive behavior unrealistic. The second form of decentralization considered, namely taxation, does not require as strong a convexity assumption as the first. Moreover, since taxes are set by the government, the assumption of competitive behavior taking taxes and subsidies as parameters is acceptable. To be sure, the weakness of this approach lies in its informational requirements. Decentralization is not only somewhat incomplete but it is also incompatible with the initial decentralization of information. The issue of the government's obtaining this information is raised because it may not be in the agents' interest to reveal their private information. Moreover, this approach creates budgetary deficits or surpluses that are dealt with by making the appropriate lump-sum transfers. If we wish to take into account a balanced-budget constraint or the impossibility of using personalized taxes, the externality problem must be couched in terms of a second-best problem (see chapter 7).

Finally, we point out that by improving the flow of information the government may encourage the creation of specific information, and by inducing competition it may provide the framework for a decentralized solution for numerous externalities. Alternatively, the government has a role to play inside organizations (firms or other types) to insure that externalities (such as pollution in the workplace) that might otherwise be ignored because of the power relations within these organizations are taken into account. Before discussing corrective measures, we must consider the validity of our theory of a liberal private-property economy.

Consider the following argument. Since the economic agents are the ones most concerned, they will be the first to become aware of their interactions and to adjust their activities so as to internalize the externalities, thus ruling out such a source of inefficiency as soon as information about the externality becomes available. On the other hand, free entry on markets induces agents to acquire this information as soon as possible. In a regime of pure and perfect competition, externalities will be internalized naturally.

Therefore, justifications for government intervention must be sought in the following:

(i) Informational and organizational advantages (in particular when the ability to exclude users is difficult or impossible[11]) accruing to the government in connection with the right of enforcement;
(ii) the malfunctioning of free entry caused by the existence of important fixed costs, imperfect capital markets and transaction costs;
(iii) the desire to use environmental policy as a redistributive tool to avoid, for example in the case of negative externalities, the agent suffering from pollution paying the polluter to reduce the level of pollution.

Finally, even if these justifications exist, the benefits of government intervention must be compared to its costs. In fact, profit-seeking behavior in a private-property economy of the sort that leads to the creation of profitable markets by intermediaries or to the integration of firms or to agreements between economic units may internalize or incorporate in market transactions numerous externalities. The advisability of government intervention to eliminate the remaining externalities can be evaluated by cost-benefit analysis (see chapter 6).

1.6* The Compatibility of Increasing Returns and Perfect Competition

Consider the following example of two firms that exhibit constant returns to scale technology when each takes the output of the other as a parameter, but exhibit globally increasing returns when both outputs vary. Both firms produce good 1 using good 2 as an input according to the technologies

$$y_1^1 \leqslant y_2^1 \cdot y_2^2 \qquad y_1^2 \leqslant y_2^2 \cdot y_2^1.$$

11. See chapter 2.

Therefore, from section 1.3, a competitive equilibrium with externalities exists.

The aggregate production set is given by

$$\{(z_1, z_2) : z_1 \leqslant 2y_2^1 \cdot y_2^2, z_2 = y_2^1 + y_2^2\},$$

from which we derive the production function

$$z_1 = z_2^2/2,$$

which indeed exhibits increasing returns. Effectively, the maximum output of good 1 from an available quantity of good 2 equal to z_2 is the solution to the problem

$$\text{Max}\{y_2^1 \cdot y_2^2 + y_2^2 \cdot y_2^1\} = 2y_2^1 y_2^2$$

subject to $y_1^1 + y_2^2 = z_2,$

from which we derive a maximum output of $z_2^2/2$.

Increasing returns are compatible with the existence of an equilibrium with externalities that is inefficient. However, merging the two firms to eliminate the inefficiency precludes the existence of a competitive equilibrium because of a nonconvexity of the aggregate production function (see chapter 3).[12]

1.7* Externalities and Game Theory

The presence of externalities introduces a difficulty to the representation of an exchange economy as a game. Effectively, what a particular coalition can realize depends (due to the externalities) on the actions of the agents who are not in the coalition. We examine the implication of this for the concept of the core.[13] A coalition is said to block an allocation if it is possible to choose activities that yield an improvement over the proposed allocation for each of its members, *regardless of the actions of those outside the coalition.* Here we are considering the traditional extremely cautious behavior (maximin) found in game theory. We call the α-core that which corresponds to this definition of a blocking coalition, that is, all the allocations that cannot be blocked by any such coalition.

12. See Laffont (1972).
13. The core is the set of allocations that cannot be blocked by a coalition of any size.

One can argue legitimally that such an attitude leads to overestimating the stability of the economic game with externalities by not giving a coalition the possibility of responding to a counter-strategy played by the others. This leads to the concept of β-core associated with the following notion of a blocking coalition. A coalition blocks an allocation if, whatever may be the action of the agents outside the coalition, the coalition has a response strategy that insures an improvement over the initial situation for all its members. Clearly the β-core is included in the α-core and it may be empty when the α-core is not. Consider the following example, due to Shapley and Shubik (1969).

The game consists of three players; each has one unit of garbage that can be irreversibly dumped in the others' areas. Let x^{ji} be the quantity of garbage dumped by player j in the area of player i so that

$$\sum_{i=1}^{3} x^{ji} = 1 \qquad \forall j.$$

Each agent also has 1 unit of money; let z^{ji} be the quantity of money given by agent j to agent i. Player i's utility is given by

$$u^i = -\sum_{j=1}^{3} x^{ji} + \sum_{j=1}^{3} z^{ji}.$$

The β-core is empty; in fact any allocation in the β-core must satisfy

(a) $u^i \geqslant -1, \quad i \in \{1, 2, 3\} = I$

(b) $u^i \geqslant \dfrac{1}{2}, \quad u^j \geqslant \dfrac{1}{2} \qquad \forall (ij) \in I \times I, \quad i \neq j$

(c) $u^1 + u^2 + u^3 = 0,$

so as not to be blocked by any coalition. However, (b) implies $u^1 + u^2 + u^3 \geqslant 3/2$, which contradicts (c). On the other hand, the α-core requires only that:

(a) $u^i \geqslant -1 \qquad \forall i \in I$
(b) $u^i \geqslant 0 \qquad\quad \forall i \in I$
(c) $u^1 + u^2 + u^3 = 0.$

Effectively, the coalition of two players, say 1 and 2, can no longer react to a strategy of agent 3 by a reallocation of money. In the β-core, if agent 3 dumps his garbage on agent 1, agent 2 may give him half his endowment of money so that each agent receives utility of $1/2$. In the α-core, the money must be distributed before it is known where agent 3 will dump his garbage. Consequently, a utility level of 0 only may be guaranteed ($+1$ from the endowment of money, -1 from the dumping of garbage by agent 3).

1.8*   A Rehabilitation of Pecuniary Externalities

We have excluded from our analysis any indirect effects transmitted by prices, that is, the so-called pecuniary externalities. Here two cases must be distinguished. When a complete system of markets with no informational asymmetries exists, the competitive equilibrium is a Pareto optimum under the assumptions of the basic model found in the introduction. Any change in the consumption or production behavior of an agent influences prices without creating resource allocation problems when all economic agents behave competitively. In this case, price movements play the role of equating supply and demand only. Inasmuch as they achieve this, competitive behavior, by equating the marginal rates of substitution and transformation, is sufficient for the realization of a Pareto optimum. Pecuniary externalities are irrelevant. As soon as we leave this Arrow-Debreu framework for the more general case, prices play additional roles that create interactions raising efficiency problems even in a competitive economy.

When information is decentralized, not only do prices equate supply and demand but they also transmit some information. Any action of an agent that influences prices alters the informational content of these prices. Consequently, such action changes the expectations of the other agents and, therefore alters their expected utilities. In this situation, one agent's action influences the other agents' utility functions by an "informational externality" through prices. Similarly, when contingent claims markets are incomplete, the price vector generates a subset of institutionally feasible consumption bundles within the set of physiologically feasible contingent consumption bundles. One agent's action, by its influence on prices, affects the other agents' consumption sets by introducing a "dimensional externality" through prices.

In the same spirit, income has only a distributional role to play in the Arrow-Debreu model. On the other hand, when increasing returns are present (see chapter 3), there exists income distributions that prevent the realization of a Pareto optimum. One agent's action by its influence on prices affects incomes and therefore may generate an income distribution that supports a Pareto optimum. Then we have a "distributional" externality. Consequently, the notion of a pecuniary externality leads to the description of many types of inefficiencies that create the potential for government intervention.

References

Aoki, M., 1971, "Two planning processes for an economy with production externalities," *International Economic Review*, 12, 403–413.

Arrow, K., 1969, "The organization of economic activity: Issues pertinent to the choice of market versus non-market allocation," in *The Analysis and Evaluation of Public Expenditures: the PPB System*, Joint Economic Committee, GPO, Washington, D.C., 47–64.

Aumann, R. J., 1967, "A survey of cooperative games without side payments," in *Essays in Mathematical Economics in Honor of O. Morgenstern*, M. Shubik, ed., Princeton University Press.

Barde, J.-Ph., 1980, *La pratique des redevances de pollution*, O.C.D.E.

Bohm, P., 1970, "Pollution, purification et théorie des effects externes," *Annales de l'INSEE*, 3, 3–21.

Coase, R. H., 1960, "The problem of social cost," *Journal of Law and Economics*, 3, 1–44.

Kolm, S. C., 1975, "Rendement qualitatif et financement optimal des politiques d'environnement," *Econometrica*, 43, 93–114.

Laffont, J.-J., 1972, "Une note sur la compatibilité entre rendements croissants et concurrence parfaite," *Revue d'Economie Politique*, 6, 1188–1112.

——— 1977, *Effets externes et théorie économique*, C.N.R.S., Paris.

Lin, S., ed., 1976, *Theory and Measurement of Economic Externalities*, Academic Press.

Milleron, J. C., 1976, "Conséquences distributives d'une politique de l'environnement," *Annales de l'INSEE*, 21, 57–83.

Shapley, L., and M. Shubik 1969, "On the core of an economic system with externalities," *American Economic Review*, 59, 678–684.

Starrett, D., 1972, "Fundamental non-convexities in the theory of externalities," *Journal of Economic Theory*, 4, 180–199.

Recommended Reading

1. Laffont 1977, chapter 1 (historical perspective).

2. Laffont 1977, chapter 2 (competitive equilibrium with externalities).

3. Laffont 1977, chapter 3; Starrett 1972; Shapley and Shubik 1969 (decentralization).

4. Laffont 1977, chapter 5; Aumann 1967; Shapley and Shubik 1969 (externalities and game theory).

5. Laffont 1977, chapter 6; Aoki 1971 (externalities and planning).

6. Bohm 1970 (pollution abatement techniques); Milleron 1976 (redistributive effects of environmental policies).

7. Barde 1980 (applications of pollution taxation).

8. Lin 1976 (advanced theory).

2 Public Goods

A national defense program, a pollution abatement program, a television program, a pool, street lighting, and the prohibition of smoking are all examples of public goods. Obviously, these quite varied economic goods cannot be produced and allocated in competitive markets. On what fundamental property is this observation based? How can we overcome the inadequacies of the market economy with better forms of social cooperation? This chapter addresses these questions.

2.1 Definitions

A good is considered *public* if its use by one agent does not prevent other agents from using it; that is, individual consumption does not exhaust the good as is the case for a private good—for example, the eating of an apple by one individual. That is, the "publicness" of a good refers to its physical nature, and indicates the potential for collective consumption. However, it is often possible to exclude some consumers from using a public good with the help of an appropriate institutional framework, such as the use of individual speakers that prevent nonpayers from enjoying a movie from outside the grounds of a drive-in. Sometimes exclusion is too costly to make it an economically feasible or even possible policy. For example, how can an individual be excluded from national defense or a pollution abatement program?

Collective consumption does not imply that the utility level of a consumer of a good is insensitive to the consumption of this good by other agents. Thus a person may enjoy watching a movie alone, or, on the contrary, he may prefer the company of other people. The utility derived from the consumption of a public good such as highway availability is clearly affected by other agents' consumption. If highway availability is the good, then highway congestion can be treated as an externality created by the simultaneous consumption of that good by many agents. The distinction between a public good and an externality is subtle. Externalities oftentime have characteristics similar to those of a public good, although this is not necessarily the case. For example, flowers in an orchard can accommodate only a limited number of bees, and pollen is certainly used up by an individual bee; however, the possibility of excluding particular bees is unlikely.

Deeper reflection indicates that the distinction between private and public goods according to the notion of exhaustibility by a single individual is superficial. Indeed, when goods are defined in an appropriate manner, individual consumption always leads to exhaustion by private use. Instead of talking about national nuclear defense, we could consider the simultaneous protection of millions of units of space. If person i occupies space l, he consumes the good "protection of space l" and prevents person j from benefiting from this good. Then *technical* and *informational* difficulties with exclusion will lead to the appropriate definition of such protection as an economic good. Since it is impossible (or at least far too costly) to exclude only one particular space l from protection, the good will be called national nuclear defense and we can say that it is not exhausted in private use.

Sometimes the costs of exclusion dictate that, although the economic good considered has a collective characteristic of not being exhausted in private use, it can nonetheless be supported by relying on a private right (defined by government mandate) because exclusion is possible. For example, consider a private club and its facilities. The goods that are exhausted by private consumption would be the multitude of services provided within the club. However, it is less costly to charge an entry fee only. Thus the economic good sold is club membership. It can be produced in a private manner inasmuch as the right of entry to the club's facilities can be reserved for club members only. Why does this good exist? Undoubtedly, in the past, the economic activity fostered by this right appeared to be desirable from an allocational or distributional perspective.

Moreover, no individual is required to consume or use a private good; rather we usually assume free choice. In fact, this "choice" does have a cost, which is nonetheless considered small enough so that it can always be ignored in an initial analysis. On the other hand, the distinction between required and optional use is important for a public good inasmuch as the decision to produce it is taken collectively; the good may therefore be imposed on certain agents against their wills. The use requirement may be of a physical nature (requiring individuals to benefit from the protection accorded by national defense) or of an institutional nature (requiring individuals to listen to a political speech after work, as in China).

To take another example, trash collection could be privatized without required subscription. However, it would be too easy for certain consumers not to buy the service and (at night) to dump their garbage into their neighbors' yards. At the same time, it would be too costly to set up a monitoring technology that would exclude some agents from this service.

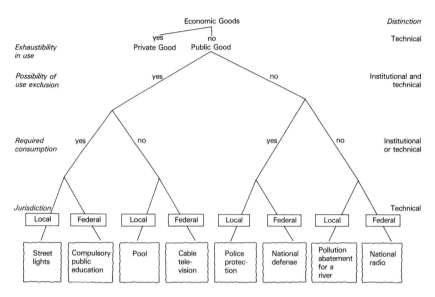

Figure 2.1
Categories of economic goods. For a private good, the possibility of use exclusion refers simply to the possibility of preventing theft. Therefore it is a purely institutional distinction. The required consumption of a private good has institutional characteristics as well.

Therefore required subscription is appropriate, with its consequent rational for the existence of a government. A good is public if it is much less costly to impose required subscription by local or national authorities ultimately supported by public mandate.

Finally, we can categorize public goods according to the group of *concerned* agents. This group might be the whole population of a country (a national defense program), of a city (the number of hospital beds), of a neighborhood (a pool), or of the workplace (a coffee-making machine). These different categories, summarized in figure 2.1, are important for determining the types of economic mechanisms and the policy instruments that are likely to yield a proper allocation of resources. The typology thus obtained is a result of the analysis rather than one given a priori. Ultimately, optimization of economic activities by property rights defines the goods to be exchanged and their different properties, namely exhaustibility or nonexhaustibility by individual use, exclusion or non-exclusion, required subscription or optional use, etc. Hence the definition of goods is endogenous, not exogenous. In this chapter we focus on problems of pure public goods with the properties: subscription is required, everyone is affected collectively, and there is no possibility of congestion.[1]

2.2   Pareto-Optimal Allocations

Consider an economy with I consumers and two goods, one private and one public. The public good is produced using the private good according to a decreasing-returns technology characterized by

$$y = g(z) \qquad g' > 0 \qquad g'' < 0,$$

where the input of the private good z is taken to be positive. For a private good, the possibility of exclusion is simply the possibility of preventing theft. Therefore the distinction is purely institutional. Required use of a private good is of a similar institutional nature. Consumer i's utility function $U^i(x^i, y)$ depends on the quantity consumed of the private good and consumption of the public good y. It is strictly concave, differentiable, and strictly increasing. Let w be the aggregate endowment of the private good. First, we characterize the Pareto-optimal allocations of resources. Pareto optima are solutions to the problem

$$\text{Max} \sum_{i=1}^{I} \alpha^i U^i(x^i, y) \qquad \alpha^i \geqslant 0 \qquad i = 1, \ldots, I$$

$$\text{subject to} \quad w - \sum_{i=1}^{I} x^i - z \geqslant 0 \tag{1}$$

$$g(z) - y \geqslant 0 \tag{2}$$

$$y \geqslant 0 \qquad z \geqslant 0 \qquad x^i \geqslant 0 \qquad i = 1, \ldots, I. \tag{3}$$

Let λ and μ be the multipliers associated with the two scarcity constraints. The first-order conditions (which are sufficient under the above convexity assumptions) are written as

$$\alpha^i \frac{\partial U^i}{\partial x^i} = \lambda \qquad i = 1, \ldots, I$$

1. For other cases, see sections 2.6* and 2.7*, and the references to this chapter.

$$\sum_{i=1}^{I} \alpha^i \frac{\partial U^i}{\partial y} = \mu$$

$$\mu g' = \lambda$$

(where $g' = dg/dz$); or, by eliminating the multipliers, as

$$\sum_{i=1}^{I} \frac{\partial U^i/\partial y}{\partial U^i/\partial x^i} = \frac{1}{g'}, \tag{4}$$

which is called the Bowen-Lindahl-Samuelson condition. Conditions (1) and (2), when satisfying the equality, combined with conditions (3) and (4) characterize the Pareto optima. In particular, we know from (4) that the sum over all consumers of the marginal rates of substitution between the public and the private good must be equal to the marginal rate of transformation in production between these two goods.

In figure 2.2a we characterize the Pareto optima in a two-agent economy with $g(z) \equiv z$ in the Kolm triangle of height w. Each triplet (x_1, x_2, z), such that $x_1 + x_2 + z = w$, can be represented as a point in the triangle because the sum of the distances to the sides is constant and equal to w.

In figure 2.2b, the indifference curves of agent 1 (resp. agent 2) are shown in the coordinate system with axes given by BA and BC (resp. CA and CB). As shown in figure 2.2c, the Pareto optima are the points of common tangency of the two sets of indifference curves.

Are there resource-allocation mechanisms that support the realization of a Pareto optimum?

2.3   A Voluntary-Contribution Equilibrium

The initial endowment of the private good characterizes private property $w^i, i = 1, \ldots, I$. We suppose that each consumer voluntarily contributes an amount z^i of the private good for production of the public good. Then the output of the public good is given by

$$y = g\left(\sum_{i=1}^{I} z^i\right).$$

Given the voluntary contributions of the other consumers $z^{-i} = (z^1, \ldots, z^{i-1}, z^{i+1}, \ldots, z^I)$, consumer i calculates his own contribution by solving the problem

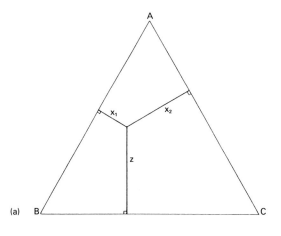

(a)

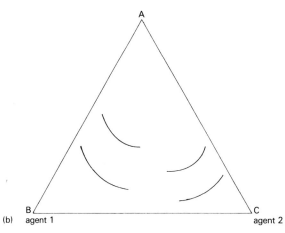

(b)

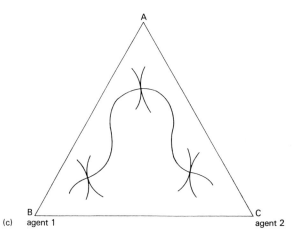

(c)

Figure 2.2

Max $U^i(x^i, y)$

subject to $x^i = w^i - z^i$

$$y = g\left(z^i + \sum_{j \neq i} z^j\right)$$

$$z^i \geq 0 \qquad x^i \geq 0,$$

or

$$\text{Max}\left[\phi^i(z^i, z^{-i}) \equiv U^i\left(w^i - z^i, g\left(z^i + \sum_{j \neq i} z^j\right)\right)\right]$$

subject to $w^i \geq z^i \geq 0$.

A *voluntary-contribution equilibrium* is a Nash equilibrium for the game defined by the objective functions $\phi^i(.)$ and the strategy spaces $\mathscr{Z}^i \equiv [0, w^i]$; that is, it is an I-tuple $(z^{*1}, \ldots, z^{*I})$ such that

$$\forall i, \quad \phi^i(z^{*i}, z^{*-i}) \geq \phi^i(z^i, z^{*-i}) \quad \forall z^i \in \mathscr{Z}^i.$$

The first-order conditions from the individual optimization problems are written as

$$\frac{\partial U^i/\partial y}{\partial U^i/\partial x^i} = \frac{1}{g'} \quad \forall i,$$

and these are clearly different from the Bowen-Lindahl-Samuelson conditions.

Agent i contributes to the production of the public good until the marginal cost of the public good measured in terms of the private good (taking the other agents' voluntary contributions as given), that is, $1/g'$, is equal to his marginal rate of substitution. He does not consider the benefit to other agents of the output he finances by his contribution. This is true for each consumer and, consequently, the consumers as a group contribute less than the amount desirable for Pareto optimality. The lack of output of the public good when voluntary contributions are relied upon may become particularly acute if the number of the agents is large, as we show in the following example.

Let

$$U^i(x^i, y) = \gamma \operatorname{Log} y + \operatorname{Log} x^i$$

$$w^i = w/I \qquad g(z) \equiv z.$$

The egalitarian Pareto optimum is obtained by maximizing

$$\sum_{i=1}^{I} [\gamma \, \text{Log} \, y + \text{Log} \, x^i]$$

subject to $\quad y + \sum_{i=1}^{1} x^i = w,$

from which we derive

$$\gamma I/y = \lambda \qquad 1/x^i = \lambda \qquad i = 1, \ldots, I$$

or

$$\hat{y} = \frac{\gamma w}{1 + \gamma} \qquad \hat{x}^i = \frac{w}{I(1 + \gamma)} \qquad i = 1, \ldots, I.$$

In the voluntary-contribution equilibrium, agent i maximizes

$$\gamma \, \text{Log} \, y + \text{Log} \, x^i$$

subject to $\quad y = z^i + \sum_{j \neq i} z^j \qquad x^i = \frac{w}{I} - z^i,$

or

$$\text{Max} \, \gamma \, \text{Log} \left(z^i + \sum_{j \neq i} z^j \right) + \text{Log} \left(\frac{w}{I} - z^i \right)$$

subject to $\quad \dfrac{w}{I} \geqslant z^i \geqslant 0,$

from which we derive the first-order condition

$$\frac{\gamma}{z^i + \sum_{j \neq i} z^j} = \frac{1}{(w/I) - z^i}$$

or

$$\frac{\gamma w}{I} = (1 + \gamma)z^i + \sum_{j \neq i} z^j.$$

By summing over i, this equality becomes

$$(I + \gamma) \sum_{i=1}^{I} z^i = \gamma w,$$

or

$$y^* = \frac{\gamma w}{I + \gamma} \qquad x^{*i} = \frac{w}{I + \gamma}.$$

The individualistic behavior assumed in these examples leads each agent to make a contribution only to the extent that it is directly beneficial to him. This is the basis for the insufficiency of output of public goods.[2]

2.4   Lindahl Equilibrium

Associate to each agent a price (personalized price) p^i for the public good. This price indicates what agent i must pay for each unit of the public good. The agent determines his "competitive" demand by solving the problem

$$\text{Max } U^i(x^i, y) \tag{5}$$

subject to $w^i - x^i - p^i y \geqslant 0$

$$x^i \geqslant 0 \qquad y \geqslant 0,$$

from which we derive the demand functions for the public good and the private good:

$$x^i(p^i) \qquad y^i(p^i).$$

Production of the public good is undertaken by a competitive firm facing a price per unit for its output of p that is equal to the sum of the personalized prices, so that

$$p = \sum_{i=1}^{I} p^i.$$

The firm's maximization problem becomes

2. For a number of writers, this is sufficient justification for the government to make decisions concerning public goods based on public preferences. Nonetheless, the origin of public preferences is unclear. See Wolfelsperger (1969) for a discussion of this institutional theory of public goods.

$$\text{Max}\left(\sum_{i=1}^{I} p^i\right) y - z \tag{6}$$

subject to $g(z) - y \geq 0$

$$y \geq 0 \qquad z \geq 0.$$

The solution to this problem determines the competitive supply curve for the public good:

$$\zeta\left(\sum_{i=1}^{I} p^i\right) = g\left((g')^{-1} \cdot \frac{1}{\sum_{i=1}^{I} p^i}\right),$$

and its associated input demand for the private good:

$$g^{-1}\left(\zeta\left(\sum_{i=1}^{I} p^i\right)\right).$$

A *Lindahl equilibrium* is a vector of personalized prices $(p^{*1}, \ldots, p^{*I})$ and a corresponding allocation such that

$$\zeta\left(\sum_{i=1}^{I} p^{*i}\right) = y^i(p^{*i}), \qquad i = 1, \ldots, I \tag{7}$$

$$\sum_{i=1}^{I} x^i(p^{*i}) + g^{-1}\left(\zeta\left(\sum_{i=1}^{I} p^{*i}\right)\right) = \sum_{i=1}^{I} w^i. \tag{8}$$

Therefore, the Lindahl equilibrium is a competitive equilibrium in the fictitious economy where the space of goods has been expanded to $(I + 1)$ goods, the private good and I personalized public goods, that is, the public goods of agent 1 through agent I. These I goods are produced "jointly," so that we must find a vector of prices for which all agents demand equal quantities of the public good. From general equilibrium theory, we know that the competitive equilibrium is a Pareto optimum in the expanded economy and, therefore, it is a Pareto optimum for the initial economy if the Pareto optima are the same in both economies. We prove directly that a Lindahl equilibrium is indeed a Pareto optimum.

The first-order conditions for problem (5) evaluated at the equilibrium can be written as

$$\frac{\partial U^i/\partial y}{\partial U^i/\partial x^i} = p^{*i}, \qquad i = 1, \ldots, I.$$

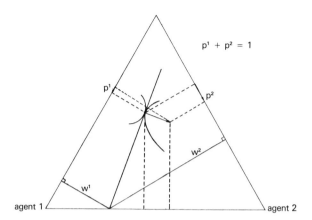

Figure 2.3

Profit maximization by the firm yields

$$\sum_{i=1}^{I} p^{*i} = \frac{1}{g'},$$

from which we derive the Bowen-Lindahl-Samuelson condition:

$$\sum_{i=1}^{I} \frac{\partial U^i/\partial y}{\partial U^i/\partial x^i} = \sum_{i=1}^{I} p^{*i} = \frac{1}{g'}.$$

The Lindahl equilibrium is represented within the Kolm triangle shown in figure 2.3.

Returning to the foregoing logarithmic example, we have

$$\text{Max}\{\gamma \, \text{Log} \, y + \text{Log} \, x^i\}$$

subject to $$\frac{w}{I} - p^i y - x^i \geq 0$$

$$y \geq 0 \qquad x^i \geq 0;$$

this yields

$$y^i(p^i) = \frac{1}{p^i} \frac{\gamma w}{(\gamma + 1)I} \qquad x^i(p^i) = \frac{w}{(\gamma + 1)I}.$$

Equation (7) requires that $p^{*i} = p^{*i'} \; \forall i, i' = 1, \ldots, I$, and the production technology requires that $\sum_{i=1}^{I} p^{*i} = 1$, from which it follows that $p^{*i} = 1/I$

$\forall i, i = 1, \ldots, I$, and

$$y^i(p^{*i}) = \frac{\gamma w}{(\gamma + 1)I} \qquad i = 1, \ldots, I,$$

which is the egalitarian Pareto-optimal allocation.

Can we design a system of competitive markets to support the Lindahl equilibrium? In the market for agent i's "public good" where the price is p^i there is necessarily a single buyer, agent i. This agent will quickly learn that he should not behave competitively (an assumption which has always been justified by the existence of a large number of market participants). He will instead react to the price vector $(1, p^i)$ without revealing his true demand for the public good, but rather he will minimize his revealed desire for the public good by contributing as little as possible to its production. Contrary to the case of private goods, where the incentive to reveal false demand functions decreases with the number of agents,[3] an increase in the number of agents here only aggravates the problem, as we can see intuitively.[4] This is the "free rider" problem. Therefore the Lindahl equilibrium seems to be more a normative prescription for the allocation of public goods than a positive description of the market mechanism.

To be sure, the government could force agent i to pay $t^{*i} = p^{*i}y^*$ as his share of financing the output of the public good that would achieve a Pareto optimum. The difficulty with this solution is the informational requirement that the preferences of the individual consumers must be discovered in order to calculate the appropriate taxes. Note that, if we could calculate these personalized taxes t^{*i}, each agent would be taxed an amount proportional to his marginal utility resulting from consuming the public good. This "benefits" approach to the theory of taxation seems appropriate from an equity perspective if the initial endowment is itself considered to be fair. Another approach to taxation (the "ability to pay" approach) would tax agents according to their endowments, that is, it would take advantage of the existence of public goods to redistribute income through their financing. Such an approach may be justifiable in a social welfare sense if lump-sum transfers supporting the realization of an optimal distribution of income are not possible. (See the theory of the second-best in chapter 7.)

3. See Postlewaite and Roberts (1976).
4. See Roberts (1976).

2.5   Cooperation and Public Goods

We have seen that the existence of public goods requires more cooperation between economic agents than a market mechanism coordinated by prices. Such cooperation can be formalized in the framework of planning procedures or politico-economic mechanisms.

2.5.1   A Planning Procedure

Consider a continuous procedure beginning at $t = 0$. In the absence of public goods, we assume that $U^i(w^i, 0) > U^i(0, y)$ $\forall y \geqslant 0$. If $[x^i(t), y(t)]$ is the allocation of private and public goods proposed to agent i at time t, we denote his marginal rate of substitution as

$$\pi^i(t) = \pi^i(x^i(t), y(t)) = \frac{\dfrac{\partial U^i}{\partial y}(x^i(t), y(t))}{\dfrac{\partial U^i}{\partial x^i}(x^i(t), y(t))}.$$

For a level of input $z(t)$, the marginal cost of the public good is denoted by

$$\gamma(t) \equiv \gamma(z(t)) \equiv \frac{1}{g'(z(t))}$$

with the additional assumption that $\gamma(0) = 0$.

The Pareto optima are characterized by the equations

$$\sum_{i=1}^{I} \pi^i(x^i, y) = \gamma(g^{-1}(y))$$

$$\sum_{i=1}^{I} x^i + g^{-1}(y) = w$$

$$y \geqslant 0 \qquad x^i \geqslant 0 \qquad i = 1, \ldots, I.$$

The allocation is governed by the system of differential equations

$$\dot{y} \equiv \frac{dy}{dt} = \sum_{i=1}^{I} \pi^i(t) - \gamma(t) \tag{9}$$

$$\dot{x}^i \equiv \frac{dx^i}{dt} = -\pi^i(t)\dot{y} + \delta^i\left(\sum_{i=1}^{I} \pi^i(t) - \gamma(t)\right)\dot{y} \tag{10}$$

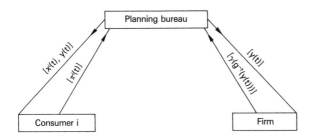

Figure 2.4

with

$$\sum_{i=1}^{I} \delta^i = 1 \qquad \delta^i \geqslant 0 \qquad i = 1, \ldots, I.$$

The messages required by this procedure are illustrated in figure 2.4. The planning bureau proposes an allocation $(x^i(t), y(t))$ to consumer i. The consumer responds by reporting his marginal rate of substitution between the public good and the private good for this allocation. The planning bureau increases the quantity of the public good so long as the sum of the marginal rates of substitution (which expresses the sum of the consumers' willingnesses to pay for an additional unit of the public good) is greater than the marginal cost. Simultaneously, the planning bureau changes the allocation of agents i's private good by making him pay the utility-equivalent amount of the private good to exactly compensate for this increase in the public good $\pi^i(t)\dot{y}$ and leaving him on the same indifference curve (since $dU^i/dt = 0 \Leftrightarrow \dot{x}^i + \pi^i(t)\dot{y} = 0$).

These payments generate a surplus $[\sum_{i=1}^{I} \pi^i(t) - \gamma(t)]\dot{y} > 0$ (this is >0 by definition of $\dot{y}$) that is then distributed amongst the consumers according to coefficients of distribution δ^i fixed ex ante. Consequently, at each point in time, the utility level of agent i can only increase; effectively,

$$\frac{dU^i}{dt}(x^i(t), y(t)) = \frac{\partial U^i}{\partial x^i}[-\pi^i(t)\dot{y} + \dot{x}^i]$$

$$= \frac{\partial U^i}{\partial x^i}\left[-\pi^i(t)\dot{y} + \pi^i(t)\dot{y} + \delta^i\left(\sum_{i=1}^{I} \pi^i(t) - \gamma(t)\right)\dot{y}\right]$$

$$= \delta^i\left[\sum_{i=1}^{I} \pi^i(t) - \gamma(t)\right]^2 \frac{\partial U^i}{\partial x^i} \geqslant 0.$$

This procedure is said to be individually rational at each point in time.

On the production side, the planning bureau transmits a level of output and the firm responds with the marginal cost associated with this level of ouput. Clearly, at each point in time, the demand for the private good equals the aggregate endowment of the private good:

$$\sum_{i=1}^{I} x^i(t) + g^{-1}(y(t)) = \sum_{i=1}^{I} w^i, \tag{11}$$

since

$$\sum_{i=1}^{I} x^i(0) = \sum_{i=1}^{I} w^i$$

and

$$\sum_{i=1}^{I} \dot{x}^i(t) + \gamma(t)\dot{y} = 0 \quad \forall t.$$

It is also obvious that a stationary solution of the system of differential equations is a Pareto optimum since $\dot{y} = 0$ implies $\sum_{i=1}^{I} \pi^i(t) = \gamma(t)$ and (11) always holds. The convergence of the procedure to a stationary solution is proved by using, as a Liapunov function, the sum of the utilities, which is always increasing and bounded above over the feasible set and the derivative of which is zero only at a stationary point.[5]

The procedure is summarized in figure 2.5 for the case of two consumers. The procedure is nonbiased in the sense that any individually rational Pareto-optimal allocation may be attained by an appropriate choice of the coefficients of distribution δ^i.[6] However, such choice is possible only if we know the preferences at the start of the procedure, whereas the procedure itself is designed to extract sufficient information concerning preferences to define a Pareto-optimal allocation.

We illustrate the unbiasedness property in the case of two consumers. Choose $\delta^1 = 1$, $\delta^2 = 0$; then

$$\frac{dU^1}{dt} = [\pi^1(t) + \pi^2(t) - \gamma(t)]^2 \frac{\partial U^1}{\partial x^1} \geq 0$$

---

5. $V(t) = \sum_{i=1}^{I} U^i(t)$ is increasing and bounded above and therefore converges: since $\lim_{t \to \infty} V(t) = K$, therefore $\lim_{t \to \infty} \dot{V}(t) = 0$. Any limit point is a stationary allocation and therefore Pareto optimal. The strict concavity of U^i implies the uniqueness of the limiting allocation and therefore the global convergence of the path defined by the system of differential equations.

6. See Champsaur (1976).

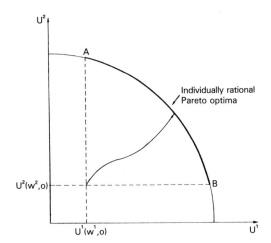

Figure 2.5

$$\frac{dU^2}{dt} = 0.$$

The procedure stops at point A. By symmetry, if $\delta^1 = 0$ and $\delta^2 = 1$ the procedure would stop at point B. Since the solution to the system of the differential equations (9) and (10) is continuous in (δ_1, δ_2), any Pareto optimum between A and B that is individually rational can be achieved by an appropriate choice of the coefficients of distribution of the surplus.

This leads us to consider the incentives that may encourage the agents to cooperate in this way. We observe that if at each point agent i transmits his real marginal rate of substitution to the planning bureau, he cannot lose utility (taking the initial situation as a benchmark). However, might he gain more utility by modifying his messages? Although the answer is yes, sometimes, truthful revelation at each point in time is a maximin[7] strategy as we show by the following argument.

Let $\psi^i(t)$ be the response of agent i perhaps different from $\pi^i(t)$ and let $X(t)$ be the sum of the responses of the others. It is sufficient to show that, for any response $\psi^i(t) \neq \pi^i(t)$, there exists a response of the others $X(t)$

7. A maximin strategy is obtained in the following manner. For each of his possible strategies, the agent considers the strategies of the other agents that are the most unfavorable to him according to the value of his objective function. The maximin strategy is the one that insures the highest value of his objective function when the most unfavorable strategies of the other agents are played.

leading to a lower utility level than would prevail for $\pi^i(t)$. Since $\pi^i(t)$ always leads to a nondecreasing utility level, it is sufficient to show that there exists an $X(t)$ leading to a decrease in the utility level. (We consider the case where $\psi^i(t) < \pi^i(t)$, leaving to the reader the case where $\psi^i(t) > \pi^i(t)$.) We have

$$\frac{dU^i}{dt} = \frac{\partial U^i}{\partial x^i} [\pi^i(t) - \psi^i(t) + \delta^i \dot{y}] \dot{y}$$

with

$$\dot{y} = X(t) + \psi^i(t) - \gamma(t).$$

It is sufficient to take

$$\gamma(t) - \psi^i(t) > X(t) > \gamma(t) - \psi^i(t) + \frac{\psi^i(t) - \pi^i(t)}{\delta^i}.$$

Therefore the iterative procedure studied has an incentive property that may induce nonstrategic behavior. However, this incentive inducement is strong only if the agents have a very large aversion to risk. (See chapter 5 for other incentive concepts.)

2.5.2   Politico-economic Equilibrium

The output decisions for public goods (government spending) and their mode of financing (government revenues) are defined simultaneously by a budgetary process culminating in the fiscal budget. As the object of study Wicksell (1896) suggested allocations generated by budgets that cannot be replaced by unanimous consent. Foley (1967) formalized this idea. We consider a model similar to the one used in this chapter with L private goods (instead of only one) and the price normalization $p_1 = 1$. Good 1 is the only one used to produce the public good according to technology $g(z)$. Each agent has an initial endowment in private goods of $w^i \in \mathbf{R}^L_+$, $i = 1, \ldots, I$, and his utility function $U^i(x^i, y)$ is now defined on $\mathbf{R}^L_+ \times \mathbf{R}_+$, with $x^i \in \mathbf{R}^L$ indicating his consumption bundle of private goods.

A *fiscal budget* is a quantity of the public good $y = g(z)$ and a distribution of its financing $(t^1, \ldots, t^I : \sum_{i=1}^I t^i = z)$, where t^i is the tax paid by agent i. Given a proposed budget $(y, t^1, \ldots, t^I)$, each agent determines his demand for private goods by solving the problem

Max $U^i(x^i, y)$

subject to $pw^i - t^i - px^i \geqslant 0$

$\qquad\qquad x^i \geqslant 0,$

where $p = (1, p_2, \ldots, p_L)$. We denote by $x^i(p, t^i, y), i = 1, \ldots, I$, the demand functions obtained from this problem.

A *politico-economic equilibrium* is a competitive equilibrium for the private goods combined with a fiscal budget that cannot be replaced by any other fiscal budget that would improve the situation of all consumers. That is, in such an equilibrium we have a price vector p^*, a quantity of the public good y^*, and a tax vector $t^* = (t^{*1}, \ldots, t^{*I})$ such that

$$\sum_{i=1}^{I} x_1^i(p^*, t^{*i}, y^*) = \sum_{i=1}^{I} w_1^i - \sum_{i=1}^{I} t^{*i}$$

$$\sum_{i=1}^{I} x_l^i(p^*, t^{*i}, y^*) = \sum_{i=1}^{I} w_l^i \qquad l = 2, \ldots, L$$

$$y^* = g\left(\sum_{i=1}^{I} t^{*i}\right);$$

furthermore, there exist no $(\tilde{y}, \tilde{t}^1, \ldots, \tilde{t}^I)$ such that

$$\tilde{y} = g\left(\sum_{i=1}^{I} \tilde{t}^i\right)$$

$$U^i(x^i(p^*, \tilde{t}^i, \tilde{y})) \geqslant U^i(x^i(p^*, t^{*i}, y^*)) \qquad i = 1, \ldots, I,$$

with at least one strict inequality.

A politico-economic equilibrium is Pareto optimal. Indeed, suppose that this were not the case. There would exist $\hat{x}^i, i = 1, \ldots, I$ and $\hat{y}$ such that

$$\sum_{i=1}^{I} \hat{x}_1^i = \sum_{i=1}^{I} w_1^i - g^{-1}(\hat{y}) \tag{12}$$

$$\sum_{i=1}^{I} \hat{x}_l^i = \sum_{i=1}^{I} w_l^i \qquad l = 2, \ldots, L \tag{13}$$

$$U^i(\hat{x}^i, \hat{y}) \geqslant U^i(x^{*i}, y^*) \qquad i = 1, \ldots, I, \tag{14}$$

with at least one strict inequality. Then we could construct a fiscal budget that is unanimously preferred to the budget (y^*, t^*) in which the quantity $\hat{y}$ of the public good is financed by the taxes $\hat{t}^i = p^*(w^i - \hat{x}^i), i = 1, \ldots, I$.

Multiplying (12) and (13) by p^* verifies that such taxes do effectively finance $\hat{y}$. Moreover, since the problem for consumer i is

Max $U^i(x^i, \hat{y})$

subject to $p^*x^i \leqslant p^*w^i - \hat{t}^i = p^*\hat{x}^i$ (15)

$\qquad\qquad x^i \geqslant 0,$

we have necessarily

Max $U^i(x^i, \hat{y}) \geqslant U^i(\hat{x}^i, \hat{y})$

subject to (15),

from which the unanimous preference for $(\hat{y}, \hat{t})$ follows from (14).

We have assumed that the only achievable fiscal budgets were those for which no unanimously preferred budget was found. This condition supposes a long and arduous procedure to discover such a budget and neglects any strategic behavior along the way. We have assumed that agents vote according to their true preferences, and we have therefore neglected the problem of manipulation. Are there voting procedures that preclude manipulation and thus provide a correct solution to the problem of choosing a fiscal budget for public goods that leads to a Pareto-efficient allocation? This question will be considered in chapters 4 and 5, within the framework of social-choice theory. Here we give an example of a voting procedure, majority voting, that allows us to choose the output level of a one-dimensional public good.

2.5.3   Majority Voting or the Law of the Median Voter

Suppose that there is only one public good and one private good and that agent i's utility function is

$$U^i(x^i, y) = x^i + \theta^i \operatorname{Log} y \qquad i = 1, \ldots, I,$$

with $\theta^i \in [0, 1]$. Moreover, agent i has an initial endowment of the private good $w^i = 1$. Finally, the production function for the public good using the private good as an input is written as

$$y = z,$$

where $z \geqslant 0$ is the input of the private good.

The (interior) Pareto optima of this economy require a production of the public good equal to

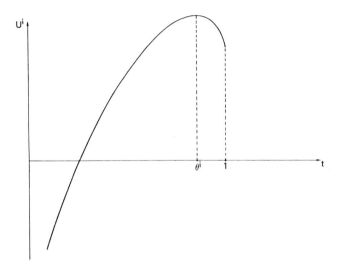

Figure 2.6

$$y = \sum_{i=1}^{I} \theta^i.$$

Suppose that social arrangements require egalitarian financing of the public good and let t be the tax rate on the private good that exactly finances the output of the public good. As a function of t, the level of utility of agent i is therefore

$$\theta^i \text{ Log } It + (1 - t).$$

Now consider the choice of t as equivalent to the choice of the public good.

The preferences are unimodal in t (figure 2.6) so that, if I is uneven, a simple majority voting procedure leads to selecting the choice made by the median voter:[8]

$$t = \theta^m \qquad y = I\theta^m.$$

In general, therefore, the collective decision is not Pareto optimal. However, if the mean of the distribution of θ coincides with the median, the choice will be Pareto optimal. At the Lindahl equilibrium for this economy,

8. See chapter 4.

$p^i = \theta^i / \sum_{j=1}^{I} \theta^j$, which corresponds to the implicit tax, $t^i = p^i y = \theta^i$. Compared to the Lindahl equilibrium the agents who like the public good more than the median agent ($\theta^i - \theta^m > 0$) benefit from majority voting.[9] Therefore, the social agreement favors these agents. If tastes vary according to the public goods considered, the agents who benefit will change and, on average, the advantages of this simple decision process (which is robust with respect to manipulation)[10] will eventually be shared equally.

2.6*   Cooperation and Game Theory

The difficulties encountered above in formalizing the types of cooperation that should take place in order to determine the output and financing of public goods suggest that it might be productive to describe possible areas of cooperation compatible with game-theoretic concepts. Champsaur (1975) proposed a clever way of associating a game with transferable utility to the economy consisting of one private good and one public good characterized in section 2.2. Let $a = (x^1, \ldots, x^I, y)$ be any allocation. To any coalition S, we associate the cost $c(a, S)$ in terms of the private good that the coalition S would have to bear if it were to assure the consumption vector (x^i, y) to each member i of the coalition. We therefore have

$$c(a, S) = \sum_{i \in S} x^i + g^{-1}(y).$$

To each utility vector $v \in \mathbf{R}^I$, we can associate the set of allocations that assure the utility level v^i to each member i of the coalition S:[11]

$$B(v, S) = \{a : U^i(x^i, y) \geqslant v^i \ \forall i \in S\}.$$

Let

$$c^*(v, S) = \inf c(a, S), a \in B(v, S)$$

be the lowest cost that allows coalition S to assure each member i the utility level v^i. Let

$$h(v, S) = c^*(v, S) - \sum_{i \in S} w^i,$$

9. See Martinez-Vasquez (1982) for an empirical application.
10. See chapter 5.
11. Where $a = [x^1, \ldots, x^I, y]$ and $u(a) = [U^1(x^1, y), \ldots, U^I(x^I, y)]$.

that is, the amount that coalition S would have to add to its own resources to be able to cover the lowest cost of financing an allocation giving each agent $i \in S$, a utility level greater than or equal to v^i.

An allocation a will be blocked by a coalition S if and only if

$$-h(u(a), S) > 0,$$

that is, if the coalition can assure its members more than $u(a)$. The core is the set of feasible allocations a such that

$$-h(u(a), S) \leqslant 0 \quad \forall S \subset \{1, \ldots, I\}.$$

For each vector v, the game with transferable utility defined by the characteristic function $-c^*(v, S)$ is convex [since $-c^*(v, S^1 \cup S^2) - c^*(v, S^1 \cap S^2) \geqslant -c^*(v, S^1) - c^*(v, S^2) \quad \forall S^1, \quad S^2 \subset \{1, \ldots, I\}$], and therefore it has a nonempty core $\mathscr{C}(v)$ (Shapley 1971).

The nonemptiness of the original core[12] follows from showing that there exists an allocation a such that $-(w^1, \ldots, w^I)$ belongs to the core $\mathscr{C}(u(a))^*$. We then have

$$-\sum_{i \in S} w^i \geqslant -c^*(u(a), S) \quad \forall S,$$

or

$$-h^*(u(a), S) \leqslant 0 \quad \forall S \subset \{1, \ldots, I\}.$$

(See Champsaur 1975 for proofs and extensions.)

Can we conclude from this that negotiations over the production and financing of public goods will necessarily lead to a core allocation? Will the agents be cooperative enough to support a core allocation and therefore a Pareto-efficient one? Recall that this game-theoretic approach has been developed for games with complete information and that the fundamental problem of public goods that we have confronted throughout this chapter is linked to the decentralized character of information. The appropriate framework for pursuing this problem further is the theory of games with incomplete information. (See Harsanyi 1967 for the theory and section 5.7* for an application to public goods.)

---

12. In fact, the core is very large since the power of the coalitions is limited by the impossibility of exclusion. When a coalition produces a public good, it cannot prevent the agents who are not in the coalition from benefiting from its use and simultaneously it cannot count on any output of the public good from these agents outside the coalition.

2.7*   "Non-Pure" Public Goods

2.7.1   Public Goods with Exclusion

It is often possible to exclude agents from some public goods, for example, cable television. Nonetheless, for a true public good without congestion, if we do not consider the informational problem of revealing Lindahl personalized prices, the social optimum precludes exclusion so that this type of good has no specificity for normative theory. However, enlightened by this chapter, we know that we must take this informational constraint into account in characterizing the social optimum. Moreover, there often exist additional institutional constraints of a political and ethical nature; for example, we might impose egalitarian contributions on financing the public good.

This problem must be posed in the general framework of the theory of the second best (chapter 7). Then the possibility of exclusion becomes an additional instrument of economic policy that usually makes possible a "second-best" optimum preferred to the one obtained if exclusion were not possible. (See exercise 3. Drèze 1980 gives a preliminary analysis.)

The possibility of exclusion is equally important when public goods give rise to *congestion*. Then it is better to divide the population into subgroups (clubs) that benefit from specific public goods.

Suppose that I agents of the economy are identical, with initial endowments w^i and with utility functions $U(x^i, y, n)$ that now depend on the number of members of the club. The optimal size of the club is then characterized by the problem

$$\underset{(x^i, z, y, n)}{\text{Max}}\ \ U(x^i, y, n)$$

subject to $nw^i - nx^i - z \geqslant 0$

$$g(z) - y \geqslant 0,$$

or

$$\underset{(z, n)}{\text{Max}}\ U\left(w^i - \frac{z}{n}, g(z), n\right).$$

When n is treated as a continuous variable, the first-order conditions are

$$n\frac{\partial U/\partial y}{\partial U/\partial x^i} = \frac{1}{g'}, \tag{16}$$

$$\frac{\partial U}{\partial n} = \frac{\partial(z/n)}{\partial n} \cdot \frac{\partial U}{\partial x^i}. \tag{17}$$

Equation (16) is the Bowen-Lindahl-Samuelson condition with identical agents. With n fixed, y is an ordinary public good. Equation (17) says that the disutility due to the congestion created by the last member added to the club exactly equals the marginal benefit that he generates by decreasing the per capita burden of financing the public good.

We mention a few of the problems posed by the theory of clubs. First, I now does have to be a multiple of n^*, the optimal size defined by (16) and (17). In general, this is a minor point that can be formally eliminated by considering a large number of agents. The nonconvexity of $U\left(w^i - \frac{z}{n}, g(z), n\right)$ in n is much more serious for descriptive theory. Clubs are likely to be fixed at sizes that are only local maxima and not the global maximum of U. Descriptive theory will depend crucially on: the method of financing the club, the behavior of the agents who change clubs, and the objective functions when agents are no longer identical. Not only do nonconvexities pose all the fundamental problems studied in chapter 3 for equilibrium theory, but the dynamics that come into play when people move are very different from the tâtonnement rules for prices to which we are accustomed.

2.7.2   Local Public Goods

The theory of local public goods has often been treated as a theory of clubs, without incorporating the scarcity of land. Tiebout (1956) proposed the following argument. Competition among "cities" to attract inhabitants and the mobility of agents leads, by a self-selection process, to the grouping of agents who have similar characteristics into the same city. The resulting uniformity of characteristics within a city alleviates the problem of preference revelation. When there is a large number of cities to which agents of each category may migrate, the result is Pareto optimal. This appealing idea, which gave rise to a few widely discussed econometric studies, is fraught with difficulties in light of the problems developed above (Bewley 1981, Pestiau 1983).

When free entry to cities (implicit in Tiebout's conception) is suppressed, we must take into account the scarcity of land. The integration of spatial economics and public economics can take place at several levels. Once the boundaries of the cities are established and the property rights to land are determined, we can analyze the distribution of agents among the various communities and the outputs of their local public goods.[13] Then the agents are influenced not only by the direct effect of the public goods on their utility functions, but also by the indirect effect these have on the value of land. If we were to make the boundaries of the cities endogenous and study the optimal division of an area into autonomous communities with respect to their decisions on local public goods, a complete theory of fiscal decentralization would be forthcoming. Here our purpose is not to summarize this vast literature but simply to draw a few lessons from Tiebout's solution to the free rider problem.

The numerous existing models differ according to:

—the method of decision-making concerning public goods within each community. These methods include all the possibilities encountered in section 2.5, along with entrepreneurial theories in which a city manager maximizes one of: the population, the value of the land, or the welfare of a representative agent. Here the community is likened to a firm, so that maximizing land value is analogous to maximizing the value of the firm's assets.

—the assumed degree of mobility and, when there is mobility, the agents' knowledge of the consequences of migration.

The hope expressed by Tiebout of resolving free rider problems by mobility has not been formalized in theory. Nonconvexities and externalities of all kinds cast legitimate doubt on the existence of a decentralized solution to the problem of the optimal distribution of economic agents among communities to procure local public goods, whether or not the size of the community is endogenous. We must point out that as soon as space constraints linked with heterogeneity of tastes or production complementarities give rise to optima with nonidentical agents, decentralization of information makes Tiebout's solution to the free rider problem inapplicable. To be sure, it is possible to construct a few special cases where Tiebout's mechanism works; but these stylized cases lack realism. At best, Tiebout's approach decreases the heterogeneity of populations living in the same locality.

Consequently, we are left to consider how the location of economic

13. See Greenberg (1983), for example.

agents depends essentially on other motives (workplace, natural advantages, exogenity of sites, etc.); then the existence of mixed communities follows. In this scenario, the fundamental problems associated with the allocation of public goods persist at the local level.

References

Bergstrom, T., D. Rubinfeld, and P. Shapiro 1982, "Micro-based estimates of demand functions for local school expenditures," *Econometrica*, 50, 1183–1206.

Bewley, T., 1981, "A critique of Tiebout's theory of local public expenditure," *Econometrica*, 49, 713–740.

Champsaur, P., 1975, "How to share the cost of a public good," *International Journal of Game Theory*, 4, 113–129.

———1976, "Neutrality of planning procedures in an economy with public goods," *Review of Economic Studies*, 43, 293–300.

Drèze, J., 1980, "Public goods with exclusion," *Journal of Public Economics*, 13, 5–24.

Drèze, J., and D. De la Vallée Poussin 1971, "A tâtonnement process for public goods," *Review of Economic Studies*," 38, 133–150.

Foley, D., 1967, "Resource allocation and the public sector," *Yale Economic Essays*, 7, 45–98.

Greenberg, J., 1983, "Local public goods with mobility: Existence and optimality of general equilibrium," *Journal of Economic Theory*, 30, 17–33.

Harsanyi, J., 1967/68, "Games with incomplete information played by 'Bayesian players'," I–III, *Management Science*, 14, 159–189, 320–334, 486–502.

Martinez-Vasquez, J., 1982, "Fiscal incidence at the local level," *Econometrica*, 50, 1207–1218.

Milleron, J. C., 1972, "Theory of value with public goods: A survey article," *Journal of Economic Theory*, 5, 419–477.

Musgrave, R. A., 1959, *The Theory of Public Finance*, McGraw-Hill.

Musgrave, R. A., and A. T. Peacock, eds., 1958, *Classics in the Theory of Public Finance*, Macmillan (translation of Wicksell 1896).

Pestieau, P., 1983, "Fiscal mobility and local public goods: A survey of the empirical and theoretical studies of the Tiebout model," in J. F. Thisse and H. G. Zoller, eds., *Locational Analysis of Public Facilities*, North-Holland.

Postlewaite, A., and J. Roberts 1976, "The incentives for price-taking behavior in large exchange economies," *Econometrica*, 44, 115–128.

Roberts, J., 1976, "The incentives for correct revelation of preferences and the number of consumers," *Journal of Public Economics*, 6, 359–374.

Samuelson, P. A., 1954, "The pure theory of public expenditure," *Review of Economics and Statistics*, 36, 387–389.

Shapley, L. S., 1971, "Cores of convex games," *International Journal of Game Theory*, 1, 11–26.

Tiebout, C. M., 1956, "A pure theory of local expenditures," *Journal of Political Economy*, 64, 416–424.

Wicksell, K., 1896, *Finanztheorie Untersuchungen Und das Steuerwesen Schwedens*, Jena (a translation is Musgrave and Peacock 1958).

Wolfelsperger, A., 1969, *Les biens collectifs*, PUF, Paris.

Recommended Reading

1. Musgrave 1959, chapters 4, 5 (history of the subject).

2. Samuelson 1954 (decentralization and Lindahl equilibrium).

3. Champsaur 1975 (public goods and game theory).

4. Drèze and De la Vallée Poussin 1971 (public goods and planning).

5. Musgrave and Peacock 1958 (in particular the papers of Lindahl and Wicksell).

6. Milleron 1972 (advanced theory).

7. Bergstrom, Rubinfeld, and Shapiro 1982 (estimates of demand for a local public good.

3 Nonconvexities

In much of economic theory, convexity assumptions play a crucial role. The convexity of preferences, represented here by the quasi-concavity of the utility functions, is justified by the "law of decreasing marginal utility" and by an interest in diversification. However, even though both may be acceptable much of the time, these properties do not represent inviolable axioms. It is easy to imagine a consumer who is indifferent between one glass of cognac and one glass of brandy but who prefers one glass of either of these liquors to a combination of half a glass of cognac and half a glass of brandy. To be sure, the argument for diversification resurfaces if we consider consumption over a longer period; however, the convexity assumption is used to establish the existence of equilibrium at each point in time. The convexity of production sets is justified by the law of decreasing returns to which it is still easier to find exceptions. Don't we often think that the larger a firm is, the more efficient it is, at least up to a certain size?

In the first part of this chapter, we consider the difficulties created by nonconvexities. In the second part, from the perspective of equilibrium and optimum theory, we see that nonconvexities are often admissible if the number of economic agents is large. (Actually, this is an implicit assumption of the theory of perfect competition.) Finally, we consider the appropriate approach when we can no longer appeal to the assumption of a large number of agents.

3.1 Consequences of Nonconvexities

3.1.1 Discontinuity of Optimal Behavior

Consider a consumer with nonconvex preferences as represented in figure 3.1. Moreover, assume that his initial endowment consists only of good 1 (point A). When the price of good 2 is p^1 (resp. p^3), he chooses the consumption vector x^1 (resp. x^3). When the price of good 2 is p^2, he is indifferent between x^2 and x'^2. Whichever way he resolves this indifference, it is important to observe that when the price goes from $p^2 + \varepsilon$ to $p^2 - \varepsilon$ his choice goes from the neighborhood of x^2 to the neighborhood of x'^2 with a discontinuity at p^2.

The agent's demand function is discontinuous. However, the proof of the existence of a perfectly competitive equilibrium uses continuous demand functions. It is not difficult to construct examples where the nonconvexity of preferences leads to the nonexistence of equilibrium. The primary re-

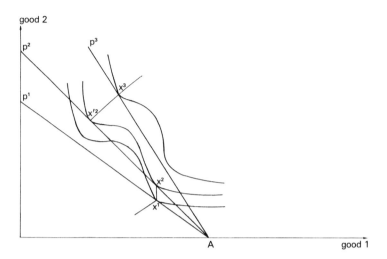

Figure 3.1

quirement of our theory, logical consistency, is not even satisfied. As the reader can see from figure 3.2, the same discontinuity phenomenon applies to a producer who maximizes his profits on a nonconvex production set.

Despite these discontinuities, if a competitive equilibrium exists, it is still a Pareto optimum (refer to the proof of this proposition not requiring a convexity assumption). But what about the case where no competitive equilibrium exists?

3.1.2 Difficulties of Decentralization

Return to figure 3.2 and assume that a planner wants the firm to maintain the outputs A and B or C. To support B (or C), he announces the price vector p^1 (or p^3) which does indeed lead a profit-maximizing firm to choose B (or C). On the other hand, there is no price vector that supports A as a decentralized optimum. Thus, the second fundamental theorem of welfare economics (that is, to any Pareto optimum we can associate prices and incomes that allow the decentralization of this optimum) does not hold.

By observation, it is possible to define a "nonlinear" system of prices $p(y)$ that would support decentralization of A by an agent maximizing $p(y)y$. In other words, we could define an objective function $\phi(y) = p(y)y$ which would yield a maximum at A (figure 3.3). The dashed curves characterize the isoprofit contours of the function $\phi(y)$. However, calculating this function $\phi(y)$ is quite complex due to its informational requirements.

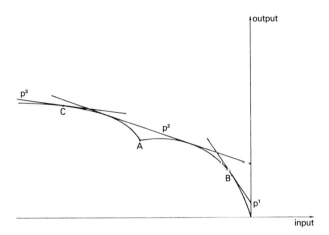

Figure 3.2

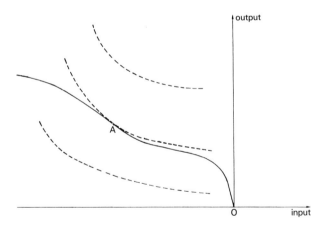

Figure 3.3

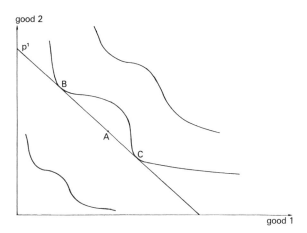

good 2

good 1

Figure 3.4

3.2   Convexity due to the Assumption of a Large Number of Agents

To demonstrate the existence of an equilibrium, the continuity of the aggregate demand function or the per capita demand function is important. Might the aggregate demand function be continuous even when individual demand functions are discontinuous? When there are a large number of agents, this is almost true.

3.2.1   Exchange Economy[1]

Imagine an economy consisting of a large number of agents I, all having the same preferences (figure 3.4) and the same initial endowment (point A). Let

$$x_B = (x_{1B}, x_{2B}); \quad w_A = (w_{1A}, w_{2A}), \quad x_C = (x_{1C}, x_{2C})$$

be the bundles of goods associated with points B, A, and C.

For the price vector p^1, each agent wants to consume the consumption bundle corresponding to either point B or point C. Can we obtain equality of supply and demand on both markets? The answer is yes if a proportion $\alpha_1 = AB/BC$ of the agents consume bundle x_C and a proportion $\alpha_2 = AC/BC$ consume bundle x_B. Then

---

1. Here our presentation is very informal. See Malinvaud (1969) or Hildenbrand and Kirman (1976) for rigorous formulations.

$$I\alpha_1 x_C + I\alpha_2 x_B = I w_A$$

or

$$I\alpha_1(x_C - w_A) = I\alpha_2(w_A - x_B);$$

that is, taking good 1,[2] we have

$$I\alpha_1(x_{1C} - w_{1A}) = I\alpha_2(w_{1A} - x_{1B})$$

$$\text{demand} = \text{supply}.$$

The price vector p^1, $I\alpha_1$ agents consuming x_C and $I\alpha_2$ agents consuming x_B, together appear to characterize a feasible competitive equilibrium. However, $I\alpha$ may not be an integer. Nonetheless, when I is very large, if $|\alpha_1 I|^3$ agents consume x_C and $|\alpha_2 I|$ agents consume x_B, we almost have an equilibrium. One agent remains, and he must consume $I w_A - |\alpha_1 I| x_C - |\alpha_2 I| x_B$, which is neither x_C nor x_B. In other words, he is left a consumption bundle that does not represent his optimal choice. If one agent out of I is not optimizing, it is almost a competitive equilibrium.[4] Observe that we have obtained the same result as we would have if we had considered the agents' indifference curves to be convex envelopes of the original indifference curves (figure 3.5).

However, note that preferences convexified in this way are not strictly convex. Demands are correspondences, not functions. Upper semicontinuity of the per capita demand correspondence is sufficient to prove the existence of an equilibrium (which is interpreted as an ε-equilibrium of the initial economy). Nonetheless we have lost one aspect of the decentralized nature of a competitive equilibrium (with respect to a situation where the preferences are strictly convex). In this model, there is nothing to explain how the correct proportion of agents who will choose B (or C) is determined. This problem is similar to that encountered when we seek decentralized firm behavior with a linear production technology.

3.2.2   Economy with Production[5]

Consider a large number of firms each with a production set as represented in figure 3.6, that is, with costs first decreasing and then increasing. By an

2. Then, supply equals demand on the market for good 2 by Walras's law.
3. $|\alpha_1 I| = $ integer part of $\alpha_1 I$.
4. Another approach consists in giving x_B or x_C to this agent at the cost that the supply-demand equilibrium is not perfect (ε-equilibrium).
5. See chapter 7 of Arrow and Hahn (1971).

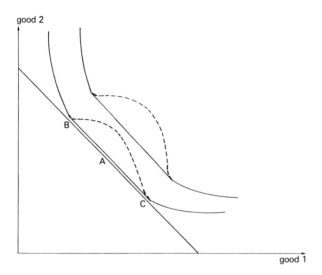

Figure 3.5

argument similar to that used above, any vector B that belongs to the convex envelope of the individual production set is a production vector that is feasible on average if a proportion $\alpha_1 = OB/OA$ of the firms produce at A and a proportion $\alpha_2 = AB/OA$ at O. A price vector normal to OA permits the decentralization of such as allocation.

Thus the assumption of a large number of agents supports the notion of an approximate competitive equilibrium that exists even with nonconvexities in consumption and production of the type represented in figures 3.4 and 3.6. While the assumption of large numbers is acceptable for consumers, it must often be rejected for producers. Moreover, there may exist firms for which average cost is always decreasing (figure 3.7) so that the foregoing argument is not applicable.

3.3   Marginal Cost Pricing

Remaining for consideration is the case of a large firm of the type characterized in figure 3.6 or of a group of firms of the type characterized in figure 3.7. Figure 3.7b corresponds to the case of a firm with a fixed cost OA and constant marginal cost. Given any price vector, the firm wishes either to produce an infinite amount or shut down. It is perfectly obvious that no

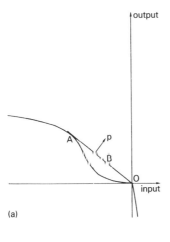

(a)

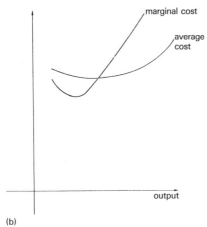

(b)

Figure 3.6

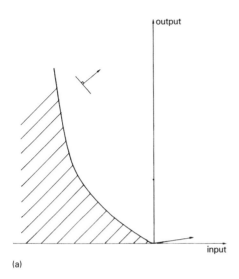

(a)

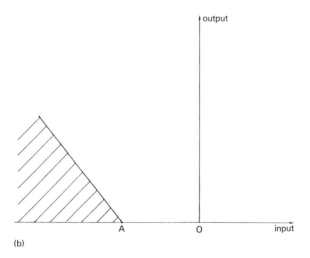

(b)

Figure 3.7

competitive equilibrium for which the firm has a nonzero level of activity
can exist. When such firms exist, their behavior must be noncompetitive
and we can try to model this economy using the concept of a monopolistic
equilibrium.[6]

However, even when such a monopolistic equilibrium exists, it is surely
not a Pareto optimum (since the firm equates its marginal revenue and not
the price of its product to its marginal cost). In a convex environment, such
an equilibrium cannot be Pareto optimal; in a nonconvex environment this
is also generally true. However, we observe that the maximization of
$p(x)x - C(x)$, where $p(x)$ is the inverse demand function and $C(x)$ the cost
function, corresponds to a particular nonlinear pricing schedule. Sometimes, by correcting this nonlinear pricing schedule with an appropriate
tax $(p(x) + t)$, we can decentralize the optimum.

Beginning with Marshall's work in 1870, recognition of the problems
faced by the competitive mechanism in the presence of increasing returns
has led to the theory of marginal cost pricing (initially developed by Lerner
1933 and Lange 1936 for socialist economies, then by Hotelling 1938, who
stated the principle that the social optimum requires selling "each thing"
at marginal cost). First we study an example.

Consider a two-good economy consisting of one consumer and one
producer with a nonconvex technology. The initial endowment, made up
solely of good 1, is w_1. The Pareto optima are characterized by the problem

Max $U(x_1, x_2)$

subject to $x_1 + g(x_2) = w_1$ with $g' > 0$,

where g^{-1} is the production function of the nonconvex producer which
yields an output of good 2 using good 1 as the input. Therefore a necessary
condition for an optimum is

$$-\frac{\partial U}{\partial x_1}\frac{\partial g}{\partial x_2} + \frac{\partial U}{\partial x_2} = 0$$

or

6. See chapter 6 of Arrow and Hahn (1971) for such an attempt; unfortunately we do not know
how to define a "proper" set of assumptions that supports the proof of the existence of a
monopolistic equilibrium (Roberts and Sonnenschein 1977). See also section 3.5*.

$$\frac{\partial U/\partial x_2}{\partial U/\partial x_1} = \frac{\partial g}{\partial x_2}.$$

As always, the marginal rate of substitution must equal the marginal rate of transformation. However, this is now only a necessary condition (figure 3.8).

Point A satisfies the first-order conditions but it is not a Pareto optimum. Can we decentralize the Pareto optimum, point O, using the rule of marginal cost pricing? Let x_2^o be the level of output associated with the optimum at point O. Consider the following rule imposed on a (public) firm: "produce the level of output x_2^o and sell at marginal cost."

Normalize the price vector so that $p_1 = 1$. Therefore, the price of good 2 is $dg/dx_2(x_2^o)$. The consumer facing prices $(1, dg/dx_2(x_2^o))$ equates his marginal rate of substitution to the price ratio, so that

$$\frac{\partial U/\partial x_2(x_1, x_2)}{\partial U/\partial x_1(x_1, x_2)} = \frac{dg}{dx_2}(x_2^o).$$

The (negative) profit of the (public) firm is given by

$$D = x_2^o \frac{dg}{dx_2}(x_2^o) - g(x_2^o).$$

If the loss is covered by a lump-sum tax on the consumer, his budget constraint is written as

$$x_1 + x_2 \frac{dg}{dx_2}(x_2^o) = w + D.$$

Therefore the optimal choice of good 1 for the consumer is $w - g(x_2^o)$, for which supply equals demand on both markets.

We note that at prices $(1, dg/dx_2(x_2^o))$, point O is not even a local maximum for the firm, so the decentralization of x_2^o cannot be achieved (with "linear" prices). The above example suggests that when decentralization of the output level is impossible, cost minimization by firms nonetheless remains as a decentralizable objective in a nonconvex environment. Arrow and Hurwicz (1960) have shown that productive efficiency may not be compatible with cost minimization.

Consider a firm having two production processes each producing good 1. With process A (resp. B), good 1 is produced using good 2 (resp. 3) according to technologies characterized by the concave inverse production

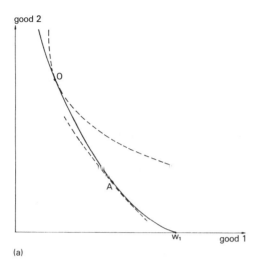

(a)

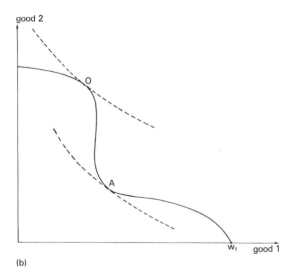

(b)

Figure 3.8

functions

$$g_A(y_1^A) \qquad g_B(y_1^B)$$

that define the quantities of good 2 and 3 required to produce y_1^A and y_1^B units of good 1. Cost minimization is written as

$$\text{Min}\{p_2 g_A(y_1^A) + p_3 g_B(y_1^B)\}$$

subject to $y_1^A + y_1^B = y_1,$

or

$$\text{Min } \psi(y_1^A) = p_2 g_A(y_1^A) + p_3 g_B(y_1 - y_1^A)$$

subject to $0 \leqslant y_1^A \leqslant y_1.$

Since ψ is a concave function, it achieves its minimum at one of the boundaries of the interval over which it is defined, that is,

$$y_1^A = 0 \qquad y_1^B = y_1$$

or

$$y_1^A = y_1 \qquad y_1^B = 0.$$

If w_2 and w_3 are the initial endowments of good 2 and 3, we have, for any $(p_2, p_3) > 0$, either

$$g_A(y_1^A) < w_2$$

or

$$g_B(y_1^B) < w_3.$$

Obviously, this contradicts the condition of optimality in production, because the problem

$$\text{Max}\{y_1^A + y_1^B\}$$

subject to $g_A(y_1^A) \leqslant w_2$

$$g_B(y_1^B) \leqslant w_3$$

yields (y_1^{A*}, y_2^{B*}) as the unique solution defined by

$$g_A(y_1^{A*}) = w_2 \qquad g_B(y_1^{B*}) = w_3.$$

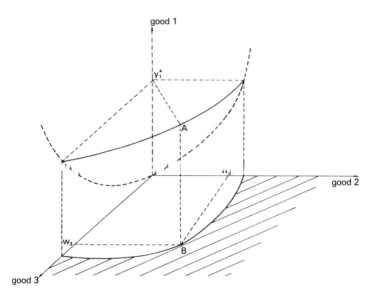

Figure 3.9

Thus optimality is not necessarily compatible with the rule of cost minimization (and therefore with the rule of marginal cost pricing, which is no
longer defined in this example).

In figure 3.9, point A represents the production optimum. The projection
onto the plane with $y_1 = 0$ of the section of the production set with output
larger than y_1^* is the nonconvex area (shaded). Point B corresponds to a cost
maximum, not a minimum. If, on the contrary, this set were convex, point
B would be decentralizable by cost minimization (see Guesnerie 1975).

More generally, consider an economy with I consumers having convex
preferences and J firms one of which, firm 1, has a nonconvex technology.
Moreover, firm 1 is the only producer of good 1, a final good. We define
an *economy with production and distribution* as one in which the gross
income of consumer i is a constant fraction δ^i of national income:[7]

$$R^i = \delta^i \left(\sum_{j=1}^{J} p \cdot y^j + p \cdot w \right).$$

Moreover, assume that the production function of firm 1, $y_1^1 = f^1(y_2^1, \ldots,$

7. This allows us to avoid the difficulties associated with financing the losses of the nonconvex
firm.

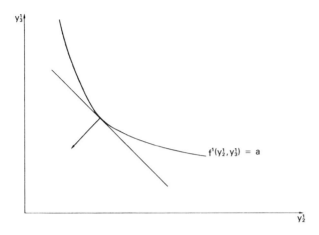

Figure 3.10

y_L^1), is continuously differentiable and, for any output level a, $B(a) = \{y^1: f^1(y_2^1, \ldots, y_L^1) \geq a\}$ is a strictly convex set.

If there is a one-to-one correspondence (given a normalization constant) between the boundary points $B(a)$ and the input price vectors $(p_2, \ldots, p_L)$ (for an example see figure 3.10), so that these points can be decentralized by cost minimization; to any price vector $(p_2 \ldots p_L)$ and any output level a, there corresponds a production vector on the boundary of the production set characterized by the solution to the problem

$$\text{Min} \sum_{k=2}^{L} p_k y_k^1 \tag{1}$$

subject to $f^1(y_2^1, \ldots, y_L^1) = a.$ \tag{2}

Solutions are characterized by (2) and

$$p_k = -\lambda \frac{\partial f^1}{\partial y_k^1}, \quad k = 2, \ldots, L. \tag{3}$$

Moreover, the Lagrangian multiplier λ is equal to marginal cost at the output level a.

The orthogonality of the price vector p to the boundary of the production set is written as

$$(p_1, p_2, \ldots, p_L) = \mu\left(1, -\frac{\partial f^1}{\partial y_2^1}, \ldots, -\frac{\partial f^1}{\partial y_L^1}\right).$$

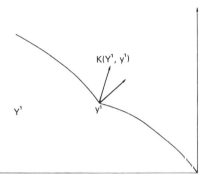

Figure 3.11

Indeed, by differentiating the production function $y_1^1 = f^1(y_2^1, \ldots, y_L^1)$ we obtain

$$dy_1^1 = \sum_{k=2}^{L} \frac{\partial f^1}{\partial y_k^1} dy_k^1$$

or

$$(dy_1^1, dy_2^1, \ldots, dy_L^2)\left(1, -\frac{\partial f^1}{\partial y_2^1}, \ldots, -\frac{\partial f^1}{\partial y_L^1}\right)' = 0.$$

Therefore, the vector $(1, -\partial f^1/\partial y_2^1, \ldots, -\partial f^1/\partial y_L^1)$ is normal to $(y_1^1, y_2^1, \ldots, y_L^1)$ on the boundary of the production set.

If $(p_2, \ldots, p_L)$ are the prices in problem (1), then $\mu = \lambda$ and $p_1 = \lambda$, that is, price is equal to marginal cost. Thus, for a firm that minimizes costs, the orthogonality of the price vector to the production set at a given point implies selling the output associated with this point at marginal cost. More generally, if the boundary of the production set is not characterized by a differentiable function, the rule of marginal cost pricing is generalizable by requiring the price vector to belong to the cone normal to Y^1 at y^1 (see figure 3.11 and Cornet 1983).

A *marginal cost pricing equilibrium* for an economy with production and distribution is a price vector $p^* \in \mathbf{R}^L$ and an allocation $(x^{*1}, \ldots, x^{*I}, y^{*1}, \ldots, y^{*J})$ such that

(a) $p^* \equiv \mu[1, -\partial f^1/\partial y_2^1(y^{*1}), \ldots, -\partial f^1/\partial y_L^1(y^{*1})]$ or $p^* \in K(Y^1, y^{*1})$;
(b) $p^* y^{*j}$ maximizes $p^* y^j$ in $Y^j, j = 2, \ldots, J$;

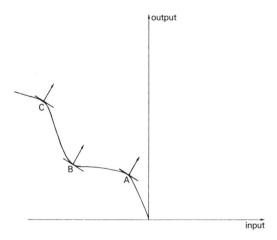

Figure 3.12

(c) x^{*i} maximizes $U^i(x^i)$ in $\{x^i : p^*x^i \leqslant R^{*i}\}$, $i = 1, \ldots, I$;
(d) supply equals demand in all markets.

Imagine the following mechanism inspired by the Walrasian tâtonnement process. Prices are proposed and then each convex agent announces his optimal consumption or production plan and each nonconvex producer announces his plans for activity levels solving the first-order conditions of profit maximization (points A, B, C of figure 3.12). We adjust prices until the announced behavior of agents yields compatible plans, that is, plans for which supply equals demand for all goods. Beato (1982) has shown that such equilibria do exist.

However, this mechanism is fraught with difficulties. As figures 3.8 and 3.12 suggest, multiple equilibria exist, of which some are not Pareto optimal. The difficulties encountered by the principle of marginal cost pricing in a general equilibrium context conform to the result of Calsamiglia (1977), who shows that decentralization in a nonconvex environment is impossible with finite-dimensional messages. Therefore, we have to set up a collective decision-making procedure that allows a transmission of information exceeding the amount that would be transmitted by a finite number of messages.

Moreover, for the case of many consumers, Guesnerie (1975) gives an example of a private property economy in which no output compatible with decentralization according to the marginal cost pricing rule is Pareto optimal. Income distributions exist for which no Pareto-optimal allocation can be achieved by a marginal cost pricing equilibrium. (Beato and Mas-Colell (1983) have even shown that when there exist several nonconvex firms, productive efficiency might not be realized). This observation is fundamental to our understanding of the nonconvex environment. Indeed, the issues of efficiency and distribution cannot be separated here as they can be in the convex environment. Any collective solution that attempts to achieve a Pareto optimum may have to modify the income distribution in nonconvex environments. Recently, Dierker (1984) and Quinzii (1980) have found sufficient conditions applying jointly to demand and supply so that a marginal cost pricing equilibrium (or all the equilibria) will be Pareto optimal.

3.4   Several Solutions

3.4.1   Politico-economic Equilibrium[8]

Consider a production economy with I consumers having convex preferences and J firms, one of which, firm 1, has a nonconvex technology. Let firm 1 be the sole producer of good 1, which is a final good. As above, we define an economy with production and distribution (E, δ) as an economy in which the gross income of consumer i is a constant fraction δ^i of national income (now excluding the nonconvex firm) so that

$$R^i = \delta^i \left[\sum_{j=2}^{J} \Pi^j(p) + p \cdot w \right] \equiv \delta^i R(r),$$

where

$$\Pi^j(p) = \text{Max } p \cdot y^j, \quad y^j \in Y^j.$$

Let r^i be the share of the loss of firm 1 that agent i must bear ($r = r^1, \ldots, r^I$); therefore the disposable income of consumer i is $\tilde{R}^i = R^i - r^i$.

A government policy proposal relative to the price vector p ($p \in R^L$, $p \geqslant 0$) is a pair (y^1, r) such that

$$py^1 + \sum_{i=1}^{I} r^i = 0, \quad y^1 \in Y^1.$$

In an economy with production and distribution (E, δ), a government

8. See Beato (1978).

policy proposal (y^1, r) relative to the price vector p is overturned by a policy proposal $(\hat{y}^1, \hat{r})$ if there exist $\hat{x}^1, \ldots, \hat{x}^I$ such that

(a) $p \cdot \hat{x}^i \leqslant \delta^i R(p) - \hat{r}^i, i = 1, \ldots, I,$
(b) $u^i(\hat{x}^i) \geqslant u^i(\bar{x}^i), i = 1, \ldots, I, \forall \bar{x}^i : p\bar{x}^i \leqslant \delta^i R(p) - r^i,$

with at least one strict inequality, and

(c) $\displaystyle\sum_{i=1}^{I} \hat{x}_1^i - \hat{y}_1^1 - w_1 = 0.$

We note that the government policy proposal is concerned with the compatibility of supply and demand only on market 1 and it assumes that prices p remain unchanged.

   A *politico-economic equilibrium* for (E, δ) is then an $(I + J + 1)$-tuple (x^i), (y^j), p of R^L and a vector r of R^I such that

(i) x^i maximizes $U^i(x^i)$ in $\{x^i : px^i \leqslant \delta^i R(p) - r^i; x^i \in X^i\}$;
(ii) $y^j \in Y^j, py^j \geqslant py'^j \quad \forall y'^j \in Y^j, j = 2, \ldots, J$;
(iii) (y^1, r) is a government policy proposal for prices p, and it cannot be overturned;
(iv) $\sum_{i=1}^{I} x^i - \sum_{j=1}^{J} y^j - w = 0.$

THEOREM 1   If $[(\bar{x}^i), (\bar{y}^j), \bar{p}, \bar{r}]$ is a politico-economic equilibrium for (E, δ), then $(\bar{x}^i)$ and $(\bar{y}^j)$ is a Pareto optimal allocation.

Proof   Assume that it is not Pareto optimal; $\exists(\hat{x}^i), (\hat{y}^j)$ for $i = 1, \ldots,$ $I : U^i(\hat{x}^i) \geqslant U^i(\bar{x}^i)$ with at least one strict equality and

$$\sum_{i=1}^{I} \hat{x}^i - \sum_{j=1}^{J} \hat{y}^j - w = 0.$$

Let $\hat{r}^i = \bar{p}\bar{x}^i - \bar{p}\hat{x}^i + \bar{r}^i$. Then

$$\sum_{i=1}^{I} \hat{r}^i = \bar{p} \sum_{i=1}^{I} \bar{x}^i - \bar{p} \sum_{i=1}^{I} \hat{x}^i + \sum_{i=1}^{I} \bar{r}^i$$

$$= \bar{p}\left(\sum_{j=1}^{J} \bar{y}^j + w\right) - \bar{p}\left(\sum_{j=1}^{J} \hat{y}^j + w\right) - \bar{p}\bar{y}^1,$$

or

$$\sum_{i=1}^{I} \hat{r}^i = \bar{p} \sum_{j=2}^{J} (\bar{y}^j - \hat{y}^j) - \bar{p}\hat{y}^1,$$

from which, since producers maximize profits, we derive

$$\sum_{i=1}^{I} \hat{r}^i + \bar{p}\hat{y}^1 \geqslant 0.$$

Therefore, $\exists (\hat{r}^1, \ldots, \hat{r}^I) \leqslant (\hat{r}^1, \ldots, \hat{r}^I)$ with

$$\sum_{i=1}^{I} \hat{r}^i + \bar{p}\hat{y}^1 = 0.$$

We note that

$$\bar{p}\hat{x}^i = \bar{p}\bar{x}^i + \bar{r}^i - \hat{r}^i \leqslant \bar{p}\bar{r}^i + \bar{r}^i \qquad \hat{r}^i{}_!$$

Therefore

$$\bar{p}\hat{x}^i \leqslant \delta^i R(\bar{p}) - \hat{r}^i.$$

Consequently, $(\bar{y}^1, \bar{r})$ is overturned by $(\hat{y}^1, \hat{r})$. Hence the contradiction. ∎

In a politico-economic equilibrium, all possible financial implications are considered but at fixed prices (p fixed), that is, by taking a linear approximation of the nonconvex production set. Then we can ask, Does a politico-economic equilibrium always exist? Since a politico-economic equilibrium is always optimal, an affirmative answer would mean that an optimum can always be achieved by selling at marginal cost and distributing the loss of the nonconvex firm. Given the problem raised by Guesnerie (1975) and mentioned in the preceding section, this would mean that redistributing income by allocating the financial burden of the loss of the nonconvex firm among the consumers would lead to the exact set of income distributions supporting Pareto optima. Such a result would be truly incredible. In fact, Malinvaud (1969) gave an example in which the only Pareto optimum is not achievable by a politico-economic equilibrium. Since any politico-economic equilibrium is Pareto optimal, we can conclude that no politico-economic equilibrium exists in his example. Thus, even if we accept the concept of a politico-economic equilibrium (for a critique of the concept, refer to chapter 2), we do not have a solution for all situations. However, this approach is interesting because it clearly shows the public-good nature of the loss of a nonconvex firm using marginal cost pricing.

3.4.2   A Planning Method

In a two-good economy, consider a planning procedure for a nonconvex firm when the planning center's objective function is $U(x_1, x_2)$. The techno-

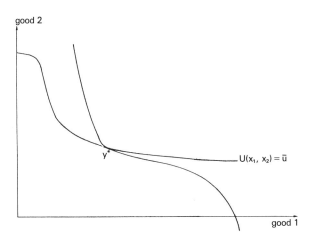

good 2

$U(x_1, x_2) = \bar{u}$

y^*

good 1

Figure 3.13

logical possibilities of the firm are represented in figure 3.13, where y^* is the optimum.

The procedure unfolds in the following manner: We assume that a vector $a \gg y^*$ is known. Starting from $Y^0 = (a - R_+^2)$, we construct a sequence of fictional production sets that contain the relevant part of Y. The center asks the firm to transmit an efficient production vector smaller than a. Let y^1 be such a vector; the center concludes that any vector larger than y^1 is not feasible and constructs a new approximation of Y, that is,

$$Y^1 = Y^0 - Y^0 \cap \{y^1 + R_+^2\},$$

which defines v^1 and v^2 (figure 3.14).

Using its objective function, the center chooses the preferred bundle from v^1 and v^2, say for example v^1. Then the center requests an efficient production vector y^2 less than v^1, and eliminates $y^2 + R_+^2$, and so forth (figure 3.15).

The subsequent production vectors obtained by maximizing U on successive approximations of the production set converge to the optimal production vector under very general conditions (Crémer 1978). The essential characteristic of this procedure is that the center must remember all the approximations to the production set, that is, the set of $\{v^i\}$ and $\{y^i\}$. Precisely because of the nonconvexity, the procedure may wander around in an irrelevant area for a few iterations. This contrasts with planning

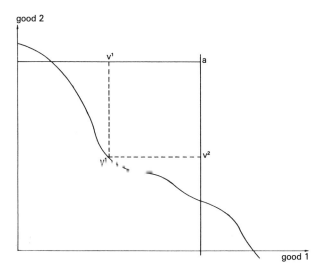

Figure 3.14

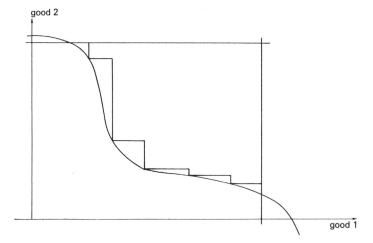

Figure 3.15

procedures in nonconvex environments that use only the last transmitted message. If we used only local information at each iteration, we would converge at best to a local optimum (Heal 1971).

3.4.3 Regulation of a Monopoly

As we have seen above, the optimal organization of an industry may require only one firm. Instead of nationalizing such an industry and organizing production itself, the government could grant monopoly rights to a firm and then control the monopolist with various instruments. Let $C(y)$ be the cost function of this firm and $p(y)$ the inverse demand function decreasing in its argument. At the optimum, price must equal marginal cost, that is,

$$p(y^*) = C'(y^*).$$

However, we also know that monopolistic behavior leads to equating marginal cost to marginal revenue given by $p(y) + p'(y)y$. We try to regulate this monopoly by using a tax t per unit of output sold. Then the monopolist will maximize

$$(p(y) - t)y - C(y),$$

from which we derive the first-order condition

$$p'(y)y + p(y) - t = C'(y),$$

and the tax which restores optimality is calculated to be

$$t^* = p'(y^*)y^* = -\frac{p(y^*)}{e(y^*)} < 0,$$

where $e(y^*)$ is the demand elasticity at y^*.

We notice, first, that the tax is in fact a subsidy. We know that a monopolist will produce less than the optimal output in order to increase profits. Therefore, the monopolist must be encouraged to produce more by subsidization. Insofar as there is no income distribution problem, this is an appropriate policy. Second, the foregoing argument, based on the first-order condition, is valid if the profit function is concave in y; but such may not be the case due either to increasing returns or even to the fact that revenue is the product of $p(y)$ and y. In this situation, productive efficiency may be impossible to establish. The intuition for this phenomenon is shown in figure 3.16.

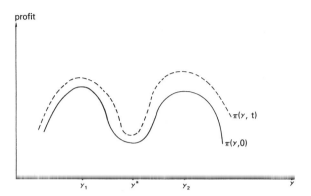

Figure 3.16

We denote by $\pi(y, t)$ the monopolist's profit as a function of the production level y and the subsidy t per unit of output. Assume that, in the absence of a subsidy, profit $\pi(y, 0)$ achieves its maximum at y_1. As the firm is subsidized, it produces a bit more output but still less than y^*. As the subsidy is increased, a level is reached where the firm is induced to produce y_2, an amount much larger than y^*, and any further increase in the subsidy yields output larger than y_2. However, there exists no value for the subsidy that will "decentralize" y^*.

Furthermore, the optimal subsidy will often be the one that increases output as much as possible before the jump to y_2 occurs, that is, in an area where small variations in the parameters of the problem give rise to large discontinuities in optimal behavior. Note that the difficulties encountered here concerning the regulation of a monopolist by taxation will resurface in any policy attempting to regulate a deviant agent who has an objective function with many local maxima. (See Guesnerie and Laffont 1978 for an in-depth study.)

If the monopolist can use a two-part pricing schedule, that is, a unit price p and a fixed premium a, he will always produce at the optimal level. By using the fixed premium, he can extract all the surplus that the consumers derive from his product; therefore it is in his self-interest to maximize this surplus net of cost. In this case, obviously only distributional considerations can justify public intervention. If the consumers have heterogeneous tastes, this two-part pricing scheme requires personalized premiums, which are in general impossible to compute (the analysis must be conducted in a framework of imperfect information, as discussed in chapter 5). Moreover, decentralizing the Pareto optima by two-part pricing schedules cannot be generalized beyond a simple two-good economy (Quinzii 1986).

When the monopolist produces many goods, the nonconvexities become quite varied. Then we can ask whether a firm is a natural monopoly for all of these goods, that is, whether or not there would be any economic loss in having many firms producing some of these goods. A firm may experience globally increasing returns, so that it is the only one that should be producing at the optimum, but all the while it may be unable to preclude competition for a particular product (see section 3.7*).

3.5*   Cournot Equilibrium with Free Entry

Perfect competition is formalized in models with a continuum of agents represented, for example, by the interval [0, 1]. Each agent corresponds to a point with measure zero in this interval, so that he can in no way influence exchange. In particular, in a competitive equilibrium the agent takes prices as given, which is the fundamental assumption of perfect competition. However, the relevance of this model depends on the answer to the question: In what respect do the results of this model approximate the results obtained in an economy with a large but finite number of economic agents? To answer this question, we must model exchange in an economy with a finite number of agents. One way to do so, in the Edgeworth tradition, consists of showing that the core allocations characterizing the results of cooperative exchange converge to the competitive equilibria. The other way, in the Cournot tradition, consists of studying the limit of oligopolistic equilibria when the number of firms in the oligopolistic industry is large.

Novshek (1980) has provided a brilliant analysis of this problem by proving the existence of Cournot equilibria with free entry that are close to "competitive exchange." This result holds even if firms have partially increasing returns as characterized by U-shaped cost curves so long as the firms are small enough with respect to the market. Let $F(.)$ be the inverse demand function (decreasing in its argument) and $C(.)$ be the average cost function available to all.

By replicating α times, the average cost function becomes $C_\alpha(.)$ with

$$C_\alpha(y) = C(\alpha y).$$

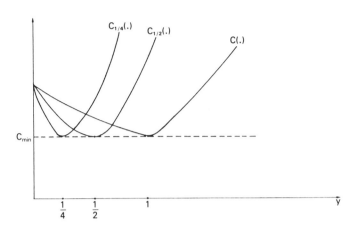

Figure 3.17

The minimum of the average cost curve remains constant as the size of the firm is reduced by replication (figure 3.17). Let n be the number of firms and $y^1, \ldots, y^n$ be the accompanying production vectors, so that

$$X = \sum_{i=1}^{n} y^i \qquad X^{-i} = \sum_{j \neq i} y^j.$$

Given $F(.)$, $C(.)$ and an α-order replication, a Cournot equilibrium with free entry is a number n^* of firms and production vectors $(y^{*1}, \ldots, y^{*n^*})$ such that

$$F(X^{*-i} + y^{*i})y^{*i} - C_\alpha(y^{*i})$$

$$\geqslant F(X^{*-i} + y^i)y^i - C_\alpha(y^i) \quad \forall y^j \in [0, \infty) \quad \forall j = 1, \ldots, n^*; \qquad \text{(a)}$$

$$F(X^* + y)y - C_\alpha(y) \leqslant 0 \quad \forall y \in [0, \infty). \qquad \text{(b)}$$

Here, (a) defines a Cournot equilibrium and (b) indicates that no firm has any interest in entering the market.

Under regularity assumptions, Novshek shows that an $\bar\alpha$ can be found such that, for any α-replication where $\alpha < \bar\alpha$, there exists a Cournot equilibrium with free entry. Moreover, the total output of the oligopolistic industry is no further than α away from the ideal competitive output, for which price is equal to the minimum of the average cost curve (a proof by contradiction). Consequently, price can only be very slightly above the minimum of the average cost curve in the Cournot equilibrium.

If we were to study the limit of Cournot equilibria by making the number of firms increase exogeneously we would find that, since the output of each firm in a symmetric Cournot equilibrium necessarily tends toward zero, price tends toward the right-hand limit of average cost as quantity tends toward zero. Therefore determining endogenously the number of firms from the condition of free entry leads to a qualitatively different result, one that formalizes the sacred economic wisdom claiming that competition leads firms to produce at the minimum of their average cost curves. The other aspect of the result, slightly more technical, is the possibility of proving the existence of Cournot equilibria with free entry as soon as firms are small enough with respect to the market. However, this is a partial-equilibrium result and significant difficulties arise when the problem is embedded in general equilibrium analysis (see Novshek and Sonnenschein 1978, Fraysse 1986).[9]

3.6*   Game Theory and Increasing Returns

One might think a priori that increasing returns facilitates the nonemptiness of the core since coalitions may benefit from more significant returns to scale, but this is not necessarily the case. (See Quinzii 1986 for sufficient conditions for the nonemptiness of the core in an economy with increasing returns.) The abovementioned marginal cost pricing poses the problem of financing losses which, in the absence of lump-sum transfers, leads to an economic loss.[10] The extreme solution consists in having Ramsey-Boiteux prices that balance the firm's budget (see section 7.1). Another solution consists in seeking an equitable sharing of costs by using prices derived from the Shapley value. (See Mirman and Taubman 1981 for a justification of this solution starting from economic axioms, and Billera, Heath, and Raanan 1978 for an example of its application.)

3.7*   Free Entry, the Theory of a Natural Monopoly, and Contestability

The analysis presented in this chapter has a major weakness: We have taken the industrial structure to be fixed. Thus, we have neglected the constraints

9. See problem 5 for a study of the control of a Cournot oligopolist.
10. This difficulty is similar to the one arising in the financing of a public good. See problem 2.

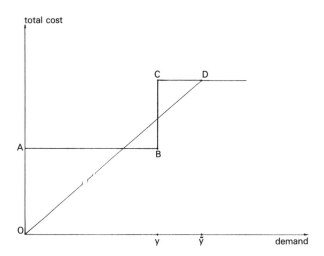

Figure 3.18

of the potential entry of competitors. The new industrial economics attempts to explain industrial structure by taking into account the possibility
of entry.

By a *natural monopoly*, we mean an industry with a cost function such
that no combination of several firms could produce at lower cost. This is
the situation if the cost function is globally strictly subadditive, that is, for
a set L of products,

$$C\left(\sum_{j=1}^{L} y^j\right) \leqslant \sum_{j=1}^{L} C(y^j) \quad \forall y^1, \ldots, y^L \in \mathbf{R}_+^L.$$

Then we can ask if there exists a price vector $p^m \in \mathbf{R}_+^L$ that allows the
monopolist to preclude the entry of competitors.

We will call such a price vector p^m *sustainable* if the profits of the
monopolist are nonnegative given p^m (when the monopolist satisfies completely all the market demand), and if there exists no price vector for an
entrant p_A^e that for a subset of goods A would permit him to attract some
demand ($p_A^e < p_A^m$) and to make profits (without his having to satisfy the
entire market demand). This definition is quite restrictive, since it does not
allow the monopolist to react and it treats the entrants in an asymmetric
way because they do not have to satisfy the entire demand.

Strict subadditivity of the cost function is necessary but not sufficient to
insure the existence of a sustainable price vector as Faulhaber's example
(figure 3.18) shows for the single-product case. The cost function is defined

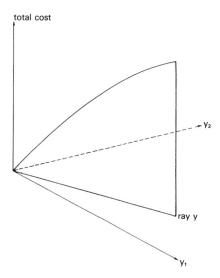

total cost

y_2

ray y

y_1

Figure 3.19

by curve $ABCD$. It is globally subadditive if $BC < OA$. At output level $\tilde{y}$, we have a natural monopoly. However, even if the monopolist makes zero profit by charging a price equal to average cost, a firm may enter, sell $y < \tilde{y}$, and make a profit by charging a price slightly less than the average cost of the monopolist.

There exist sufficient conditions to insure sustainability. The function must have *decreasing average cost along any ray* (see figure 3.19), that is,

$C(\gamma y) < \gamma C(y)$ for $\gamma > 1$ $\forall y \neq 0$.

The cost function must exhibit "economies of scale" indicating complementarities in production (figure 3.20). This will be the case if the cost function is *transversally convex* along the hyperplane

$$\sum_{l=1}^{L} a_l y_l = k \quad a_l > 0,$$

that is if $\forall y^a$, y^b on this hyperplane,

$C(\lambda y^a + (1 - \lambda)y^b) \leqslant \lambda C(y^a) + (1 - \lambda)C(y^b)$ for $0 \leqslant \lambda \leqslant 1$.

The assumptions of decreasing average cost along any ray and of transverse convexity insure the existence of sustainable prices (Baumol, Panzar, and Willig 1982).

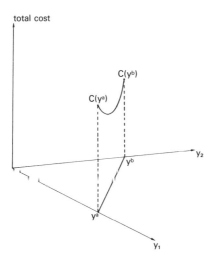

total cost

$C(y^b)$

$C(y^a)$

y^b

y_2

y^a

y_1

Figure 3.20

The notion of sustainability described here corresponds to a very strong concept of free entry. Its generalization leads to the notion of *contestable* markets. A market is contestable if entry into the market and exit from the market are absolutely costless (Baumol 1982). We are then immediately led to the conclusion that, as soon as there is more than one firm, pricing is at marginal cost and the equilibrium is an optimum. However, Baumol's analysis is superficial in two respects. First, the question of the existence of an equilibrium is taken too lightly. Second, a general theory requires a more symmetric treatment of firms and a more precise specification of an entry game. Furthermore, the analysis becomes very sensitive to the extensive form chosen to represent the entry game (Sharkey 1982, Encaoua and Moreaux 1985).

References

Arrow, K., and F. Hahn 1971, *General Competitive Analysis*, Holden-Day.

Arrow, K., and L. Hurwicz 1960, "Decentralization and computation in resource allocation," in R. W. P. Fouts, ed., *Essays in Economics and Econometrics*, University of North Carolina Press, 34–104.

Baumol, W., 1982, "Contestable markets: an uprising in the theory of industry structure," *American Economic Review*, 72, 1–15.

Baumol, W., J. Panzar, and R. Willig 1982, *Contestable Markets and the Theory of Industry Structure*, Harcourt Brace Jovanovich.

Beato, P., 1978, unpublished Ph.D. thesis, University of Minnesota.

—— 1982, "The existence of marginal cost pricing equilibria with increasing returns," *Quarterly Journal of Economics*, 97, 669–688.

Beato, P., and A. Mas-Colell, 1983, "Gestion au coût marginal et efficacité de la production agrégée: un exemple," *Annales de l'INSEE*, 51, 39–46.

Billera, L. J., D. C. Heath, and J. Raahan, 1978, "Internal telephone billing rates: A novel application of non-atomic game theory," *Operations Research*, 26 (Nov.–Dec.).

Brown, D., and G. Heal, 1979, "Equity, efficiency and increasing returns," *Review of Economic Studies*, 46, 571–585.

Calsamiglia, X., 1977, "Decentralized resource allocation and increasing returns," *Journal of Economic Theory*, 14, 263.

Cornet, B., 1983, "Existence of equilibria in economies with increasing returns," mimeo, Berkeley.

Crémer, J., 1978, "A quantity-quantity algorithm for planning under increasing returns to scale," *Econometrica*, 46, 1339–1348.

Dierker, E., 1984, "When does marginal cost pricing lead to Pareto efficiency?," mimeo.

Encaoua, D., and M. Moreaux, 1985, "Concurrence par les prix et élimination des profits: une nouvelle approche de la théorie des marchés contestables," G.R.E.M.A.Q. (*Annales d'Economie et de Statisque*, forthcoming).

Fraysse, J., 1986, "Existence d'équilibre de Cournot: un tour d'horizon," *Annales d'Economie et de Statistique*, 1, 9–33.

Grossman, S., 1981, "Nash equilibrium and the industrial organization of markets with large fixed costs," *Econometrica*, 49, 1149–1172.

Guesnerie, R., 1975, "Pareto optimality in non-convex economies," *Econometrica*, 43, 1–30.

Guesnerie, R., and J. J. Laffont, 1978, "Taxing price makers", *Journal of Economic Theory*, 19, 423–455.

Heal, G., 1971, "Planning prices and increasing returns," *Review of Economic Studies*, 38, 281–294.

Hildenbrand, W., and A. Kirman, 1976, *Introduction to Equilibrium Analysis*, North-Holland.

Hotelling, H., 1938, "The general welfare in relation to problems of taxation and of railway and utility rates," *Econometrica*, 6, 242–269.

Lange, O., 1936, "On the economic theory of socialism," *Review of Economic Studies*, 1, 1936–1937.

Lerner, A. P., 1936, "A note on socialist economics," *Review of Economic Studies*, 1, 157–175.

Malinvaud, E., 1969, *Leçons de Théorie Micro-économique*, Dunod, Paris.

Mirman, L., and Y. Tauman, 1981, "Valeur de Shapley et répartition équitable des coûts de production," *Cahiers du Séminaire d'Econométrie*, no. 23, C.N.R.S., Paris.

Novshek, W., 1980, "Cournot equilibrium with free entry," *Review of Economic Studies*, 47, 473–486.

Novshek, W., and H. Sonnenschein, 1978, "Cournot and Walras equilibrium," *Journal of Economic Theory*, 19, 223.

Quinzii, M., 1986, *Rendements croissants et équilibre général*, thesis, Paris II.

Roberts, J., and H. Sonnenschein, 1977, "On the foundations of the theory of monopolistic competition," *Econometrica*, 45, 101–113.

Sharkey, W., 1982, *The Theory of Natural Monopoly*, Cambridge University Press.

Recommended Reading

1. Malinvaud 1969; Hildenbrand and Kirkman 1976; Arrow and Hahn 1971 (nonconvexities and large number of agents).

2. Beato 1982 (existence of equilibrium with marginal cost pricing).

3. Crémer 1978 (planning and increasing returns).

4. Guesnerie 1975 (decentralization of Pareto optima).

5. Novshek 1980; Fraysse 1986 (Cournot equilibrium with free entry).

6. Quinzii 1986 (general equilibrium and marginal cost pricing).

4 Collective Choice Theory

The Pareto-optimal criterion allows us to consider a subset of states of the economy among which society should reasonably choose.[1] A fundamental question of welfare economics deals with the criterion used to make this choice. The economic theory presented so far was based on an ordinal representation of preferences and on the assumption that the preferences of different agents in the economy are non-comparable. As we shall see below, welfare economics forces us rather quickly to take into account more detailed information on individual preferences.

In section 4.1 we define the various informational structures under consideration in welfare economics. In section 4.2, essentially dealing with Arrow's theorem, we demonstrate the impossibility of finding a satisfactory way to aggregate preferences if we remain within the framework of ordinal preferences and non-comparability as defined above. In sections 4.3 and 4.4 we examine several methods leading to a less ambitious aggregation than that suggested by Arrow. Finally, in section 4.5 we reflect on the role social choice theory plays in the various concepts of government used by economists.

4.1 Informational Structures of Welfare Economics[2]

We consider a finite set of agents indexed by $i = 1, \ldots, I$ and a set A of social states that contains at least three elements. A social state is a complete description of the activities of the agents and of their environment. For example, in an exchange economy, a social state is a set of feasible consumption bundles for all the consumers. In the case of public goods, the quantities of public goods and the method of financing them must be specified.

Agent i's preferences are represented by a utility function $U^i(.)$ defined on the set of social states A. Let $\Sigma(A)$ be the class of admissible utility functions $U^i(.)$ on A. Let $(U^1, \ldots, U^I) = U$ be a generic element of $[\Sigma(A)]^I$, and call it a preference profile. $S(A)$ is a set of admissible social preorderings on A.

DEFINITION   A social welfare function (or social ranking) $\mathscr{F}$ is a function of $[\Sigma(A)]^I$ in $S(A)$ that maps any admissible profile into an admissible social preordering.

---

1. See also the theory of the second best (chapter 7).
2. See Sen (1977b).

The social decision maker wishes to aggregate individual preferences in order to construct a social preordering. If he is incapable of distinguishing between two utility functions U^i and $\tilde{U}^i$ for agent i, the social welfare function must not be changed when U^i is replaced by $\tilde{U}^i$. For example, if the social decision maker is capable of identifying only individual pre-orderings, $\mathcal{F}$ must be invariant with respect to any increasing transformation of its arguments.

We next distinguish five different concepts of invariance associated with five possible informational structures. These examples help us to understand under which informational assumptions certain welfare functions can be legitimately used.

4.1.1   Cardinal Preferences—Total Comparability

Total comparability means that the social decision maker is capable of comparing the utility levels as well as the variations in utility of the different agents. Cardinal preferences, however, means that utility functions are defined only up to a constant affine transformation, that is, the social decision maker has no absolute measure of utility.

The social welfare function must be invariant to the same increasing affine transformation of its arguments.

EXAMPLE   Benthamite social welfare function (or utilitarian criterion) $\sum_{i=1}^{I} U^i(.)$.

Clearly, if we replace each $U^i(.)$ by the same affine transformation $\alpha + \beta U^i = \tilde{U}^i$, then

$$\mathcal{F}(\tilde{U}^1(.), \ldots, \tilde{U}^I(.)) = I\alpha + \beta \sum_{i=1}^{I} U^i(.)$$

defines the same social preordering on A as $\sum_{i=1}^{I} U^i(.)$.

We observe that $\sum_{i=1}^{I} U^i(.)$ defines the same social preordering as $(\sum_{i=1}^{I} U^i(.))/I$. The latter criterion can be interpreted as the expected utility of an agent who, in an initial situation where he does not know his future identity, has probability $1/I$ of being characterized by the utility function $U^i(.)$, $i = 1, \ldots, I$ (see Harsanyi 1953).

4.1.2   Ordinal Preferences—Comparability of Utility Levels

Individual utility functions are defined only up to an increasing transformation; however, the social decision maker is capable of comparing the utility levels of the different agents. Therefore the social welfare function must be invariant with respect to the same increasing transformation of the individual functions.

EXAMPLE   Rawlsian criterion $\mathscr{F}(U^1, \ldots, U^I) = \text{Min}_i\, U^i(.)$.

If we consider $\Phi(U^1)$, ..., $\Phi(U^I)$, with Φ an increasing function, $\text{Min}_i\, \Phi(U^i(.))$ is achieved for the same agent so that the social preordering generated by $\mathscr{F}$ remains unchanged. In the same spirit as Harsanyi's interpretation of the utilitarian criterion, the maximin criterion or Rawlsian criterion can be considered as the social preordering of an agent who is in an initial situation where he does not know his future identity, and where, because of his very large aversion to risk, he fears having the worst lot in society.

4.1.3   Cardinal Preferences—Comparability of Variation in Utility

This means that the social decision maker is capable of comparing an increase in the utility of agent i with an increase in the utility of agent j, but he can not say anything about their utility levels. Linked with the assumption of cardinal preferences, this implies that the social welfare function must be invariant to an affine transformation of the type

$$\tilde{U}^i = \alpha^i + \beta U^i(.) \qquad \beta > 0 \quad i = 1, \ldots, I$$

EXAMPLE   Generalized Nash criterion

$$\mathscr{F}(U^1, \ldots, U^I) = \prod_{i=1}^{I} (U^i(.) - U^i(\tilde{a}))^{\delta^i} \qquad \sum_{i=1}^{I} \delta^i = 1 \quad \delta^i \geqslant 0 \quad i = 1, \ldots, I,$$

where $\tilde{a}$ is a social state representing the status quo. $\mathscr{F}(\tilde{U}^1, \ldots, \tilde{U}^I) = \beta \mathscr{F}(U^1, \ldots, U^I)$ indeed represents the same preordering as $\mathscr{F}(U^1, \ldots, U^I)$.

4.1.4   Cardinal Preferences—Non-Comparability

The social decision maker is incapable of comparing the variations in or the levels of utility of the various agents. However, there exists a cardinal representation of the preferences. Therefore the social welfare function must be invariant for any I-tuple of affine transformations

$$\tilde{U}^i = \alpha^i + \beta^i U^i \qquad i = 1, \ldots, I.$$

EXAMPLE   Nash criterion $\mathscr{F}(U^1, \ldots, U^I) = \prod_{i=1}^{I} (U^i(.) - U^i(\tilde{a}))$.

4.1.5   Ordinal Preferences—Non-Comparability

The social welfare function must be invariant to any I-tuple of increasing transformations of its arguments, that is, it must depend only on the preorderings of individual preferences.

EXAMPLE   Borda's rule: Each agent ranks social states, and attributes points to the various states: 1 for the state he prefers, 2 for the next preferred state, etc. Then a_1 is socially preferred to a_2 if and only if a_1 receives less total points than a_2. Clearly this rule depends only on individual preorderings.

In the above paragraphs, we examined the type of information required by a social decision maker to make various social welfare functions informationally coherent. The richest informational structure is cardinal preference with total comparability. This leaves us with a large family of invariant social welfare functions to compare. Figure 4.1, where the shaded

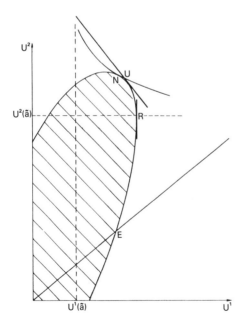

Figure 4.1
Social welfare functions. N indicates the choice according to the Nash criterion when the status quo is defined by $(U^1(\tilde{a}), U^2(\tilde{a}))$; U indicates choice according to the Benthamite criterion; R indicates choice according to the Rawlsian criterion; and E indicates the best egalitarian choice.

area represents feasible utility levels, illustrates this comparison in the case of two agents. From this figure we see that the Rawlsian maximin criterion is the most egalitarian criterion compatible with Pareto efficiency.[3]

It may appear useful to construct a social choice rule that does not require interpersonal utility comparisons, since these comparisons are very delicate or impossible in certain cases. Our first task is to study to what degree this construction is possible.

4.2 Aggregation of Preferences in the Structure: Non-Comparable Ordinal Preferences

The agents' preferences are now represented by orderings[4] P^i, $i = 1, \ldots, I$. Here $\Sigma(A)$ is the class of admissible orderings for each agent. First we note that a requirement of collective rationality is implicit in the definition of a social welfare function. Indeed, the definition requires that social choice be representable by a preordering (rather than a less structured binary relation). As early as 1785, the Marquis de Condorcet noted that simple majority rule (denoted MS) does not define a social welfare function since it does not always lead to a transitive binary relation.

Consider the example of three agents and three social states with the profiles

$$a_1 \; P^1 \; a_2 \; P^1 \; a_3$$
$$a_3 \; P^2 \; a_1 \; P^2 \; a_2$$
$$a_2 \; P^3 \; a_3 \; P^3 \; a_1.$$

Then

$$a_1 \; MS \; a_2 \qquad a_2 \; MS \; a_3 \qquad a_3 \; MS \; a_1,$$

where a_i MS a_j indicates that a_i beats a_j by a simple majority.

Arrow (1951) generalized this result by showing that there exists no social ranking satisfying a set of conditions considered reasonable. We briefly describe these conditions.

A social ranking satisfies the assumption of universal domain (UD) if $\Sigma(A)$ is the class of all the orderings on A.

---

3. For a more complete discussion of this point, see Kolm (1974).
4. To simplify the presentation, we assume that the preferences of agents and of society are strict. Recall that we always consider total binary relations.

The assumption of universal domain does not permit restrictions to be placed on individual preferences. We seek to construct a social ranking that would be valid for any group of agents.[5]

A social ranking satisfies the Pareto principle (PP) if, when some social state a_1 is preferred to some other social state a_2 by all the agents, the social preordering ranks a_1 above a_2. Formally,

$$\forall \mathbf{P} = (P^1, \ldots, P^I) \in [\Sigma(A)]^I \text{ and } \forall a_1 \in A, \forall a_2 \in A:$$

$$a_1 P^i a_2, \forall i = 1, \ldots, I, \Rightarrow a_1 \mathscr{F}(\mathbf{P}) a_?$$

This assumption is harmless if we accept that social choices must be based on individual choices.[6]

A social ranking satisfies the assumption of independence of irrelevant alternatives (IIA) if the ranking of two social states by the social preordering depends on the ranking of only *these* states by the agents. Formally,

$$\forall a_1, a_2 \in A, \forall \mathbf{P} = (P^1, \ldots, P^I) \in [\Sigma(A)]^I \text{ and } \mathbf{P}':(P'^1, \ldots, P'^I) \in [\Sigma(A)]^I:$$

$$(a_1 P^i a_2 \Leftrightarrow a_1 P'^i a_2 \forall i) \Rightarrow (a_1 \mathscr{F}(\mathbf{P}) a_2 \Leftrightarrow a_1 \mathscr{F}(\mathbf{P}') a_2).$$

Without even specifying the assumption of invariance in the structure of non-comparable ordinal preferences (as we are doing, following Arrow, in this section), the assumption of independence of irrelevant alternatives is a formal way of excluding any possibility that the social ranking could take into account the intensities of preferences. Indeed, two preference profiles that represent the same individual orderings must lead to the same social ordering.

A social ranking is dictatorial if there exists an agent whose preferences determine the social ordering. That is,

$$i \in \{1, \ldots, I\} \text{ is a dictator} \Leftrightarrow \forall (P^1, \ldots, P^I) \in [\Sigma(A)]^I, \mathscr{F}(P^1, \ldots, P^I) = P^i.$$

THEOREM 1 (Arrow 1951)[7]   Any social ranking that satisfies assumptions PP, IIA, and UD is dictatorial, if $I \geq 2$ and $|A| \geq 3$.

Proof   Given a set of agents S, we call S barely decisive for the ordered pair (a_1, a_2) if

---

5. Restricting ourselves only to convex preferences without externalities is not sufficient to invalidate Arrow's result (see Maskin 1976).
6. However, if a concept of proximity can be defined on preferences, we can ask for only approximative optimality.
7. See chapter 3 of Sen (1970). Theorem 1 is often called Arrow's impossibility theorem.

$\forall \mathbf{P} = (P^1, \ldots, P^I) \in [\Sigma(A)]^I$, $a_1 P^i a_2$, $\forall i \in S$ and $a_2 P^j a_1$, $\forall j \notin S$

$\Rightarrow a_1 \mathcal{F}(\mathbf{P}) a_2$.

A set of agents S is said to be decisive for the ordered pair (a_1, a_2) if

$\forall \mathbf{P} = (P^1, \ldots, P^I) \in [\Sigma(A)]^I$, $a_1 P^i a_2$, $\forall i \in S \Rightarrow a_1 P a_2$.

By definition,

$D^j(a_1, a_2)$ if j is barely decisive for (a_1, a_2)

$\bar{D}^j(a_1, a_2)$ if j is decisive for (a_1, a_2).

LEMMA 1   Under the assumptions PP, UD, and IIA, there exists an agent who is barely decisive for an ordered pair of social states.

Proof   For any pair (a_1, a_2), the set of all the agents is decisive (and therefore barely decisive) due to PP.

We consider the smallest set of agents, denoted S, that is barely decisive for a pair of states (formed by varying the pairs).

If S contains a single agent, the proof is finished.

If S contains more than one agent, consider a partition of S, $S_1 \cup S_2$ where S_1 contains a single agent. Let S_3 be the set of agents who are not in S.

Consider the profile UD:

For $i \in S_1$, $a_1 P^i a_2 P^i a_3$

For $j \in S_2$, $a_3 P^j a_1 P^j a_2$

For $k \in S_3$, $a_2 P^k a_3 P^k a_1$.

Since S is barely decisive for (a_1, a_2) and since a_1 is preferred to a_2 by each agent of S and since each agent who is not in S prefers the opposite,

$a_1 P a_2$.

If $a_3 P a_2$, then S_2 is a barely decisive group for (a_3, a_2) by invoking IIA, thus contradicting the definition of S.

If on the contrary, $a_2 P a_3$, the transitivity requirement on P implies that $a_1 P a_3$; then S_1 is a barely decisive group for (a_1, a_3) from IIA, thus contradicting the definition of S. ■

LEMMA 2   Under the assumptions PP, IIA, and UD, if there exists an agent j who is barely decisive for an ordered pair of social states, j must be a dictator.

Proof   Let (a_1, a_2) belonging to A be the pair of social states for which j is barely decisive. First, consider a social triplet (a_1, a_2, a_3) and assume that

$$a_1 P^j a_2 P^j a_3$$

$$a_2 P^i a_1 \text{ and } a_2 P^i a_3 \quad \forall i \neq j.$$

Since j is barely decisive for (a_1, a_2), $a_1 P a_2$.
From PP, $a_2 P a_3$.
By transitivity, $a_1 P a_3$.
Therefore $a_1 P a_3$ independently of the rankings of the agents $i \neq j$ over (a_1, a_3).
Also $a_1 P a_3$ is independent of the rankings of (a_1, a_2) and (a_2, a_3) by IIA.
Therefore, $a_1 P a_3$, regardless of the preferences of agents $i \neq j$.
Therefore, j is decisive for $(a_1, a_3): \bar{D}^j(a_1, a_3)$.
Similarly, by interchanging the role of (a_1, a_2) with (a_3, a_1) and by choosing the appropriate profile using UD, we show that j is decisive for (a_3, a_2), that is, $\bar{D}^j(a_3, a_2)$.
To summarize, given three social states $a_\alpha, a_\beta, a_\gamma$, we have

$$D^j(a_\alpha, a_\beta) \dashrightarrow \bar{D}^j(a_\alpha, a_\gamma)$$

$$\dashrightarrow \bar{D}^j(a_\gamma, a_\beta).$$

The sign $\dashrightarrow$ means "implied by the reasoning above."
On the other hand, by definition

$$\bar{D}^j(a_\alpha, a_\beta) \xrightarrow{d} D^j(a_\alpha, a_\beta).$$

By repeating the above argument, we have

$$D^j(a_1, a_2) \dashrightarrow \bar{D}^j(a_1, a_3)$$
$$\downarrow d$$
$$D^j(a_1, a_3) \dashrightarrow \bar{D}^j(a_2, a_3)$$
$$\downarrow d$$
$$D^j(a_2, a_3) \dashrightarrow \bar{D}^j(a_2, a_1)$$
$$\downarrow d$$
$$\bar{D}^j(a_3, a_1) \dashleftarrow D^j(a_2, a_1)$$
$$\downarrow d$$
$$\bar{D}^j(a_3, a_2) \dashleftarrow D^j(a_3, a_1)$$
$$\downarrow d$$
$$\bar{D}^j(a_1, a_2) \dashleftarrow D^j(a_3, a_2)$$

Therefore agent j is a dictator for any set of three social states containing (a_1, a_2).

Consider a set of social states larger than (a_1, a_2) and let (u, v) be any pair of social states in the set. Then either

(i) (u, v) is the same as (a_1, a_2), in which case $\bar{D}^j(a_2, a_1)$ (see above); or
(ii) u is equal to a_1 without v being equal to a_2 (or any other case of this type).

Choose the triplet $(u = a_1, a_2, v)$.

$D^j(a_1, a_2) \nrightarrow \bar{D}^j(a_1, v) \Rightarrow \bar{D}^j(v, a_1)$ by the schema above, or

(iii) if u and v are different from a_1 and a_2, we proceed as follows.

First consider the triplet (a_1, a_2, u).

$D^j(a_1, a_2) \nrightarrow \bar{D}^j(a_1, u) \xrightarrow{d} D^j(a_1, u)$.

Then consider the triplet (a_1, u, v)

$D^j(a_1, u) \nrightarrow \bar{D}^j(v, u) \rightarrow \bar{D}^j(u, v)$ by the schema above.

Therefore, $D^j(a_1, a_2) \Rightarrow \bar{D}^j(u, v)$ for any ordered pair (u, v).
Therefore, j is a dictator. ∎

Therefore, lemmas 1 and 2 provide a proof of Arrow's theorem. ∎

The force of Arrow's theorem lies in the statement that any imaginable aggregation procedure violates at least one of the assumptions. Take for example Borda's rule. It satisfies PP and UD and is nondictatorial (ND); therefore, it violates IIA. For an example, consider three states a_1, a_2, and a_3. Agent 1 gives 1 point to a_1, 2 points to a_2 and 3 points to a_3, whereas agent 2 gives 1 point to a_3, 2 points to a_1, and 3 points to a_2. Then a_1 receives 3 points, a_2 receives 5 points, a_3 receives 4 points. Therefore $a_3 P a_2$. If the ordering of agent 1 is changed to $a_2 P'^1 a_1 P'^1 a_3$ and that of agent 2 to $a_3 P'^2 a_2 P'^2 a_1$, then a_3 receives 4 points and a_2 receives 3 points. Therefore $a_2 P a_3$.

Even though the rankings of a_2 and a_3 are unchanged for the two agents, the social choice between a_2 and a_3 is changed.

The simple majority rule satisfies IIA (because it is a binary procedure), PP, UD, and ND, but it does not yield a transitive binary relation (refer to Condorcet's Paradox). The rule of unanimity satisfies IIA, PP, UD, and

ND, but it does not yield a total binary relation. Let $\tilde{P}$ be a fixed preordering that represents "tradition,"

$$\forall \mathbf{P} = (P^1, \ldots, P^I) \in [\Sigma(A)]^I, \mathscr{F}(\mathbf{P}) = \tilde{P}.$$

It does not satisfy PP.

4.3   Several Paths of Study

(1) A first direction consists of observing that, for the purpose of public economic, it may not be necessary to construct a social preordering. Although it is crucial to be able to make coherent decisions, it may not be necessary to compare all social states with a social preordering.

Let us weaken the requirements of collective rationality to the existence of a social binary relation that allows choice in all circumstances. Let R be a binary relation on A such that P indicates strict preference and I indicates indifference and let B be a subset of A.

A social state a belonging to B is a preferred choice in B for R if and only if

$$\forall b \in B \Rightarrow aRb$$

Let $C(B, R)$ be the set of preferred choices in B for R. If $C(B, R) \neq \varnothing$ for all B contained in A, we have a well-defined choice function $C(., R)$, a mapping from partitions of A, $\mathscr{P}(A)$, into itself.

What conditions on R imply the existence of a well-defined choice function derived from R? First of all, R must be reflexive and complete.

If a notR a, then $C(\{a\}, R) = \varnothing$; therefore R must be reflexive.

If a notR b, and b notR a, then $C(\{a, b\}, R) = \varnothing$; therefore R must be complete.

We say that R is acyclic on A if and only if

$$\forall (a_1, \ldots, a_j) \in A; [a_1 Pa_2, a_2 Pa_3, \ldots, a_{j-1} Pa_j] \Rightarrow a_1 Ra_j.$$

Then we have

THEOREM 2   If R is reflexive and complete, a necessary and sufficient condition for $C(., R)$ to be well defined on a finite set A is that R be acyclic.

Proof   Necessity: Suppose that R is not acyclic; then there exists a subset of states $(a_1, \ldots, a_j)$ belonging to A such that $a_1 Pa_2 \ldots a_{j-1} Pa_j$ and $a_j Pa_1$. Then $C(\{a_1, \ldots, a_j\}, R) = \varnothing$.

Sufficiency: Suppose that there exists B such that $C(B, R) = \varnothing$ and that B has k elements. Let x_1 be any element of B. Since $C(B, R) = \varnothing$, there exists in B an x_2 such that $x_2 P x_1$. Since P is asymmetric $x_2 \neq x_1$. Since $C(B, R) = \varnothing$, there exists $x_3 \in B$ such that $x_3 P x_2$ ($x_3 \neq x_2$). Furthermore, $x_3 \neq x_1$, otherwise $x_1 P x_2$ and $x_2 P x_1$ from which it follows that $x_1 P x_1$ which is impossible. We continue in the same manner: There exists x_4 belonging to B such that $x_4 P x_3$. We have $x_4 \neq x_3$, $x_4 \neq x_2$; otherwise $x_2 P x_3$ and $x_3 P x_2$ from which it follows that $x_2 P x_2$. $x_4 \neq x_1$, otherwise $x_1 P x_3$ and $x_3 P x_2$ and $x_2 P x_1$ from which it follows that $x_1 P x_1$. In proceeding thus, we exhaust the k elements of B. Since $C(B, R) = \varnothing$, there exist $x_{k+1} \in B$ such that $x_{k+1} P x_k$ and we show that B must have $k + 1$ distinct elements contradicting the initial assumption that B has k elements. ∎

Reflexivity, completeness, and acyclicity (which is weaker than transitivity) emerge as the minimal conditions necessary to impose on the social binary relation so that a decision can be made in all circumstances. Define the social decision function as a mapping that associates to every I-tuple of individual preorders a binary relation which is reflexive, complete, and acyclic. Completing the Pareto rule by considering as indifferent all social states that are not ordered by the Pareto criterion defines a nondictatorial social decision function that satisfies UD, PP, and IIA. Obviously the problem with this social ranking is that it includes too much indifference. One way of interpreting the various positive results obtained for the informational structure of non-comparable ordinal preferences is that we obtain either nondemocratic procedures (oligarchy or agents with veto rights), or procedures that result in too much indifference. (Gibbard 1969, Mas-Colell and Sonnenschein 1972).

(2) An alternative way consists of constructing a social ranking for a particular society or a set of particular societies in which the agents have numerous points in common. We have prior information on the agents' preferences and we recognize the futility of trying to construct social rankings that would be valid for all possible societies as is implicit in the condition of universal domain.

Suppose for example that we have the following information about the set of admissible preorderings $\Sigma(A)$, assumed to be strict. The social states can be arranged on a straight line in such a way that, for any $P^i \in \Sigma(A)$, there exists a social state a^{*i} such that

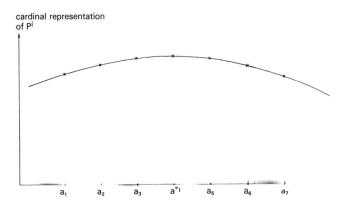

Figure 4.2

$$\forall a_h, a_k \in A : a_h < a_k < a^{*i} \Rightarrow a^{*i} P^i a_k P^i a_h$$

$$\forall a_h, a_k \in A : a^{*i} < a_k < a_h \Rightarrow a^{*i} P^i a_k P^i a_h.$$

We call such preferences unimodal (UM) (see figure 4.2).

Under the assumptions UM, PP, and IIA, the simple majority rule leads to a social preordering when the number of agents is odd. It is sufficient to show that this social ranking defines a transitive binary relation. One agent is the median voter if his preferred choice is the median in the set of preferred choices of agents ordered on R according to the ranking defined above. It is easy to show that the preferred choice of the median voter is chosen above any other social state by a majority vote. Let us eliminate this state. The socially preferred state by the new median voter is chosen above all other outcomes by a majority vote. We construct the social preordering in this manner.

Although very restrictive because it is based on the possibility of a unidimensional ranking of social states over which the agents have uni-modal preferences, this result has been used extensively by an American school of thought (the Public Choice Society) as a theory of public decision-making. Public choices correspond to the preferred choices of the median voter because of a democratic aggregation of preferences according to majority rule. (see section 2.5.3) This somewhat excessive interpretation of the above result has nevertheless the advantage of concreteness; it reflects the need for a theory of public choice to answer numerous questions in public economics. However, it points out the lack of progress made by neoclassical economic thought on this subject—perhaps because it is considered by many to be outside the realm of economics.

Majority rule, which plays a central role in the theory of social choice, can be characterized rather easily. Let $N(aPb)$ be the number of agents who prefer a to b:

$$aMSb \Leftrightarrow [N(aPb) \geqslant N(bPa)].$$

We call an aggregation function (that is a function which associates a binary relation to an I-tuple of individual preorderings) *anonymous* (A) if it is invariant to a permutation of individual preorderings. An aggregation function is *neutral* (N) if it is invariant to a permutation social states $\forall a,b,c,d, \in A$:

$$\forall i : aR^i b \Leftrightarrow cR^i d \text{ and } bR^i a \Leftrightarrow dR^i c$$
$$\Rightarrow aRb \Leftrightarrow cRd \text{ and } bRa \Leftrightarrow dRc.$$

Finally we say that an aggregation function *responds positively* (RP) if and only if

$$\forall a,b \in A$$

$$\forall i, aP^i b \Rightarrow aP'^i b$$

$$aI^i b \Rightarrow aR'^i b$$

and

$$\exists k : aI^k b \text{ and } aP'^k b$$

or

$$bP^k a \text{ and } aR'^k b;$$

then

$$aRb \Rightarrow aP'b.$$

That is, if the new preferences between a and b are such that a is at least as well thought of by all agents and gives a strict improvement for at least one agent, the social preferences make a preferable to b. In particular if a is indifferent to b, then $aP'b$.

First of all we note that neutrality implies the independence of irrelevant alternatives (it suffices in the definition of neutrality to take $c = a$ and $d = b$):

$N \Rightarrow IIA$.

Anonymity obviously implies the absence of a dictator:

$A \Rightarrow ND$.

Neutrality and positive response imply the Pareto principle:

$N + RP \Rightarrow PP$.

Indeed neutrality implies that if aI^ib, $\forall i, aIb$. Positive response implies that if $\forall i : aR^ib$ and $\exists j : aP^jb$ then aPb.

Consequently, UD, A, N, and $RP \Rightarrow$ UD, IIA, ND, and PP.

Therefore we can deduce from Arrow's theorem the nonexistence of a social welfare function under UD, A, N, and RP.

We can show that in fact UD, A, N, and RP characterize majority rule, which we know from Condorcet leads to a nontransitive binary relation. Thus a slight strengthening of Arrow's assumptions leads to a very simple proof of the impossibility theorem.

THEOREM 3 (May)   UD, A, N, and RP are, together, necessary and sufficient for majority rule MS.

Proof   It is evident that majority rule has these properties.

Since $N \Rightarrow IIA$, it is sufficient to examine individual preferences over a and b to determine social preference over a and b.

The assumption of anonymity implies that the preference of a over b cannot depend on the number of agents who prefer a to b.

If $N(aPb) = N(bPa)$, then aIb by neutrality.

Furthermore, if $[N(aPb) > N(bPa)]$, then aPb by positive response.

This is indeed majority rule. ∎

Numerous results have been obtained by restricting the domain of preferences (see chapter 10 of Sen 1970, for various results concerning majority rule, Grandmont 1978 for a study of the idea of the median voter in the multidimensional case, and Kalai and Muller 1976 for a characterization of domains of preferences that allow the construction of a social ranking).

(3) When the social states are multidimensional, we must recognize that the concrete results obtained above are not robust. Then we are led inescapably to requiring some comparability of individual preferences if we wish to rank

social outcomes in sufficiently varied situations. Many economists refuse to admit the possibility of such comparisons (the criteria of Kaldor and Scitovsky are typical examples of an attempt to compare social states without appealing to interpersonal comparisons; see chapter 6). Other economists observe that society must make choices and therefore it implicitly uses a social decision function (see Guesnerie et al. 1972 for a study which attempts to define the preferences implicit in the planning bureau). They admit the necessity of utility comparisons but often reject the appropriateness of these comparisons in the political domain.

Social choice theory has only recently crossed the Rubicon of interpersonal comparison of utilities; yet many results have already been obtained. In the following, we give two examples of such results (see Sen 1977a, b for a remarkable synthesis).

Hammond (1976) considers the informational structure of totally comparable cardinal preferences. Preferences are represented by utility functions, and the social welfare function must be invariant to the same affine transformation of utility functions. The definitions of UD, IIA, A, and the Pareto principle can be adapted immediately to this context.

First of all we define the leximin criterion (LM). Given a social state a, we consider a ranking of individuals by ordering them according to their level of utility starting from the least favored individual: $1(a), 2(a), \ldots, I(a)$:

$$aP_{LM}b \Leftrightarrow \exists j \in \{1, \ldots, I\} \text{ such that } j = j(a) = j(b)$$

$$U^{j(a)}(a) > U^{j(b)}(b)$$

and

$$U^{i(a)}(a) = U^{i(b)}(b) \qquad \forall i(a) = i(b) < j(a) = j(b)$$

$$aI_{LM}b \Leftrightarrow U^{i(a)}(a) = U^{i(b)}(b) \qquad \forall i(a) = i(b).$$

Thus we have a lexicographic ordering starting with the least favored individual. Hammond (1976) introduces an axiom of equity (E):

If, for any pair of social states (a, b) and for an I-tuple of utility functions, $\{U^i\}$, we have for two agents j and k

$$U^j(b) < U^j(a) < U^k(a) < U^k(b)$$

and

$$U^i(a) = U^i(b) \qquad \forall i \neq j, k,$$

then

aRb.

Priority is given to *a* because the agent who prefers *a* to *b* is less favored both in *a* and *b*. We have the following characterization result.

THEOREM 4   In the informational structure of totally comparable cardinal preferences, a social welfare function that satisfies the properties UD, IIA, A, PP,[8] and E must be equivalent to the leximin criterion.

Several authors have provided a characterization of the utilitarian criterion as well.

THEOREM 5   In the informational structure of cardinal preferences with comparability of variations in utility, a social welfare function that satisfies the properties UD, IIA, A, and PP[8] must be equivalent to the utilitarian criterion.

To conclude this section, I mention the complexity of the condition IIA. The strength of this condition depends greatly on the informational structure in which we work. As it was presented by Arrow, this condition conveyed simultaneously an aspect of independence and an aspect of excluding interpersonal utility comparisons. In specifying the informational structure beforehand, we can separate these two roles so that IIA becomes only a condition of independence. To do this it suffices to define the condition for a social welfare function only, that is, for profiles of utility functions but not for profiles of preorderings. Remaining, for example, in a structure of non-comparable ordinal preferences, the elimination of the IIA condition leads to Borda's rule. The latter makes implicit utility comparisons, the normative character of which is not clear. For public economics, it is undoubtedly more interesting to impose normative properties on explicit utility comparisons.

4.4   Measures of Inequality and Social Welfare Functions

Consider prices to be fixed. Then a social welfare function of the Bergson-Samuelson type $\tilde{W}(U^1(x^1), \ldots, U^I(x^I))$ can be expressed as a function of incomes by using the indirect utility functions: $W(R^1, \ldots, R^I)$.

8. A strict version of the Pareto principle is needed.

The purpose of inequality measures is to compare distributions of income. The first question to be asked concerns the existence of partial criteria for comparing income distributions that are compatible with reasonable qualitative restrictions on social welfare functions. The Lorenz-curve criterion is a good example of such a result.

The Lorenz curve associates to every proportion of the population x the percentage of total income held by this population group (including the least favored ones). Let two income distributions be ordered as

$$(R^1 \leqslant R^2 \leqslant \cdots \leqslant R^I) \equiv \mathbf{R}$$

$$(R'^1 \leqslant R'^2 \leqslant \cdots \leqslant R'^I) \equiv \mathbf{R'},$$

and let

$$\mu = \frac{1}{I} \sum_{i=1}^{I} R^i \quad ; \quad \mu' = \frac{1}{I} \sum_{i=1}^{I} R'^i.$$

The Lorenz curve corresponding to $\mathbf{R}$ never lies below the one corresponding to $\mathbf{R'}$ (and it is therefore at least as egalitarian by the Lorenz measure $\Leftrightarrow \mathbf{R} \geqslant_L \mathbf{R'}$) if and only if

$$\frac{1}{\mu} \sum_{i=1}^{k} R^i \geqslant \frac{1}{\mu'} \sum_{i=1}^{k} R'^i \qquad k = 1, \dots, I.$$

Certainly, the Lorenz criterion is only partial.

Consider the following "reasonable" restrictions on $W(.)$.

(1) *Monotonicity*: $W(.)$ is nondecreasing in each of its arguments. We define a constant-mean progressive transfer (TP) between two agents whose incomes are R^j and R^i with $R^j \geqslant R^i$ as a quantity $\Delta \geqslant 0$ such that the agents' new incomes are $\tilde{R}^j = R^j - \Delta$

$$\tilde{R}^j = R^j - \Delta$$

$$\tilde{R}^i = R^i + \Delta \qquad \text{with} \quad \tilde{R}^j \geqslant \tilde{R}^i.$$

From a result of Hardy, Littlewood, and Polya (1952), a distribution $\mathbf{R'}$ can be obtained from a distribution $\mathbf{R}$ with the help of a sequence of constant-mean progressive transfers if and only if:

$$\mathbf{R'} = B\mathbf{R},$$

where B is a bistochastic[9] matrix, from which we derive the following restriction.

(2) *Egalitarian Desire*: $\forall \mathbf{R}$, $W(B\mathbf{R}) \geqslant W(\mathbf{R})$ for any bistochastic matrix B.[10] Then we can show:

If $\mu = \mu'$; $\mathbf{R} \geqslant_L \mathbf{R}'$ if and only if $W(\mathbf{R}) \geqslant W(\mathbf{R}')$
for any $W(.)$ satisfying (1) and (2).

If $\mu \neq \mu'$ and $\mathbf{R} \geqslant_L \mathbf{R}'$,   then $W(\mathbf{R}) \geqslant W(\mathbf{R}')$
for any $W(.)$ satisfying (1).

See Shorrocks (1983) for some extensions.

An index of inequality is an index of dispersion. A social welfare function will depend at least on two statistics, the mean of the distribution and an index of dispersion. Therefore, we cannot hope to associate in a general one-to-one way social welfare functions and inequality indices. At most we can hope for some coherent connections. Nonetheless there exists a way to construct inequality indices that achieve a one-to-one mapping (up to a constant increasing transformation) with social welfare functions.

Let $\mathbf{R}^e = (R^e, \ldots, R^e)$ be the egalitarian distribution of income equivalent to $\mathbf{R}$ for the social welfare function $W(.)$:

$$W(\mathbf{R}^e) = W(\mathbf{R}).$$

Then define the inequality index for distribution $\mathbf{R}$ by

$$I(\mathbf{R}) = \frac{\mu - R^e}{\mu}.$$

Reciprocally, given $I(\mathbf{R})$, define the social welfare function

$$W(\mathbf{R}) = F(\mu(1 - I(\mathbf{R}))),$$

where F is any increasing function. More generally, we call the social welfare function $W(R)$ compatible with the index of inequality $I(\mathbf{R})$, if there exists a function F increasing in μ and decreasing in I such that

$$W(\mathbf{R}) = F(\mu, I(\mathbf{R})).$$

---

9. See mathematical definitions, p. ix.
10. We say that W is S-concave.

Then we can ask: Does there exist a social welfare function compatible with the Gini index? The Gini index is given by

$$G(\mathbf{R}) = \frac{1}{2I^2\mu} \sum_{i=1}^{I} \sum_{j=1}^{I} |R^i - R^j|.$$

As a first response, we use the construction

$$W(\mathbf{R}) = F(\mu(1 - G(\mathbf{R}))).$$

As a second response, we propose

$$W(\mathbf{R}) = \text{Log } \mu - G(\mathbf{R}).$$

Indeed, there obviously exists an infinite number of possible functions. They are all equivalent when we compare distributions with the same mean. Unfortunately, they may differ and lead to conflicting conclusions as soon as the distributions have different means.

4.5   Conclusion: Public Economics and Theories of Government

Social choice theory is incorporated in a contractual theory of government associated with the philosophical tradition of Rousseau, Locke, and, more recently, Rawls and Nozick. In the social contract, agents agree on collective decision rules; the theory of preference aggregation considers the possibility of designing a satisfactory procedure of coherent collective decision making starting from individual preferences. One lesson to be learned from this theory is that, in the absence of common moral values that permit us to make use of important information on individual preferences (by making interpersonal comparisons), it is impossible to aggregate satisfactorily in diverse situations. When aggregation is possible, the degree to which it can form a social consensus remains to be determined. For this purpose, it is often useful to consider an initial state in which agents do not know their own identity (Rawls and Harsanyi). However, a fundamental problem arises: How can one evaluate the future if one does not know one's own tastes? Conceptually, it is easier to imagine instead a repeated application of the obtained social ranking and to look for conditions under which it would be individually rational on average for each agent to accept the framework of the social ranking.

This approach can be criticized from the positivist perspective. For the applied economist, it is more important to know how the government actually operates rather than how it should function in the name of a contractual notion of society. When he makes recommendations in the political arena, must the economist consider normative theory, or the government as it actually exists? It is interesting to note that the positivist critique of the government comes from very diverse political camps.

The current liberal extremists (for example, Brennan and Buchanan 1977) see the government as a Leviathan maximizing its size and from which individuals must protect themselves by imposing limits on this expansion. This critique does not really contradict the contractual approach. Nonetheless, this school recognizes that the government has its own innate dynamic laws and recommends that these be taken into account by the social contract. For Marx, the government is endogenous to the class conflict and serves the most powerful interest group. In order to act correctly, one must take into account the historical explanation for the existence of the government. The solution is not to set normative rules on the behavior of the government but rather to seize power (see Foley 1978 for some implications of this point of view in public economics). From the Marxist critique, one can retain the endogenous character of the government and try to describe the problem of public decision making with the help of the theory of games using concepts like the core. This model can be contrasted with the traditional normative models of which the optimal-taxation literature is the most extreme example.

The idealistic vision of the government implicit in numerous contributions in public economics captures the aggregation of individual preferences, either in a democratic way or not, by the choice of a particular social welfare function. Then the economist can define optimal policies from the perspective of this criterion. Unfortunately, struggles for power bear more and more on the choice of economic policy instruments, thus making this determination endogenous.[11] The economist's role in shaping economic policy is not very clear in this scenario; in order for his opinion to be heard, the economist must become an adviser to one or the other of the important political parties. In this conclusion, which in many respects is a caricature, my intent has been to sensitize the reader to different visions of government. In effect, a particular theory of public economics corresponds to each theory of government.

11. In this vein, see a study of Guesnerie and Oddou (1979).

References

Arrow, K., 1951, *Social Choice and Individual Values*, Wiley. See also the second edition, 1963.

Brennan, G., and J. Buchanan 1977, "Towards a tax constitution for Leviathan," *Journal of Public Economics*, 8, 255–273.

Foley, D., 1978, "State expenditures from a Marxist perspective," *Journal of Public Economics*, 9, 221–235.

Gibard, A., 1976, "Intransitive social indifference and the Arrow dilemma," unpublished ms.

Grademont, J. M., 1978, "Intermediate preferences and the majority rule," *Econometrica*, 16, 317–330.

Guesnerie, R., and C. Oddou 1979, On economic games which are not necessarily super-additive, *Economic Letters*, 3, 301–306.

Guesnerie, R., and P. Malgrange 1972, "Formalisation des objectifs à moyen terme: application au VIe Plan," *Revue Economique*, 23, 442–491.

Hammond, P., 1976, Equity, Arrow's conditions and Rawls' difference principle, *Econometrica*, 44, 793–804.

Hardy, G., J. Littlewood, and R. Polya 1952, *Inequalities*, Cambridge University Press.

Harsani, J. C., 1955, "Cardinal welfare, individualistic ethics, and interpersonal comparisons," *Journal of Political Economy*, 63, 309.

Kalai, K., and E. Muller 1977, "Characterization of domains admitting non-dictatorial social welfare functions and non-manipulable voting procedures," *Journal of Economic Theory*, 16, 457–469.

Kolm, S. C., 1974, "Sur les consequences économiques des principes de justice et de justice pratique," *Revue d'Economie Politique*, 84, 80–107.

Mas-Colell, A., and H. Sonnenschein 1972, "General possibility theorem for group decisions," *Review of Economic Studies*, 39, 185–192.

Maskin, E., 1976, "Social welfare functions for economics," mimeo, Harvard University.

Nozick, R., 1974, *Anarchy, State and Utopia*, Blackwell.

Rawls, J., 1971, *A Theory of Justice*, Harvard University Press.

Sen, A., 1973, *On Economic Inequality*, Oxford University Press.

———— 1977a, "Social choice theory: a reexamination, *Econometrica*, 45, 53–90.

———— 1977b, "On weights and measures: Informational constraints in social welfare analysis, *Econometrica*, 45, 1539–1572.

Shorrocks, A. F., 1983, "Ranking income distributions," *Economica*, 50, 3–17.

Recommended Reading

1. Arrow 1951 (the basic work).

2. Kolm 1974 (reflections on Rawls' criterion).

3. Sen 1970, 1977a, 1977b (research in the theory of social choice).

4. Guesnerie and Malgrange 1972 (objective function of the planning bureau).

5. Brennan and Buchanan 1977; Foley 1978; Nozick 1974; Rawls 1971 (theories of the state).

5 Incomplete Information and Public Economics

A fundamental characteristic of economic systems is decentralization of information. When a collective decision must be taken, whether it be the choice of the level of a tax that internalizes an externality, the choice of the level of output of a public good, the choice of the level of output for a firm exhibiting increasing returns, or even the choice of a social welfare function, the social decision maker must collect information that is by its nature decentralized since each agent possesses aspects of this information which he alone knows. A problem of strategic behavior arises with respect to this private information. Given a social choice function that associates a collective decision desirable from the perspective of the social decision maker or center with the information characteristics of the agents, how can this decision be implemented? In other words, can a game be found for which the strategic equilibria lead to the desired outcome? The purpose of this chapter is to point out the general problematic nature of implementation and to offer several solutions to classic problems in public economics.

5.1 The Implementation Notion

Consider a society made up of I agents and let A be the set of feasible social states. The preferences of agent i are represented by a preordering R^i. It will sometimes be useful to constrain the space of admissible preferences of agent i. Let Θ^i be a space of characteristics for agent i; to each $\theta^i \in \Theta^i$ is associated a preordering for agent i, $R^i(\theta^i)$, by applying a function $R^i(.)$ that is common knowledge.

EXAMPLE $\Theta^i = \mathbf{R}^2$; $(\theta_1^i, \theta_2^i) \xrightarrow{R^i(.)}$ preordering representing the utility function $x^{\theta_1^i} \cdot y^{\theta_2^i}$.

If there are no restrictions on the admissible preorderings, then Θ^i represents the space of preorderings on A and $R^i(.)$ is an identity.

The true value of the characteristic θ^i is known only to agent i, so that information is decentralized. The center must choose a social state on the basis of messages that are transmitted to him by the agents concerning their private characteristics. Given that each agent attempts to take advantage of the center's ignorance of his own characteristics, incentive theory studies the feasible actions of the center using mechanisms designed to overcome this informational gap at the lowest cost. The following definitions will allow us to specify more precisely this construction.

A *social choice function f* is a mapping that associates to each vector of characteristics, $\theta \equiv (\theta^1, \ldots, \theta^I) \in \Theta \equiv \prod_{i=1}^{I} \Theta^i$, a feasible social state $f(\theta) \in A$.

A *mechanism* is an *I*-tuple of message spaces $\mathbf{M} \equiv (M^1, \ldots, M^I)$ and a function $g(.)$ that associates to each *I*-tuple of messages $\mathbf{m} \equiv (m^1, \ldots, m^I)$ a feasible social state $g(m)$ belonging to A. Agent i must transmit a message m^i knowing that the center will use the mechanism to choose the social state while, at the same time, he himself is ignorant of the characteristics of other agents. Therefore, a mechanism defines a game with incomplete information for which we must choose an equilibrium concept, denoted by c.

Let $E_{g,c}(.)$ be the mapping that associates to each *I*-tuple of true characteristics θ, the equilibrium messages of this game for the equilibrium concept c.

A mechanism (M, g) implements a social choice function $f(.)$ for the equilibrium concept c if $\forall \theta \in \Theta$, $g(E_{g,c}(\theta)) \equiv f(\theta)$. The concept of implementation can be illustrated by the following schema, due to Mount and Reiter:

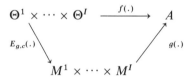

Two examples of equilibrium concepts will illuminate this schema.[1]

(i) Dominant equilibrium: $c \equiv d$. An *I*-tuple of messages $(m^{*1}, \ldots, m^{*I}) \in M$ is a dominant equilibrium if and only if

$$\forall i = 1, \ldots, I \qquad g(m^{*i}, m^{-i}) R^i(\theta^i) g(m^i, m^{-i})$$

$$\forall m^i \in M^i$$

$$\forall m^{-i} \in \prod_{j \neq i} M^j.$$

where

$$m^{-i} \equiv (m^1, ., m^{i-1}, m^{i+1}, \ldots, m^I)$$

$$(m^i, m^{-i}) \equiv (m^1. \ldots m^{i-1}, m^i, m^{i+1}, \ldots .m^I).$$

1. See also section 5.7*

Regardless of the messages of the other agents, agent i's choice of message m^{*i} leads to a social state that is preferred or indifferent to all other social states obtainable by sending any other message. For each $\theta \in \Theta$, $E_{g,d}(\theta)$ gives the set of dominant equilibria. The function $g(.)$ translates the equilibrium messages into social states.

(ii) Nash equilibrium: $c = n$. An I-tuple of messages $(m^{*1}, \ldots, m^{*I})$ is a Nash equilibrium if and only if

$$\forall i = 1, \ldots, I \qquad g(m^{*i}, m^{*-i}) R^i(\theta^i) g(m^i, m^{*-i})$$

$$\forall m^i \in M^i,$$

Given the equilibrium messages of the other agents, m^{*-i}, the choice of message m^{*i} is at least as good for agent i as any other message that he could choose. For each $\theta \in \Theta$, $E_{g,n}(\theta)$ gives the set of I-tuples of Nash equilibrium messages.

The equilibrium concept chosen determines the type of incentive compatibility of the implementation obtained. Thus implementation in dominant equilibria appears to be most satisfactory in the sense that if the agents really have dominant messages, it is reasonable to expect they will use them. The agents have very strong incentives to behave in the expected manner. On the other hand, implementation in Nash equilibria appears much weaker. Can we be sure that the agents will arrive at a Nash equilibrium in a game with incomplete information? When the equilibrium concept used is the dominant-message equilibrium, incentive theory is greatly simplified by the principle of revelation.

We say that a mechanism is *direct* if the space of messages of agent i, M^i, coincides with the space of his characteristics Θ^i for all $i = 1, \ldots, I$. A direct mechanism is said to be *revealing* if $\theta \in E_{g,c}(\theta)$ for each $\theta \in \Theta$, that is to say, if transmitting true characteristics is an equilibrium message. We say that a direct mechanism *implements by revelation* the social choice function $f(.)$ in dominant equilibria (or in Nash equilibria) if the direct mechanism is revealing and if $g(\theta) = f(\theta)$ for each $\theta \in \Theta$.

We note that implementation by revelation is a weaker concept than implementation since there may exist other equilibria that do not lead to the allocation characterized by $f(.)$.

THEOREM 1   The Revelation Principle (Gibbard 1973). Let (g, M) be a mechanism that implements the social choice function $f(.)$ for the dominant equilibrium concept. Then there exists a direct mechanism (Ψ, Θ) that implements by revelation $f(.)$ in dominant equilibria.

Proof Let $m^{*1}(\theta^1), \ldots, m^{*I}(\theta^I)$ be an I-tuple of dominant messages for (g, M). Define $\Psi(.)$ by

$$\Psi(\theta) \equiv g(E_{g,d}(\theta)).$$

By definition, $\Psi(\theta) \equiv f(\theta)$; (Ψ, Θ) is indeed a direct mechanism. Suppose that the transmission of his true characteristic is not a dominant message strategy for agent i. Then there exists $(\tilde{\theta}^i, \theta^{-i}) \in \Theta$ such that

$$\Psi(\tilde{\theta}^i, \theta^{-i}) P^i(\theta^i) \Psi(\theta^i, \theta^{-i}), \tag{1}$$

where $P^i(\theta^i)$ is the strict preference relation associated with $R^i(\theta^i)$.

By definition, (1) can be rewritten as

$$g(E_{g,d}(\tilde{\theta}^i, \theta^{-i})) P^i(\theta^i) g(E_{g,d}(\theta^i, \theta^{-i})). \tag{2}$$

Let $(m^{*1}, \ldots, m^{*i}, \ldots, m^{*I}) \in E_{g,d}(\theta^i, \theta^{-i})$; (2) indicates that there exists

$$(m^{*1}, \ldots, m^{*(i-1)}, \tilde{m}^i, m^{*(i+1)}, \ldots, m^{*I}) \in E_{g,d}(\tilde{\theta}^i, \theta^{-i})$$

such that

$$g(m^{*1}, \ldots, m^{*(i-1)}, \tilde{m}^i, m^{*(i+1)}, \ldots, m^{*I}) P^i(\theta^i) g(m^{*1}, \ldots, m^{*i}, \ldots, m^{*I}),$$

which contradicts the assumption that $(m^{*1}, \ldots, m^{*i}, \ldots, m^{*I}) \in E_{g,d}(\theta^i, \theta^{-i})$. ∎

Thus all social choice functions that can be implemented by dominant equilibria of complex messages can also be implemented by direct revelation mechanisms. Therefore it is sufficient to limit ourselves to direct revelation mechanisms when we study implementation in dominant strategy equilibria.

The general point that I wish to emphasize here is that the considerable weakening of incentive compatibility when we move from dominant equilibria to Nash equilibria is significant and fruitful only if the message spaces are more general than the spaces of characteristics.[2] Indeed, the following theorem illustrates this point.

---

2. The possibility of implementation in Nash equilibria by direct mechanisms when the agents lie also arises.

THEOREM 2   A social choice function $f(.)$ is implemented by revelation in a Nash equilibrium if and only if it is implemented by revelation in dominant equilibria by a direct mechanism.

Proof   The sufficient condition is obvious by definition. To establish the necessary condition, we write that $f(.)$ is implemented in Nash equilibria by a direct revelation mechanism (g, Θ) as

$$\forall i = 1, \dots, I$$

$$\forall \theta^i \in \Theta^i, \quad \forall \theta^{-i} \in \prod_{j \neq i} \Theta^j \tag{3}$$

$$g(\theta^i, \theta^{-i}) R^i(\theta^i) g(\tilde{\theta}^i, \theta^{-i}), \quad \forall \tilde{\theta}^i \in \Theta^i.$$

(3) can be rewritten immediately as

$$\forall i = 1, \dots, I$$

$$g(\theta^i, \theta^{-i}) R^i(\theta^i) g(\tilde{\theta}^i, \theta^{-i}), \quad \forall \tilde{\theta}^i \in \Theta^i, \quad \forall \theta \in \Theta,$$

but this is the definition that θ^i is a dominant strategy for agent i. ∎

In the following section, we show that in the absence of prior restrictions on the characteristics, implementation in dominant equilibria is essentially impossible.

5.2   Characterization of Social Choice Functions That Are Implementable in Dominant Equilibria under the Assumption of Universal Domain

Recall the example of chapter 4 that allowed us to present the paradox of Condorcet and consider the social choice function characterized by the simple majority voting procedure for the pair (a_1, a_2) and a simple majority vote between the one chosen in the first vote and a_3. If the agents vote according to their true preferences, a_1 is the winner in the first round and a_3 in the second. However, agent 1 can manipulate the procedure by voting for a_2 in the first round, thus assuring the victory of a_2 in the first round as well as in the second round. We generalize this result by showing that any social choice function (SCF) that has universal domain and is nondictatorial will be manipulable; that is, in the language of section 5.1, the SCF is not implementable in dominant equilibria.[3] Following the revelation principle, it is sufficient to focus on direct revelation mechanisms.

Let $\Sigma(A)$ be the set of orderings on A.[4] Let $(g, \Sigma(A))$ be a direct revelation mechanism; since $g(.)$ must coincide with the social choice function $f(.)$, we shall use $f(.)$ only. The profile $\mathbf{P} = (P^1, \ldots, P^I)$ plays the role of the vector θ in the previous section.

A SCF f is *manipulable* at $\mathbf{P} = (P^1, \ldots, P^I) \in [\Sigma(A)]^I$ if there exists $P'^i \in \Sigma(A)$ such that

$$f(P^1, \ldots, P'^i, \ldots, P^I)P^i f(P^1, \ldots, P^i, \ldots, P^I).$$

If we consider P^i to represent his true preferences, manipulation indicates that agent i can insure an outcome which he prefers by announcing P'^i.

A SCF f is *incentive-compatible* (or implementable in dominant equilibria by a direct revelation mechanism) if there exists no profile of preferences for which it is manipulable. In other words, for all the orderings announced by the other agents, agent i's true ordering is a dominant strategy for all i:

$$\forall \mathbf{P} = (P^1, \ldots, P^I) \in [\Sigma(A)]^I, \quad \forall P'^i \in \Sigma(A)$$

$$\Rightarrow f(P^1, \ldots, P^i, \ldots, P^I)P^i f(P^1, \ldots, P'^i, \ldots, P^I).$$

If f is a SCF and has an image on $A' \subseteq A$, we say that f is a SCF with image on A'.

A SCF with image on A' is *dictatorial* if there exists an agent whose favored social state in A' is always the social choice, that is, $i \in \{1, \ldots, I\}$ is a *dictator*, if for any $\mathbf{P} \in [\Sigma(A)]^I$, and any $a \in A'$ such that $a \neq f(\mathbf{P})$, then $f(\mathbf{P})P^i a$.

THEOREM 3 (Gibbard 1973, Satterthwaite 1975)   If A' has at least three elements, then a social choice function with image on A' that has universal domain and is incentive-compatible must be dictatorial.

Proof[5]

LEMMA 1   If there exists $i \in \{1, \ldots, I\}$ such that

$$f(P^1, \ldots, P^i, \ldots, P^I) = a_1$$

---

3. The dimension of the set of states that can be obtained for at least one profile of preferences must be greater than or equal to 3, as in Arrow's theorem. With two states only simple majority voting is nonmanipulative and nondictatorial. Nonetheless A is assumed to be finite.
4. To simplify the argument, the analysis is restricted to orderings.
5. We owe this particular proof to Schmeidler and Sonnenschein.

$$f(P^1, \ldots, P'^i, \ldots, P^I) = a_2, a_1 \neq a_2$$

and if

$$a_2 P^i a_1 \quad \text{or} \quad a_1 P'^i a_2$$

then f is manipulable at $(P^1, \ldots, P^i, \ldots, P^I)$ or at $(P^1, \ldots, P'^i, \ldots, P^I)$.

Proof   If $a_1 P'^i a_2$, then

$$f(P^1, \ldots, P^i, \ldots, P^I) P'^i f(P^1, \ldots, P'^i, \ldots, P^I).$$

If $a_2 P^i a_1$, then

$$f(P^1, \ldots, P'^i, \ldots, P^I) P^i f(P^1, \ldots, P^i, \ldots, P^I). \quad \blacksquare$$

LEMMA 2   If f has an image on $A' \subseteq A$ and if $B \subseteq A'$ and if **P** is a profile so that for any pair of states, a_1, a_2, with $a_1 \in B$, $a_2 \in A'$ and $a_2 \notin B$, $a_1 P^i a_2$, for all i, then $f(P^1, \ldots, P^I) \in B$.

Proof   Assume the contrary; let $f(P^1, \ldots, P^I) = a_2 \notin B$. Since $B \subset A'$, there exist $(P'^1, \ldots, P'^I) \in [\Sigma(A)]^I$ such that $f(P'^1, \ldots, P'^I) = a_1 \in B$.

Then consider the set of social states

$$\{a_3^i\}_{i=0}^{i=I}$$

defined by

$$a_3^i = f(P'^1, \ldots, P'^i, P^{i+1}, \ldots, P^I),$$

and let j be the first integer such that $a_3^j \in B$. Then

$$f(P'^1, \ldots, P'^j, P^{j+1}, \ldots, P^I) = a_3^j \in B$$

$$f(P'^1, \ldots, P'^{(j-1)}, P^j, \ldots, P^I) = a_3^{j-1} \notin B$$

and

$$a_3^j P^j a_3^{j-1},$$

which implies that f is manipulable at $(P'^1, \ldots, P'^{(j-1)}, P^j, \ldots, P^I)$. $\blacksquare$

The basic idea of this proof is to start from the social choice function f and to construct a social ranking $\mathscr{F}$ that satisfies the assumptions of Arrow's impossibility theorem. This allows us to conclude that $\mathscr{F}$ is dictatorial, and hence f is dictatorial.

Given a profile $(P^1, \ldots, P^I)$ and a pair or states (a_1, a_2), we construct a modified profile $(\tilde{P}^1, \ldots, \tilde{P}^I)$ as follows: $\tilde{P}^i$ is derived from P^i by replacing a_1 and a_2 at the top of the list and by keeping the ordering P^i on $\{a_1, a_2\}$ and on $\{a/a \in A,\ a \neq a_1,\ a \neq a_2\}$. Let $\phi_{a_1, a_2}(P^i)$ be the ordering $\tilde{P}^i$ constructed in this way.

For the pair (a_1, a_2), we then define $a_1 P a_2$ if $a_1 = f(\tilde{P}^1, \ldots, \tilde{P}^I)$.

Repeating this process for every pair of social states yields a binary relation P and repeating it for each admissible profile yields a potential social ranking, that is, a function that associates to each profile a binary relation.

$\mathscr{F}$ satisfies the assumption of universal domain by definition.

$\mathscr{F}$ satisfies PP on A' by lemma 2.

$\mathscr{F}$ satisfies IIA, otherwise an argument similar to that of lemma 2 shows that f is manipulable. It remains to show that P is an ordering. The fact that P is complete and asymmetric is obvious.

Suppose that P is not transitive, then there exists $P^1, \ldots, P^I, a_1, a_2, a_3$ with

$$a_1 = f[\phi_{a_1 a_2}(P^1), \ldots, \phi_{a_1 a_2}(P^I)] \Leftrightarrow a_1 P a_2$$

$$a_2 = f[\phi_{a_2 a_3}(P^1), \ldots, \phi_{a_2 a_3}(P^I)] \Leftrightarrow a_2 P a_3$$

$$a_3 = f[\phi_{a_1 a_3}(P^1), \ldots, \phi_{a_1 a_3}(P^I)] \Leftrightarrow a_3 P a_1.$$

Let $(P'^1, \ldots, P'^I)$ be the profile defined by placing (a_1, a_2, a_3) at the top of the list and keeping the orderings P^i on the sets $\{a_1, a_2, a_3\}$ and $\{a/a \in A,\ a \neq a_1, a \neq a_2, a \neq a_3\}$. Then suppose that $a_1 = f(P'^1, \ldots, P'^I)$.

Let $(P''^1, \ldots, P''^I)$ be the profile obtained by replacing a_3 in the third position of each of the orderings P'^i. Since $a_1 P^i a_3 \Leftrightarrow a_1 P''^i a_3$, $a_3 P a_1$ and the property IIA implies $a_3 = f(P''^1, \ldots, P''^I)$.

Let $a_4^i = f(P''^1, \ldots, P''^i, P'^{(i+1)}, \ldots, P'^I)$, $i = 0, \ldots, I$, and let j be the first integer such that $a_4^j \neq a_1$.

If $a_4^j = a_3$, then f is manipulable by lemma 1.

If $a_4^j = a_2$, then f is manipulable by j at $(P''^1, \ldots, P''^j, P'^{(j+1)}, \ldots, P'^I)$.

By Arrow's theorem, $\mathscr{F}$ is dictatorial. The dictator for $\mathscr{F}$ is obviously a dictator for f. ∎

Starting from this fundamental negative result, we look in several directions for positive results. As for Arrow's impossibility theorem itself, we can examine restrictions on the preferences that lead to nonmanipulable social choice functions. Closely related to the restrictions that allow the

construction of a social ranking in Arrow's problem are those that allow
the construction of a nonmanipulable social choice function (see Kalai and
Muller 1976). We know that the majority voting procedure for unimodal
preferences yields a social welfare function satisfying Arrow's assumptions.
It is easy to show that the best choice for the median voter is a nonmanipulable social choice function. Indeed, any lie that does not change the
median voter has no effect and any lie that changes the median voter
changes him in the wrong direction.[6] In the following section we shall see
how restricting ourselves to additively separable utility functions also
facilitates the construction of nonmanipulable social choice functions.
Another direction to take consists of weakening the notion of nonmanipu-
lability and seeking implementation by equilibria other than dominant
equilibria,[7] for example, Nash equilibria.

A social choice function $f(.)$ is *monotonic* if

$$\forall \mathbf{R}, \tilde{\mathbf{R}} \in [\Sigma(A)]^I, \quad \forall a \in A, \quad a \in f(\mathbf{R})$$

$$\forall i \in I, \quad \forall b \in A, \quad aR^i b \Rightarrow a\tilde{R}^i b$$

$$\Rightarrow a \in f(\tilde{\mathbf{R}}).$$

That is, if a is chosen for the profile $\mathbf{R}$ and if a is an improvement for all
agents in the profile $\tilde{\mathbf{R}}$, then a must be chosen for the profile $\tilde{\mathbf{R}}$. The social
choice function $f(.)$ does not recognize *veto power*, if and only if for a profile
$\mathbf{R}$ such that

$$\forall j \neq i, \quad \forall b \in A, \quad aR^j b \quad \Rightarrow \quad a \in f(\mathbf{R}).$$

The following fundamental theorem allows us to characterize implementable social choice functions in Nash equilibria.

THEOREM 4 (Maskin 1977)   Consider a social choice function of $[\Sigma(A)]^I$
on A with $|A| \geq 3$. If f is implementable for Nash equilibria, it is monotonic.
Furthermore, if $f(.)$ is monotonic and it does not recognize veto power, it
is implementable in Nash equilibria.

6. Hervé Moulin (1980) has shown that the only nonmanipulable social choice functions are
those with positional dictators. Recall that, in this structure, the social states are ordered on
a straight line and becoming positional dictator i is the best choice of the agent whose best
choice is the ith starting from the left. Majority rule corresponds to the choice of positional
dictator $(I + 1)/2$.
7. See chapter 5 of Green and Laffont (1979) and Dasgupta, Hammond, and Maskin (1979).

The proof of this theorem is by construction and consists of designing a mechanism for the message spaces $M^i = \prod_{j=1}^{I} \Theta^j$, $\forall i$, that is, where each agent announces characteristics for all the agents. This highlights, in an extreme way, the weakness of the concept of implementation for Nash equilibria because nothing is said about the way in which the Nash equilibria are obtained in games with incomplete information. However, in the above mechanism, agent i announces characteristics for all the agents in society at Nash equilibria. Indeed, this notion is adapted to the case where agents do not know the characteristics when they choose the mechanism but do know them when they play the game of transmitting messages.

5.3 A Nonmanipulable Mechanism for Determining the Output of Public Goods

The intuition for this mechanism can be developed from a Vickrey auction. Consider an indivisible commodity that is auctioned off among a group of I agents. These agents' true willingness to pay for the commodity can be obtained by the following procedure. Require each agent to make his offer by sealed bid knowing that the commodity will be given to the highest bidder but that he will have to pay only the second highest bid price. That the true willingness to pay is a dominant strategy for each agent can be shown easily.

Without loss of generality consider agent 1 and differentiate two cases according to whether telling the truth v^1 leads the agent to have the highest bid (first case) or not (second case). In the first case, he receives the commodity and pays the second highest bid price, call it w^2. It is never in his self-interest to bid anything other than v^1. As long as his bid $w^1 > w^2$, nothing changes, he neither gains nor loses anything. If his bid $w^1 < w^2$, he no longer receives the commodity so that he pays nothing. However, he loses utility $(v^1 - w^2)$ that he would have secured had he told the truth. In the second case, so long as his bid w^1 is smaller than the highest bid w^2, nothing changes for him. If his bid $w^1 > w^2$, he receives the commodity and pays w^2 so that he has a loss of utility equal to $(w^2 - v^1)$, which is positive by assumption.

The following mechanism exploits the same idea in the context of public goods. We assume that the utility functions are quasi-linear, that is, *private good* ↓   *public good,* $y = \{0,1\}$

$$U^i(x^i, y) = x^i + v^i(y) \qquad i = 1, \ldots, I,$$

where x^i is the consumption of the single private good and y is the available quantity of the public good. Let $\bar{x}$ be the aggregate endowment of the private good. Consider the case in which the public good is produced at zero cost and there is a unique possible level of public good, $y = 1$. Therefore, $y = \{0, 1\}$ and we adopt the normalization

$$v^i(0) = 0, \quad \text{with} \quad v^i(1) = v^i \qquad i = 1, \ldots, I.$$

A correct decision is defined by

$$y = 1 \Leftrightarrow \sum_{i=1}^{I} v^i \geqslant 0.$$

We ask each agent to reveal his willingness to pay for the public good, w^i. Let $\mathbf{w} = (w^1, \ldots, w^I)$. The social decision is taken according to the rule

$$y(w) = 1 \Leftrightarrow \sum_{i=1}^{I} w^i \geqslant 0,$$

and by announcing to agent i a transfer in terms of the private good[8] of:

$$t^i(w) = \left| \sum_{j \neq i} w^j \right| \quad \text{if} \quad \left(\sum_{j \neq i} w^j \right) \left(\sum_{i=1}^{I} w^i \right) < 0$$

$$= 0 \quad \text{otherwise.} \tag{4}$$

It is easy to show that the truth $w^i = v^i$ is a dominant strategy for each agent.

We calculate below the variation in utility Δ^i between the true response v^i and any other response for all possible cases:

First case: $\sum_{j \neq i} w^j > 0.$

(a) $\sum_{j \neq i} w^j + v^i \geqslant 0 \qquad \sum_{j \neq i} w^j + w^i \geqslant 0$

$\Delta^i = v^i - v^i = 0.$

---

8. When he changes the social decision by his response, the agent must pay the cost which he imposes on others. The Vickrey auction exhibits this property also: when the agent takes the commodity (that is, bids higher than the others), he pays the cost that he imposes on the others (that is, the second highest price).

(b) $\sum_{j\neq i} w^j + v^i > 0 \qquad \sum_{j\neq i} w^j + w^i < 0$

$$\Delta^i \doteqdot v^i - \left(-\sum_{j\neq i} w^j\right) = v^i + \sum_{j\neq i} w^j > 0$$

(c) $\sum_{j\neq i} w^j + v^i < 0 \qquad \sum_{j\neq i} w^j + w^i < 0$

$$\Delta^i = -\sum_{j\neq i} w^j - \left(-\sum_{j\neq i} w^j\right) = 0$$

(d) $\sum_{j\neq i} w^j + v^i < 0 \qquad \sum_{j\neq i} w^j + w^i > 0$

$$\Delta^i = -\sum_{j\neq i} w^j - v^i = -\left(v^i + \sum_{j\neq i} w^j\right) > 0$$

Second case: $\sum_{j\neq i} w^j < 0.$

(same type of calculations)

Notice that without changing the above reasoning, we can add to the function $t^i(w)$ any function of the responses of the other agents. Thus, we obtain the family of Groves mechanisms, for which the transfers can be rewritten:[9]

$$t^i(w) = \sum_{j\neq i} w^j + h^i(w^{-i}) \quad \text{if } \sum_{i=1}^{I} w^i \geqslant 0$$

$$\qquad = h^i(w^{-i}) \qquad\qquad \text{if } \sum_{i=1}^{I} w^i < 0,$$

where $h^i(.)$ is an arbitrary function of w^{-i}.

In this class of mechanisms, there exist feasible mechanisms in the sense that $\sum_{i=1}^{I} t^i(w) \leqslant 0$, that is, they yield a budgetary surplus rather than deficit for the social decision maker. An example is the mechanism described in (4) above. Here the set of social outcomes A is the set of feasible consumption levels of the private good and an achievable quantity of the public good

$$A = \left\{ y, (x^1, \ldots, x^I) : y \in \{0, 1\}, \sum_{i=1}^{I} x^i \leqslant \bar{x} \right\}.$$

9. It is necessary to add to (4): $\text{Min}(0, -\sum_{j\neq i} w^j) + h^i(w^{-i})$.

The mapping

$$(v^1, \ldots, v^I) \xrightarrow{f} \begin{cases} y(v) \\ t^1(v) \\ \ldots \\ t^I(v) \end{cases}$$

of R^I in A describes a social choice function that is implementable in dominant equilibria.

In general, however, there do not exist functions $h^i(.)$ such that $\sum_{i=1}^I t^i(w) = 0$, that is, those for which the budget of the social decision maker is exactly balanced. Consequently, it is not possible to implement with dominant messages a Pareto-optimal social choice function even under the very strong restriction of quasi-linearity. Decentralization of information is incompatible with Pareto optimality and the center's problem must be explicitly formulated in terms of the second best as we shall see in an example in section 7.4. Otherwise, we must weaken the notion of incentive compatibility (see section 5.7*). As a step in this direction, we study the differentiable method in the next section.

5.4   The Differentiable Method

In this section, we use a constructive method to obtain mechanisms with dominant messages for the problem of the preference revelation discussed in the preceding section. Suppose that the public good is now divisible and that the function of willingness to pay of agent i for public good y is parametrized by $\theta^i \in R$ and written as $v^i(y, \theta^i)$, where v^i is continuously differentiable. The center knows the form of the function $v^i(.\,,.)$ for all i but not the true value of the parameter θ^i. It designs a direct mechanism where $\tilde{\theta}^i$, which could be different from θ, is announced by agent i and the social outcome is determined by a decision function for the public good $y^*(\tilde{\theta})$ and by transfers in terms of the private good $t^i(\tilde{\theta})$, $i = 1, \ldots, I$, where $\tilde{\theta} = (\tilde{\theta}^1, \ldots, \tilde{\theta}^I)$.

For it to be in agent i's self-interest to tell the truth, $\tilde{\theta}^i = \theta^i$ must be a solution to the problem

$$\underset{\tilde{\theta}^i}{\text{Max}} \ [v^i(y^*(\tilde{\theta}^i, \tilde{\theta}^{-i}), \theta^i) + t^i(\tilde{\theta}^i, \tilde{\theta}^{-i})],$$

for which the first-order condition is (under the appropriate assumptions of differentiability)

$$\frac{\partial v^i}{\partial y}(y^*(\tilde{\theta}^i, \tilde{\theta}^{-i}), \theta^i)\frac{\partial y^*}{\partial \theta^i}(\tilde{\theta}^i, \tilde{\theta}^{-i}) + \frac{\partial t^i}{\partial \theta^i}(\tilde{\theta}^i, \tilde{\theta}^{-i}) = 0. \tag{5}$$

A necessary condition for $\tilde{\theta}^i = \theta^i$ to be a solution to (5) for any announcements from the other agents $\tilde{\theta}^{-i} \in \prod_{j \neq i} \Theta^j$ is

$$\frac{\partial v^i}{\partial y}(y^*(\theta^i, \tilde{\theta}^{-i}), \theta^i)\frac{\partial y^*}{\partial \theta^i}(\theta^i, \tilde{\theta}^{-i}) + \frac{\partial t^i}{\partial \theta^i}(\theta^i, \tilde{\theta}^{-i}) = 0. \tag{6}$$

If we want the mechanism to reveal the truth, whatever the truth may be, (6) must hold for any θ^i. Therefore (6) becomes an identity in θ that we can rewrite as

$$\frac{\partial v^i}{\partial y}(y^*(\theta), \theta^i)\frac{\partial y^*}{\partial \theta^i}(\theta) + \frac{\partial t^i}{\partial \theta^i}(\theta) \equiv 0; \tag{7}$$

by integration we have

$$t^i(\theta) = -\int_0^{\theta^i} \frac{\partial v^i}{\partial y}(y^*(s^i, \theta^{-i}), s^i)\frac{\partial y^*}{\partial s^i}(s^i, \theta^{-i})\,ds^i + \tilde{h}^i(0^{-i}) \qquad \forall i, \tag{8}$$

where $\tilde{h}^i(\theta^{-i})$ is an arbitrary function of θ^{-i}.

If the decision function for the public good that we seek to implement, $y^*(\theta)$, is the one that maximizes $\sum_{i=1}^{I} v^i(y, \theta^i)$ (that is, the decision function of the public good that corresponds to an interior Pareto optimum), then

$$\frac{\partial v^i}{\partial y}(y^*(\theta), \theta^i) = -\sum_{j \neq i} \frac{\partial v^j}{\partial y}(y^*(\theta), \theta^j)$$

and (8) becomes

$$t^i(\theta) = \sum_{j \neq i} v^j(y^*(\theta), \theta^j) + h^i(\theta^{-i}),$$

which turns out to be the Groves mechanism in the case of a divisible public good. We know that this necessary form of transfers $t^i(.)$ yields mechanisms for which telling the truth is truly a dominant strategy. We can verify that

$$v^i(y^*(\theta^i, \theta^{-i}), \theta^i) + \sum_{j \neq i} v^j(y^*(\theta^i, \theta^{-i}), \theta^j) + h^i(\theta^{-i})$$

$$\geq v^i(y^*(\tilde{\theta}^i, \theta^{-i}), \theta^i) + \sum_{j \neq i} v^j(y^*(\tilde{\theta}^i, \theta^{-i}), \theta^j) + h^i(\theta^{-i})$$

by definition of $y^*(.)$.

The method described above is one of the most convenient tools in the theory of incentives. It consists of integrating a system of differential equations that give a necessary condition for a mechanism to be revealing in dominant strategies. In general, supplementary conditions must be imposed on the solutions for them to satisfy second-order conditions as well. In the case considered here, all the solutions obtained by integration are valid when $y^*(.)$ maximizes $\sum_{i=1}^{I} v^i(.)$. However, the comments at the end of section 5.3 still apply.

5.5   An Application to Planning Procedures

Reconsider the procedure MDP studied in chapter 2 and assume for simplification that the cost of the public good is zero but that the agents can either like or dislike the public good. Denote the marginal rate of substitution by $\theta^i(t) = \dfrac{\partial U^i/\partial y}{\partial U^i/\partial x^i}$. It is easy to characterize the planning procedures for which truth will be a dominant strategy at each point in time.

At each point in time, agent i transmits his marginal rate of substitution and the planning procedure that begins at time $t = 0$ for which $x^i(t) = w^i$, $i = 1, \ldots, I$, and $y(t) = 0$, revises the allocation according to the system of differential equations

$$\frac{dy}{dt}(t) = \dot{y} = Y(\theta^1(t), \ldots, \theta^I(t)) \tag{9}$$

$$\frac{dx^i}{dt}(t) = \dot{x}^i = T^i(\theta^1(t), \ldots, \theta^I(t)) \qquad i = 1, \ldots, I. \tag{10}$$

At each point in time agent i wishes to maximize, with respect to the announcement $\tilde{\theta}^i$, the speed of increase of his utility function proportional to[10] $\theta^i Y(\tilde{\theta}^i, \theta^{-i}) + T^i(\tilde{\theta}^i, \theta^{-i})$. Consequently, we say that the agent behaves myopically.

A necessary condition for telling the truth to be a dominant strategy is therefore

10. Because $\dfrac{dU^i}{dt} = \dfrac{\partial U^i}{\partial x^i}(x^i(t), y(t))[\theta^i(t)\dot{y} + \dot{x}^i]$.

$$\theta^i \frac{\partial Y}{\partial \theta^i}(\theta^i, \theta^{-i}) + \frac{\partial T^i}{\partial \theta^i}(\theta^i, \theta^{-i}) = 0 \qquad \text{for all } \theta^i \text{ and } \theta^{-i},$$

from which it follows that

$$T^i(\theta) = -\int_0^{\theta^i} s^i \frac{\partial Y}{\partial s^i}(s^i, \theta^{-i}) \, ds^i + h^i(\theta^{-i}). \qquad (11)$$

The necessary second-order condition is written as:

$$\theta^i \frac{\partial^2 Y}{(\partial \theta^i)^2}(\tilde{\theta}^i, \theta^{-i}) + \frac{\partial^2 T^i}{(\partial \theta^i)^2}(\tilde{\theta}^i, \theta^{-i}) \leqslant 0 \quad \text{in } \tilde{\theta}^i = \theta^i \text{ for any } \theta^{-i}.$$

Using the identity given by the first-order condition, the above necessary condition can be rewritten as

$$\frac{\partial Y}{\partial \theta^i}(\theta^i, \theta^{-i}) \geqslant 0 \qquad \forall \theta^i, \quad \forall \theta^{-i}.$$

In fact, this condition is sufficient as well because:

$$\theta^i Y(\theta^i, \theta^{-i}) + T^i(\theta^i, \theta^{-i}) \geqslant \theta^i Y(\tilde{\theta}^i, \theta^{-i}) + T^i(\tilde{\theta}^i, \theta^{-i}) \quad \text{for all } (\tilde{\theta}^i, \theta^{-i}).$$
$$(12)$$

Indeed, using (11), (12) can be written as

$$(\theta^i - \tilde{\theta}^i) Y(\tilde{\theta}^i, \theta^{-i}) \leqslant \int_{\tilde{\theta}^i}^{\theta^i} Y(s^i, \theta^{-i}) \, ds^i,$$

which follows from the weak monotonicity of $Y(.)$.

   This class of procedures contains only one member of the class of MDP[11] procedures in the case where $I = 2$. Then

$$Y(\theta) = \theta^1 + \theta^2$$

$$T^1(\theta) = -\theta^1 Y(\theta) + \tfrac{1}{2}[Y(\theta)]^2$$

$$T^2(\theta) = -\theta^2 Y(\theta) + \tfrac{1}{2}[Y(\theta)]^2,$$

which turns out to be the MDP procedure with egalitarian sharing of the surplus.

11. That is, the procedure proposed by Malinvaud (1972) and Drèze and De la Vallée Poussin (1971).

5.6   An Application to Externalities

Consider the following example: A firm pollutes the environment by its activity. It can adjust the amount of its pollution x by using an antipollution activity having the associated cost function $C(x, \theta)$, which is decreasing in x, and where θ ($\theta \in R$) represents a parameter known only to the firm. The damage created by an amount of pollution x is $D(x)$.

The social optimum corresponds to an amount x^* such that

$$D(x^*) + C(x^*, \theta) = \min_{x} [D(x) + C(x, \theta)].$$

Suppose that this amount is unique for all θ and that the functions $D(.)$ and $C(.)$ are continuously differentiable. What social choice functions are implementable in dominant messages?

Characterize a social outcome by an amount of pollution x and a transfer payment to the firm by

$$f(\theta) = \begin{cases} x(\theta) \\ t(\theta) \end{cases}.$$

By adopting the differentiable method, we see that $(x(\theta), t(\theta))$ must satisfy

$$\frac{\partial C}{\partial x}(x(\theta), \theta)\frac{\partial x}{\partial \theta}(\theta) + \frac{\partial t}{\partial \theta}(\theta) \equiv 0,$$

from which it follows that

$$t(\theta) = \int_0^\theta \frac{\partial C}{\partial x}(x(t), t)\frac{\partial x}{\partial t}(t)\, dt + K.$$

The local second-order condition is

$$\frac{\partial x}{\partial \theta}(\theta)\frac{\partial^2 C}{\partial x \partial \theta}(x(\theta), \theta) \leqslant 0 \qquad \forall \theta.$$

Suppose that we seek to implement the amount of pollution corresponding to the social optimum. Then

$$\frac{d}{dx}D(x) + \frac{\partial C}{\partial x}(x, \theta) = 0$$

implicitly defines $x(\theta)$, and

$$t(\theta) = -\int_0^\theta \frac{d}{dx} D(x) \frac{\partial x}{\partial t}(t)\, dt + K$$

$$= -D(x(\theta)) + K'.$$

The local second-order condition is satisfied and a particular case of the Groves mechanism emerges.

If we tell the agent that he must pay (up to an arbitrary constant) the total amount of damage he creates, he is led to reveal his true cost parameter. Interestingly, this nonlinear price or this non-Pigouvian tax allows us to resolve simultaneously the difficulties due to the nonconvexity of negative externality described in chapter 1 and to the asymmetry of information. Generally speaking, the nonlinear optimal tax does not restore a complete information optimum (see problem 7).

5.7*   Bayesian Equilibria

In many cases, implementation in dominant equilibria is too demanding. Therefore, we appeal to the concept of Bayesian equilibria proposed by Harsanyi (1967–68). Consider the structure of section 5.1. Call $\mu^i(\theta^{-i}/\theta^i)$ the expectations of agent i concerning the characteristics of the other agents, $i = 1, \ldots, I$. We say that the functions $(m^{*1}(\theta^1), \ldots, m^{*I}(\theta^I))$ of $\prod_{i=1}^I \Theta^i$ in $\prod_{i=1}^I M^i$ form a Bayesian equilibrium if

$$\int_{\Theta^{-i}} U^i(g(m^{*i}(\theta^i), m^{*-i}(\theta^{-i})))\, d\mu^i(\theta^{-i}/\theta^i)$$

$$\tag{13}$$

$$\geqslant \int_{\Theta^{-i}} U^i(g(m^{*i}(\tilde{\theta}^i), m^{*-i}(\theta^{-i})))\, d\mu^i(\theta^{-i}/\theta^i) \qquad \forall \tilde{\theta}^i \in \Theta^i \quad \forall i = 1, \ldots, I,$$

where the notation $m^{*-i}(\theta^{-i})$ means $m^{*1}(\theta^1), \ldots, m^{*i-1}(\theta^{i-1}), m^{*i+1}(\theta^{i+1}), \ldots, m^{*I}(\theta^I)$.

Given his expectations, the strategy $m^{*i}(\theta^i)$ maximizes the expected utility of agent i with characteristic θ^i who believes that the other agents will employ strategies $(m^{*j}(.))$ and who has expectations $\mu^i(./\theta^i)$ concerning their characteristics. Aspremont and Gerard-Varet (1979) have proposed the following incentive concept for the problem of allocating public goods. Reconsider the structure of section 5.4. Truthful revelation strategies make up a Bayesian equilibrium if

θ^i maximizes $\displaystyle\int_{\Theta^{-i}} \{v^i(y^*(\tilde{\theta}^i, \theta^{-i}), \theta^i) + t^i(\tilde{\theta}^i, \theta^{-i})\}\, d\mu^i(\theta^{-i}/\theta^i)$

with respect to $\tilde{\theta}^i$, or

$$-E_{\Theta^{-i}}\frac{\partial v^i}{\partial y}(y^*(\theta^i, \theta^{-i}), \theta^i)\frac{\partial y^*}{\partial \theta^i}(\theta^i, \theta^{-i}) = E_{\Theta^i}\frac{\partial t^i}{\partial \theta^i}(\theta^i, \theta^{-i}) \tag{14}$$

by using the differentiable approach.

For example, consider the transfer payments, written as

$$t^i(\theta) = r^i(\theta^i) - \frac{1}{(I-1)}\sum_{\substack{j=1 \\ j \neq i}}^{I} r^j(\theta^j), \tag{15}$$

which sum to zero by construction. From (14) it follows that

$$\frac{dr^i}{d\theta^i} = -E_{\Theta^{-i}}\frac{\partial v^i}{\partial y}(y^*(\theta^i, \theta^{-i}), \theta^i)\frac{\partial y^*}{\partial \theta^i}(\theta^i, \theta^{-i})$$

$$r^i(\theta) = \int_0^{\theta^i} -E_{\Theta^{-i}}\frac{\partial v^i}{\partial y}(y^*(s^i, \theta^{-i}), s^i)\frac{\partial y^*}{\partial s^i}(s^i, \theta^{-i})\, ds^i + K^i. \tag{16}$$

If we wish to implement the function y^* that maximizes $\sum_{i=1}^{I} v^i(y, \theta^i)$, switching integrals in (16) yields

$$r^i(\theta^i) = E_{\Theta^{-i}}\sum_{j \neq i} v^*(y^*(\theta^i, \theta^{-i}), \theta^i) + K^i.$$

The mechanisms formed from function $y^*(.)$ and the transfer payments in (15) implement the Pareto optimum for Bayesian equilibria. Not only is the decision for the public good Pareto optimal, but the transfer payments also net out to zero. Hence, some gain over the Groves mechanism is achieved by weakening the incentive concept to a Bayesian equilibrium.

References

Aspremont, C. d', and L. A. Gerard-Varet 1979, "Incentives and incomplete information," *Journal of Public Economics*, 11, 225–45.

Dasgupta, P., P. Hammond, and E. Maskin 1979, "The implementation of social choice rules. Some general results on incentive compatibility," *Review of Economic Studies*, 66, 185–216.

Drèze, J., and D. De la Vallée Poussin 1971, "A tâtonnement process for public goods," *Review of Economic Studies*, 38, 133–150.

Gibbard, A., 1973, "Manipulation for voting schemes," *Econometrica*, 41, 587–601.

Green, J., and J.-J. Laffont 1979, *Incentives in Public Decision Making*, vol. 1, Studies in Public Economics, North-Holland.

Harsanyi, J. C., 1967/68, " Games with incomplete information played by 'Bayesian players'," *Management Science*, 14, 159–189, 320–334, 486–502.

Kalai, E., and E. Muller 1976, "Characterization of domains admitting non-dictatorial social welfare functions and non-manipulable voting procedures," *Journal of Economic Theory*, 16, 457–469.

Laffont, J.-J., 1985, "Incitations dans les procédures de planification," *Annales de l'INSEE*, 58, 3–36.

Laffont, J.-J., and E. Maskin 1980, "A differential approach to dominant strategy mechanisms," *Econometrica*, 48, 1507–1520.

———— 1982, "The theory of incentives: an overview," chapter 2 of W. Hildenbrand, ed., *Advances in Economic* Theory, Cambridge University Press.

Malinvaud, E., 1972, "Prices for individual consumption, quantity indicators for collective consumption," *Review of Economic Studies*, 39, 385–405.

Maskin, E., 1977, "Nash equilibrium and welfare optimality," mimeo.

Moulin, H., 1980, "On strategy proofness and single peakedness," *Public Choice*, 35, 437–455.

Satterthwaite, M., 1975, "Strategy-proofness and Arrow's conditions: Existence and correspondence theorems for voting procedures and social welfare functions," *Journal of Economic Theory*, 10, 187–217.

Recommended Reading

1. Gibbard 1973 (the fundamental paper).

2. Dasgupta, Hammond, and Maskin 1979 (a remarkable synthesis of incentive theory and social choice theory).

3. Green and Laffont 1979 (a monograph on Clarke-Grove mechanisms).

4. Laffont and Maskin 1980 (the differential approach to incentive compatibility).

5. Laffont and Maskin 1982 (a survey of incentive theory).

6. Laffont 1985 (incentives and planning).

Preface to Chapter 6
Duality in Consumer Theory

Consider a consumer in an economy with L commodities; let $X = \mathbf{R}^L_+$ be his consumption set and $U(x)$ be his utility function defined on X. Assume

HO: $U(x)$ is strictly increasing, strictly quasi-concave, and twice continuously differentiable.

Let $p \in R^L_+$ be the vector of prices and R be the income of the consumer.
   The Walrasian or *Marshallian demand function* $x(p, R)$ is the solution to the problem

Max $U(x)$
$_r$

subject to $R - px \geqslant 0$

$$x \geqslant 0.$$

   The *compensated demand* or *Hicksian demand function* $\Psi(p, u)$ is the solution to the problem

Min px
$_x$

subject to $U(x) \geqslant u$

$$x \geqslant 0.$$

This function characterizes the consumption bundles that allow the consumer to achieve, at the lowest cost, the utility level u when the vector of prices is given by p.
   The *cost* or *expenditure function* $C(p, u)$ specifies the minimum cost that allows an agent to achieve the utility level u given the vector of prices p. $C(p, u)$ is the value of the objective function at the optimum in the above problem, that is,

$C(p, u) = p\Psi(p, u).$

THEOREM   Under HO, for all $p \in R^L_+$ such that $C(p, u) > 0$,
(a) $\Psi(p, u)$ is a continuous function and
(b) $C(p, u)$ is a differentiable function that is increasing in u and strictly increasing and concave in p. Furthermore,

$$\frac{\partial C}{\partial p_h}(p, u) \equiv \Psi_h(p, u).$$

Proof   (a) follows immediately from the strict quasi-concavity of $U(.)$ and from the maximum theorem.[1] That $C(p, u)$ is increasing in u and p follows from the definition of $C(.,.)$.

(b) Proof that $C(p, U)$ is strictly concave in p:

Let

$p \in R_+^L$ and $p' \in R_+^L$, $p \neq p'$

$C(p, u) = \min\{px : U(x) \geq u \text{ and } x \geq 0\} = p\Psi(p, u)$

$C(p', u) = \min\{p'x : U(x) \geq u \text{ and } x \geq 0\} = p'\Psi(p', u)$

$C(\lambda p + (1 - \lambda)p', u) = \min\{(\lambda p + (1 - \lambda)p')x : U(x) \geq u \text{ and } x \geq 0\}$

$$= [\lambda p + (1 - \lambda)p']\Psi(\lambda p + (1 - \lambda)p', u)$$

Therefore, the definition of Ψ implies

$p\Psi(\lambda p + (1 - \lambda)p', u) \geq p\Psi(p, u)$

and

$p'\Psi(\lambda p + (1 - \lambda)p', u) \geq p'\Psi(p', u),$

from which it follows that

$C(\lambda p + (1 - \lambda)p', u) = [\lambda p + (1 - \lambda)p']\Psi(\lambda p + (1 - \lambda)p', u)$

$$\geq \lambda p\Psi(p, u) + (1 - \lambda)p'\Psi(p', u)$$

$$= \lambda C(p, u) + (1 - \lambda)C(p', u).$$

Proof that $C(p, u)$ is differentiable in p:

Let

$h \in R^L$, $p + h > 0$, $h \neq 0$

$C(p + h, u) = (p + h)\Psi(p + h, u) \leq (p + h)\Psi(p, u) = p\Psi(p, u) + h\Psi(p, u)$

$$\leq C(p, u) + h\Psi(p, u)$$

$C(p, u) = p\Psi(p, u) \leq p\Psi(p + h, u) = (p + h)\Psi(p + h, u) - h\Psi(p + h, u)$

$$\leq C(p + h, u) - h\Psi(p + h, u),$$

1. See Berge (1959) or the mathematical results, page ix.

from which it follows that

$$\frac{h[\Psi(p + h, u) - \Psi(p, u)]}{|h|} \leqslant \frac{C(p + h, u) - C(p, u) - h\Psi(p, u)}{|h|} \leqslant 0. \tag{1}$$

Since Ψ is continuous in p, the left-hand side of (1) tends toward zero when h tends toward zero and

$$\lim_{h \to 0} \frac{C(p + h, u) - C(p, u) - h\Psi(p, u)}{|h|} = 0.$$

Therefore $C(., u)$ is differentiable in p and

$$\frac{\partial C}{\partial p_h}(p, u) \equiv \Psi_h(p, u) \qquad h = 1, \ldots, L. \blacksquare$$

By strengthening the assumptions, we can show that $x(p, R)$ and $\Psi(p, u)$ are C^1 and that $C(p, u)$ is C^2 in p and C^1 in u (see Guesnerie 1980). By definition of the compensated demand function, we have

$$\Psi(p, u) \equiv x(p, C(p, u)) \quad \text{with} \quad R = C(p, u), \tag{2}$$

from which it follows that

$$\frac{\partial \Psi_k}{\partial p_h}(p, u) = \frac{\partial x_k}{\partial p_h}(p, R) + \frac{\partial x_k}{\partial R}(p, R)\frac{\partial C}{\partial p_h}(p, u).$$

From the above theorem and (2) we have

$$\frac{\partial C}{\partial p_h}(p, u) = \Psi_h(p, u) = x_h(p, R).$$

Therefore

$$\frac{\partial \Psi_k}{\partial p_h}(p, u) = \frac{\partial x_k}{\partial p_h}(p, R) + x_h(p, R)\frac{\partial x_k}{\partial R}(p, R),$$

where u is the utility level achieved given the parameters (p, R).

Observe that $\dfrac{\partial \Psi_k}{\partial p_h}(p, u)$ is nothing other than what is often denoted by $\dfrac{\partial x_k}{\partial p_h}\bigg|_{u=cte}$. If the cost function is C^2 in p, Young's theorem yields

$$\frac{\partial^2 C}{\partial p_h \partial p_k} = \frac{\partial^2 C}{\partial p_k \partial p_h},$$

from which it follows that

$$\frac{\partial \Psi_h}{\partial p_k}(p, u) = \frac{\partial \Psi_k}{\partial p_h}(p, u).$$

Furthermore,

$$\frac{\partial x_h}{\partial p_k}(p, R) + x_k \frac{\partial x_h}{\partial R}(p, R) = \frac{\partial x_k}{\partial p_h}(p, R) + x_h \frac{\partial x_k}{\partial R}(p, R),$$

which are none other than the Slutsky equations that we can characterize by saying that the Slutsky matrix $\nabla_p \Psi(p, u)$ is symmetric.

Since $C(p, u)$ is concave in p, $\nabla_p \Psi(p, u)$ is negative semidefinite and we have in particular

$$\frac{\partial x_h}{\partial p_h}(p, R) + x_h(p, R) \frac{\partial x_h}{\partial R}(p, R) \leqslant 0 \qquad \forall h = 1, \ldots, L.$$

Finally, we recall that $\Psi(., u)$ is homogeneous of degree zero in p so that we have

$$\sum_{h=1}^{L} p_h \frac{\partial \Psi_k}{\partial p_h}(p, u) = 0 \qquad k = 1, \ldots, L.$$

or, from the symmetry of $\nabla_p \Psi$,

$$\sum_{h=1}^{L} p_h \frac{\partial \Psi_h}{\partial p_k}(p, u) = 0 \qquad k = 1, \ldots, L.$$

The indirect utility function $V(p, R)$ is obtained by substituting the Walrasian demand function into the utility function as follows:

$$V(p, R) \equiv U(x(p, R)).$$

We have

$$\Psi_h(p, V(p, R)) \equiv x_h(p, R) \tag{3}$$

$$R \equiv C(p, V(p, R)). \tag{4}$$

Differentiating (4) with respect to R and p_h, we have

$$\frac{\partial C}{\partial u}(p, V(p, R)) \frac{\partial V}{\partial R}(p, R) \equiv 1$$

and

$$\frac{\partial C}{\partial p_h}(p, V(p, R)) + \frac{\partial C}{\partial u}(p, V(p, R))\frac{\partial V}{\partial p_h}(p, R) \equiv 0,$$

which yields

$$-\frac{\dfrac{\partial V}{\partial p_h}(p, R)}{\dfrac{\partial V}{\partial R}(p, R)} \equiv \frac{\partial C}{\partial p_h}(p, V(p, R))$$

$$\equiv \Psi_h(p, V(p, R)).$$

Thus we obtain Roy's identity:

$$x_h(p, R) = -\frac{\dfrac{\partial V}{\partial p_h}(p, R)}{\dfrac{\partial V}{\partial R}(p, R)}.$$

A function is *homothetic* if it is an increasing transformation of a homogeneous of degree 1 function. Therefore, to characterize the behavior of a consumer with a homothetic utility function, we can assume that his utility function is homogeneous of degree 1. We denote by $U(x)$ such a function and show that its Engel curves are linear and go through the origin.

First of all, observe that the cost function is linear in utility, that is, $C(p, u) = c(p)u$. In fact, $C(p, u) = \text{Min}\{p \cdot x : U(x) = u\}$. By the homogeneity of degree 1 of U, λu is derived from λx and, therefore, it can be obtained at a cost λ times higher. However, since $R = C(p, V(p, R))$

$$V(p, R) = \frac{R}{c(p)}; \tag{5}$$

furthermore,

$$\Psi_l(p, u) = \frac{\partial C}{\partial p_l}(p, u) = \frac{\partial c}{\partial p_l}(p)u \qquad \forall l.$$

Therefore

$$x_l(p, R) = \Psi_l(p, V(p, R)) = \frac{\dfrac{\partial c}{\partial p_l}(p)}{c(p)}R \equiv a_l(p)R \qquad \forall l \tag{6}$$

Finally, we prove that if we can find a representation of preferences so that the marginal utility of income is independent of income, then such a utility function yields linear Engel curves that do not necessarily go through the origin as they did in the homothetic case. Suppose that an increasing function f exists such that $\tilde{V}(p, R) = f(V(p, R))$ and

$$\frac{\partial}{\partial R}\left(\frac{\partial \tilde{V}}{\partial R}(p, R)\right) = 0. \tag{7}$$

Equation (7) can be written as

$$f''\left(\frac{\partial V}{\partial R}\right)^2 + f'\left(\frac{\partial^2 V}{\partial R^2}\right) = 0$$

or

$$\frac{f''}{f'} = -\frac{\partial^2 V/\partial R^2}{(\partial V/\partial R)^2} = \frac{\partial}{\partial R}\left(\frac{1}{\partial V/\partial R}\right). \tag{8}$$

However

$$-\frac{\partial^2 V/\partial R^2}{(\partial V/\partial R)^2} = \frac{\partial^2 C/\partial u^2}{(\partial C/\partial u)}.$$

Indeed, $C(p, V(p, R)) = R$ implies that

$$\frac{\partial C}{\partial u}\cdot\frac{\partial V}{\partial R} = 1 \quad \text{and} \quad \frac{\partial}{\partial R}\left(\frac{1}{\partial V/\partial R}\right) = \frac{\partial}{\partial R}\left(\frac{\partial C}{\partial u}(p, V(p, R))\right) = \frac{\partial^2 C}{\partial u^2}\cdot\frac{\partial V}{\partial R}$$

$$= \frac{\partial^2 C/\partial u^2}{\partial C/\partial u}.$$

Equation (8) can be written as

$$\frac{f''(u)}{f'(u)} = \frac{\dfrac{\partial^2 C}{\partial u^2}(p, u)}{\dfrac{\partial C}{\partial u}(p, u)}, \tag{9}$$

which yields by integration

$$C(p, u) = A(p)f(u) + B(p) \tag{10}$$

or

$$\Psi(p, u) = C_p(p, u) = A_p(p)f(u) + B_p(p)$$

$$x(p, R) = A_p(p)f(V(p, R)) + B_p(p)$$

$$= A_p(p)\left(\frac{R - B(p)}{A(p)}\right) + B_p(p) \qquad \text{by (10)}$$

$$= R\frac{A_p(p)}{A(p)} + \left(B_p(p) - B(p)\frac{A_p(p)}{A(p)}\right),$$

from which it follows that the Engel curves are linear.

Conversely, we have

$$\tilde{V}(p, R) = f(V(p, R)) = \frac{R - B(p)}{A(p)}$$

by (10), which yields $\dfrac{\partial}{\partial R}\left(\dfrac{\partial \tilde{V}}{\partial R}\right) = 0.$

References

Berge, C., 1959, *Espaces Topologiques*, Dunod, Paris.

Guesnerie, R., 1980, *Modèles de l'Economie Publique*, C.N.R.S, Paris.

6 Cost-Benefit Analysis

We have identified many instances in which public intervention has both advantages and disadvantages that must be compared in order to evaluate its effectiveness. Is it necessary to create a market for pollution rights, to specify the output of a public good, or to determine the level at which a firm exhibiting increasing returns should produce? The allocation and distribution of resources will be influenced by these economic policies; the welfare levels of different economic agents will be affected either favorably or unfavorably. In this chapter, we assume that the information about the consequences of an economic decision that takes us from one state to a second state is known perfectly and we focus on two types of questions. Under what circumstances can we say that a given agent prefers state 1 to state 2? When will society prefer state 1 to state 2?[1]

6.1 Partial Equilibrium Analysis

Consider a consumer who maximizes his utility level taking prices and income as fixed under the classical assumptions.

6.1.1 "Parallel" Preferences

First, we consider an economy with two goods and we assume that the consumer has the following quasi-linear, quasi-concave, increasing utility function:

$$u(x_1, x_2) = x_1 + v(x_2).$$

There is no income effect on the demand for good 2; furthermore, we choose a normalization of the utility function yielding a constant marginal utility equal to 1 for good 1.[2] The consumer's decision set is determined by his income R and by the vector of prices $(1, p)$ where the price of good 1 is normalized to 1.

A change in income with prices fixed has an unambiguous effect on utility. If income increases (decreases), the choice set expands (contracts) and the level of maximal utility for the consumer given the budget constraint increases (decreases). The change in income, ΔR, provides a monetary

---

1. The differentiability assumptions necessary for our argument will not be made explicit.
2. Good 1 can be considered to be an aggregate consumption good (see the Hicks-Leontief theorem).

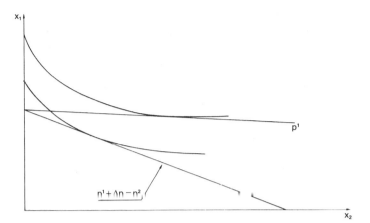

Figure 6.1

evaluation of the change in utility in terms of the constant marginal utility of good 1.

For income fixed at R^1, consider a change in the price of good 2 from p^1 to $p^2 = p^1 + \Delta p$ (see figure 6.1). When income R^1 is large enough,[3] the demand for good 2 is derived from the following first-order condition, which is independent of income:

$$v'(x_2) = p \quad \text{or} \quad x_2 = x_2(p).$$

The change in utility between the two states[4] is written as

$$\Delta u = u(x_1^2, x_2^2) - u(x_1^1, x_2^1)$$

$$= x_1(p^1 + \Delta p, R^1) + v[x_2(p^1 + \Delta p)] - x_1(p^1, R^1) - v(x_2(p^1)),$$

or, by using the budget constraint, as

$$\Delta u = v[x_2(p^1 + \Delta p)] - v[x_2(p^1)] - [(p^1 + \Delta p)x_2(p^1 + \Delta p) - p^1 x_2(p^1)]$$

$$= \int_{x_2(p^1)}^{x_2(p^1 + \Delta p)} v'(x)\, dx - [(p^1 + \Delta p)x_2(p^1 + \Delta p) - p^1 x_2(p^1)].$$

This is none other than the shaded area in figure 6.2, and it can be rewritten as

3. We exclude a corner solution in which $v'(R/p) > 1$.
4. In this section, the superscript indicates the state.

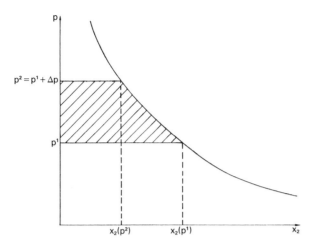

Figure 6.2

$$\Delta u = -\int_{p^1}^{p^1+\Delta p} x_2(p)\, dp, \tag{1}$$

that is, the integral under the demand function between p^1 and $p^1 + \Delta p$. When the change in price is very small, (1) can be approximated:

$$\Delta u \approx -\Delta p \cdot x_2(p^1),$$

that is, *the change in value of the vector of commodities consumed by the agent in state 1.* To be sure, a more precise approximation (see figure 6.2) is

$$\Delta u \approx -\Delta p x_2(p^1) - \tfrac{1}{2}\Delta p[x_2(p^2) - x_2(p^1)]$$

$$= -\Delta p x_2(p^1) - \tfrac{1}{2}\Delta p \Delta x_2.$$

This involves replacing $v(.)$ by a linear approximation between $x_2(p^1)$ and $x_2(p^2)$; $v'(x_2)$ is the marginal utility of good 2 when the quantity consumed equals x_2. Here the consumer is willing to pay $v'(x_2)$ units of good 1 to consume an additional unit of good 2. If he pays p to obtain this unit of good 2, the difference $v'(x_2) - p$ may be called the *marginal surplus*. For a quantity consumed x_2^1 of good 2, the sum of these marginal surpluses when x_2 varies between 0 and x_2^1 measures the consumer surplus for good 2 (shaded area in figure 6.3):

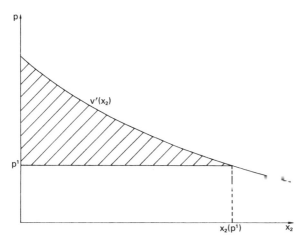

Figure 6.3

$$S = \int_0^{x_2^1} v'(x_2)\, dx_2 - p^1 x_2^1$$

$$= v(x_2^1) + x_1^1 - R^1 = u(x_1^1, x_2^1) - R^1.$$

If we consider a change in price with income fixed, the change in utility is equivalent to the change in surplus. We now provide an economic interpretation of this change in surplus. If, for example, the price of good 2 decreases from p^1 to p^2, the consumer gains $-\Delta p x_2(p^1)$ on the units of good 2 which he was previously buying. On the other hand, his surplus increases by

$$\int_{x_2(p^1)}^{x_2(p^2)} [v'(x_2) - p^2]\, dx_2$$

on the additional units that he buys, so that

$$\Delta S = -\Delta p x_2(p^1) + \int_{x_2(p^1)}^{x_2(p^2)} (v'(x_2) - p^2)\, dx_2.$$

Similarly, if the price of good 2 increases from p^1 to p^2 as in figure 6.2, he loses $\Delta p x_2(p^2)$ on the units which he is still consuming and

$$\int_{x_2(p^2)}^{x_2(p^1)} [v'(x_2) - p^1]\, dx_2$$

on the units that he no longer buys. In each case he gains

$$\int_{x_2(p^1)}^{x_2(p^2)} v'(x_2)\, dx_2 - [p^2 x_2(p^2) - p^1 x_2(p^1)],$$

which is in fact (1).

Thus, when the marginal utility of a good is constant, it is possible to
to evaluate changes in utility by the surplus measured in units of marginal
utility of this good. When this good is also the numéraire for the economy,
the marginal utility of this good can be interpreted as the marginal utility
of income. We are consequently tempted to consider ΔS as proportional
to a change in income, which is the first step toward an interpersonal
comparison of surplus (see section 6.2).

We repeat that the surplus is measured in units of the (constant) marginal
utility of good 1. These results can be generalized immediately to the case
of L goods so long as there exists a good with constant marginal utility. If

$$u(x_1, \ldots, x_L) = x_1 + v(x_2, \ldots, x_L)$$

and if we move from state $(1, p_2^1, \ldots, p_L^1, R^1)$ to state[5] $(1, p_2^2, \ldots, p_L^2; R^2) =$
$(1, p_2^1 + \Delta p_2, \ldots, p_L^1 + \Delta p_L; R^1 + \Delta R)$, then

$$\Delta u = \Delta R + \int_{state\ 1}^{state\ 2} \sum_{l=2}^{L} v_l'(x)\, dx_l - \left[\sum_{l=2}^{L} p_l^2 x_l(p^2) - \sum_{l=2}^{L} p_l^1 x_l(p^1) \right].$$

If the change in states is small, then

$$\Delta u \approx dR - \sum_{l=2}^{L} x_l^1\, dp_l$$

$$\approx dR - \sum_{l=2}^{L} x_l^1\, dp_l - \frac{1}{2} \sum_{l=2}^{L} dx_l^1\, dp_l,$$

whether we take a first- or second-order approximation.

6.1.2   Marginal Changes in the Parameters

When the change in the parameters is small, it is not restrictive to assume
that these exists a good with constant marginal utility, because

5. The integral $\int_{state\ 1}^{state\ 2} \sum_{l=2}^{L} v_l'(x)\, dx_l$ is well defined, that is, it is independent of the path

of integration if $\dfrac{\partial v_l'}{\partial x_k} = \dfrac{\partial v_k'}{\partial x_l}$ which follows from $v(.)$ being twice differentiable.

$$du = \sum_{l=1}^{L} \frac{\partial u}{\partial x_l}(x^1)\, dx_l,$$

which, by choosing an arbitrary good (good 1 for example), can be written as

$$du = \frac{\partial u}{\partial x_1}(x^1) \sum_{l=1}^{L} \frac{\dfrac{\partial u}{\partial x_l}(x^1)}{\dfrac{\partial u}{\partial x_1}(x^1)}\, dx_l$$

$$= \frac{\partial u}{\partial x_1}(x^1) \sum_{l=1}^{L} p_l\, dx_l = \frac{\partial u}{\partial x_1}(x^1)\left[dR - \sum_{l=1}^{L} x_l^1\, dp_l \right],$$

where p_l is the relative price of good l to good 1 and R is income measured in the system of normalized prices with $p_1 = 1$. Therefore we have

$$\frac{du}{\dfrac{\partial u}{\partial x_1}(x^1)} = dR - \sum_{l=2}^{L} x_l^1\, dp_l.$$

The marginal utility in state 1 of any good, take for example the numéraire, can be used as a unit of measure since for small variations in the state considered it remains essentially constant. What can we say about a discrete change in the parameters when there is no good with constant marginal utility, in other words, the general case?

6.1.3   The General Case

Let $V(p, R)$ be the indirect utility function for the consumer under consideration. Recall that V is increasing in R and decreasing in p. Let (p^1, R^1) be the parameters in the initial state (or state 1) and (p^2, R^2) be the parameters in the final state (or state 2).

The *compensating income variation* C is the amount that must be added to the initial level of income so that, for the new vector of prices p, the agent can attain the same level of utility as he did in the initial state. In other words, C is the change in income which just compensates the agent for the changes in prices, that is, $V(p^1, R^1) = V(p^2, R^1 + C)$. Clearly if $R^2 > R^1 + C$, the utility of the agent increases, because

$$V(p^2, R^2) \gtreqless V(p^1, R^1) \Leftrightarrow R^2 \gtreqless R^1 + C.$$

The *equivalent income variation E* is the amount that must be subtracted from the initial level of income so that, for the initial vector of prices, the agent attains the same level of utility as he does with the vector of final prices and the *initial* level of income. In other words, the change in income is equivalent to the change in prices, so that[6]

$$V(p^1, R^1 - E) = V(p^2, R^1).$$

By definition of the expenditure function $C(.,.)$, we have

$$V(p, C(p, u^1)) = V(p^1, R^1) \qquad \text{for any } p,$$

where u^1 is the level of utility associated with (p^1, R^1), such that $C(p^1, u^1) = R^1$.

Then we can redefine the foregoing concepts as:

$$C = C(p^2, u^1) - C(p^1, u^1)$$

$$E = C(p^2, u') - C(p^1, u'),$$

where u' is the level of utility associated with (p^2, R^1).

Now consider the change in a single price p_1, that is,

$$p^1 = (p_1^1, p_2^1, \ldots, p_L^1)$$

$$p^2 = (p_1^2, p_2^1, \ldots, p_L^1).$$

Then we have:[7]

$$C = C(p^2, u^1) - C(p^1, u^1) = \int_{p_1^1}^{p_1^2} \frac{\partial C}{\partial p_1}(p, u^1)\, dp_1 = \int_{p_1^1}^{p_1^2} \Psi_1(p, u^1)\, dp_1$$

$$E = C(p^2, u') - C(p^1, u') = \int_{p_1^1}^{p_1^2} \frac{\partial C}{\partial p_1}(p, u')\, dp = \int_{p_1^1}^{p_1^2} \Psi_1(p, u')\, dp,$$

where Ψ_1 is the (Hicksian) compensated demand function for good 1 (see the graphical presentation in figure 6.4).

If we assume that only Walrasian demand functions are observable, some relationship between both C and E and the integral under the Walrasian demand function, A, is useful to establish (see figure 6.4a).

---

6. When the utility function is quasi-linear, we observe immediately that $C = E$.

7. In fact, we know that $\dfrac{\partial C}{\partial p_1}(p, u^1) = \Psi_1$ from the theorem in the Preface to Chapter 6.

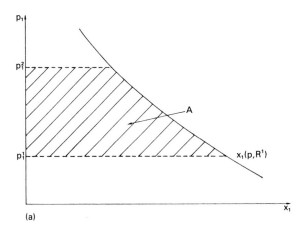

(a)

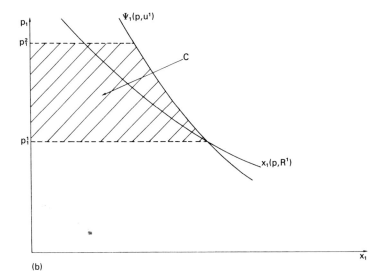

(b)

Figure 6.4

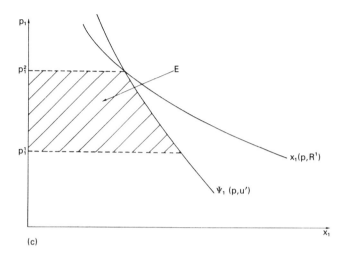

Figure 6.4 (continued)

For $p_1^2 > p_1^1$, the curve $\Psi_1(p, u^1)$ is above the curve $x_1(p, R^1)$ if the good is not inferior (consider the Slutsky equation) (see figure 6.4b). For $p_1^2 > p_1^1$, the curve $\Psi_1(p, u')$ is below the curve $x_1(p, R^1)$ if the good is not inferior (see figure 6.4c). So,

If good 1 is not inferior, $C \geqslant A \geqslant E$;
If good 1 is inferior, $E \geqslant A \geqslant C$;
If there is no income effect, $E = A = C$.

Therefore, partial but unambiguous evaluations of utility changes can be obtained by using the foregoing inequalities. For example, if the good is not inferior and if $R^2 < R^1 + A < R^1 + C$, we know that the utility of the agent has decreased. We can also consider the possibility of approximating the compensating and equivalent variations in income from observable variables. Information about the income elasticity of the Walrasian demand function allows us to make such an approximation.

First, take the case where the income elasticity can be considered to be constant:

$$\frac{\partial x_1(p, R)}{\partial R} \cdot \frac{R}{x_1(p, R)} = \eta \neq 1.$$

By integrating the differential equation $\dfrac{\partial x_1(p, R)}{x_1(p, R)} \equiv \eta \dfrac{\partial R}{R}$ we obtain

$\text{Log } x_1(p, R) = \eta \text{ Log } R + C^{te}$

which yields

$\text{Log } x_1(p, R^1) = \eta \text{ Log } R^1 + C^{te},$

so that

$$x_1(p, R) = x_1(p, R^1) \left[\frac{R}{R^1} \right]^\eta.$$

On the other hand we have

$$\frac{\partial C(p, u^1)}{\partial p} = x_1(p, C(p, u^1)) = x_1(p, R^1) \left[\frac{C(p, u^1)}{R^1} \right]^\eta,$$

or

$$\frac{dC(p, u^1)}{[C(p, u^1)]^\eta} = \frac{x_1(p, R^1)}{(R^1)^\eta} dp_1.$$

Integrating this differential equation with the given initial condition $C(p^1, u^1) = R^1$ yields

$$\frac{[C(p^2, u^1)]^{1-\eta} - [C(p^1, u^1)]^{1-\eta}}{1 - \eta} = (R^1)^{-\eta} \int_{p_1^1}^{p_1^2} x_1(p, R^1) \, dp_1$$

or

$$C(p^2, u^1) = R^1 \left[1 + \frac{(1 - \eta)}{R^1} \int_{p_1^1}^{p_1^2} x_1(p, R^1) \, dp_1 \right]^{1/(1-\eta)}.$$

In this case, the compensating income variation is exactly equal to[8]

$$C = R^1 \left[1 + \frac{1 - \eta}{R^1} \int_{p_1^1}^{p_1^2} x_1(p, R^1) \, dp_1 \right]^{1/(1-\eta)} - R^1$$

and is expressed only in terms of the observable variables.

If we denote by A the integral under the Walrasian demand function, $A = \int_{p_1^1}^{p_1^2} x_1(p, R^1) \, dp_1$, and if we use the approximation

$$(1 + l)^{1/(1-\eta)} \approx 1 + \frac{l}{1 - \eta} + \frac{\eta l^2}{2(1 - \eta)^2},$$

8. Analogous calculations for $\eta = 1$ yield $C = R^1 \left[\exp \left\{ \frac{1}{R^1} \int_{p_1^1}^{p_1^2} x_1(p, R^1) \, dp_1 \right\} - 1 \right]$.

then

$$C \approx A + \frac{\eta A^2}{2R^1},$$

which yields

$$\frac{C - A}{A} \approx \frac{\eta A}{2R^1}.$$

Similarly, we obtain

$$\frac{A - E}{A} \approx \frac{\eta A}{2R^1}.$$

For example, if

$$R^2 \geq A + \frac{\eta A^2}{2R^1} + R^1,$$

we can conclude that the agent's utility level has increased in moving from state 1 to state 2 or, alternatively, that we must give him at least $A + (\eta A^2 / 2R^1)$ to insure that he is better off in state 2 than in state 1.

If we know that the income elasticity is not constant but that it lies between $\underline{\eta}$ and $\bar{\eta}$, we can construct approximations of C and E. In this manner, Willig (1976) obtains

$$\frac{R^1}{A}\left[\left(1 + (1 - \underline{\eta})\frac{A}{R^1}\right)^{1/(1-\underline{\eta})} - 1 - \frac{A}{R^1}\right] \leq \frac{C - A}{A}$$

$$\leq \frac{R^1}{A}\left[\left(1 + (1 - \bar{\eta})\frac{A}{R^1}\right)^{1/(1-\bar{\eta})} - 1 - \frac{A}{R^1}\right].$$

When the change envisioned is small enough, the approximation becomes

$$\frac{\underline{\eta} A}{2R^1} \leq \frac{C - A}{A} \leq \frac{\bar{\eta} A}{2R^1}.$$

These approximations allow us to make unambiguous evaluations of changes in utility. For example, if

$$R^2 \geq A + \frac{\bar{\eta} A^2}{2R^1} + R^1,$$

then the agent's utility level increases by moving from state 1 to state 2.

The foregoing results may be generalized to the case of simultaneous changes in several prices. The compensating income variation is written as

$$C = \int_{p^1}^{p^2} \sum_{l=1}^{L} \frac{\partial C}{\partial p_l}(p, u^1)\, dp_l = \int_{p^1}^{p^2} \sum_{l=1}^{L} \Psi_l(p, u^1)\, dp_l.$$

This expression is well defined since the differential $\sum_{l=1}^{L} \Psi_l(p, u^1)\, dp_l$ is total due to the equality of the cross partial derivatives of the compensated demand functions (Slutsky equations). Approximations for C can be developed as above (see Willig 1973).[9]

On the other hand, the integral under the Walrasian demand functions, given by

$$\int_{p^1}^{p^2} \sum_{l=1}^{L} x_l(p, R)\, dp_l,$$

is not mathematically well defined in the general case because it depends on the path of integration from p^1 to p^2. In certain particular cases, it will be mathematically well defined and this brings out a second problem, namely, its economic meaning. Note that

$$\sum_{l=1}^{L} x_l(p, R)\, dp_l$$

is a total differential if and only if

$$\frac{\partial x_l}{\partial p_k} = \frac{\partial x_k}{\partial p_l} \qquad \forall k, l; k \neq l.$$

On the other hand from the Slutsky conditions we have

$$\frac{\partial x_l}{\partial p_k} + x_k \frac{\partial x_l}{\partial R} = \frac{\partial x_k}{\partial p_l} + x_l \frac{\partial x_k}{\partial R}$$

from which it follows that

$$\frac{\partial x_l}{\partial R} \cdot \frac{R}{x_l} = \frac{\partial x_k}{\partial R} \cdot \frac{R}{x_k} = k(p, R) \qquad \forall k, l. \tag{2}$$

If the prices of all the goods in the economy change, they will all appear in the differential $\sum_{l=1}^{L} x_l\, dp_l$. Therefore, by the budget constraint,

9. See also section 6.4*.

$$\sum_{l=1}^{L} p_l x_l(p, R) = R, \tag{3}$$

from which it follows that

$$\sum_{l=1}^{L} p_l \frac{\partial x_l}{\partial R}(p, R) = 1$$

and, from (2) and (3), $k(p, R) = 1$ or

$$\frac{\partial x_l/\partial R}{x_l} = \frac{1}{R} \quad l = 1, \dots, L,$$

from which it follows by integration that $x_l = \Psi_l(p)R$ and $x_l/x_k = \Psi_l(p)/\Psi_k(p)$ with $x_l = 0 \quad \forall l$ if $R = 0$.

The Engel curves are straight lines passing through the origin (that is the utility functions that generate them are homothetic).[10] Nonetheless, the conditions of symmetry $\partial x_l/\partial p_k = \partial x_k/\partial p_l$ can be applied only to the prices that change. Consequently, in the above case of two goods, if only one price changes, the condition is automatically satisfied. When a single good is subject to income effects (quasi-linear functions), this good can be chosen as a numéraire and the conditions of symmetry do not imply homotheticity.

More generally, these conditions can be applied to the subset of goods for which prices change. Only condition (1) is required for the Marshallian surplus to be mathematically well defined. In the absence of income effects, this surplus is economically meaningful because it coincides with the equivalent and compensating income variations. Furthermore, Dixit and Weller (1979) provide conditions under which the Marshallian surplus is bounded by the compensating and equivalent variations as in the case when only one price changes (see above). In the same spirit, Seade (1978)[11] has shown that, for utility functions yielding linear Engel curves (not necessarily passing through the origin), it is possible to construct precise relationships between the compensating and equivalent income variations and the derivatives of the Walrasian (observable) demand:

$$C = \int_{p^1}^{p^2} \exp\left\{-\int_{p^2}^{p} \frac{\partial x}{\partial R} \cdot dp'\right\} x \cdot dp. \tag{4}$$

10. See Preface to Chapter 6.
11. See also section 6.3*.

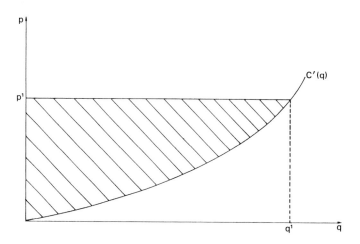

Figure 6.5

This case is an interesting generalization of the homothetic case ($\partial x/\partial R = x/R$), for which

$$C = R\left(\exp\left\{-\frac{1}{R}\int_{p^2}^{p^1} x\cdot dp\right\} - 1\right),$$

generalizing to the case of many goods the formula given in footnote 7.

Remark Producer Surplus: Consider the supply curve of a competitive producer that is determined by equating price to marginal cost. Producer surplus is the shaded area in figure 6.5. More formally,

$$\int_0^{q^1} [p^1 - C'(q)]\, dq = p^1 q^1 - C(q^1),$$

or, in other words, aggregate profit. The change in producer surplus will be equal to the change in aggregate profit. Nonetheless, a more complete analysis should take into account the distribution of these profits to the consumers.

In concluding this section, we assert that the concepts of compensating or equivalent income variations have a precise meaning for individual demand functions. The economist who possesses the appropriate information concerning individual demand functions can provide approximations to these variations. However, information is not available if econometric analysis furnishes the applied economist with only aggregate demand functions (see, however, section 6.2.4).

6.2   Social Welfare Measures

Consider two states of the economy, state 1 and state 2. Either the Pareto criterion allows us to rank these two states or it does not. In the former case, a comparison of the surplus for each agent allows us to choose unambiguously between the two states (if we accept the Pareto criterion). In the latter case, in order to rank the two states, it is necessary to make interpersonal utility comparisons.

One possible remedy is to specify a social welfare function, that is, a rule for aggregating the utility levels of the individuals. The other path taken consists essentially in equating a dollar for agent A with a dollar for agent B; in other words,

—for marginal changes, assume that the problem of distributing income has been solved before analyzing the project under consideration;
—for discrete changes, ignore the income distribution problem.

In the following, consider an exchange economy where $w \in R_+^L$ is the vector of initial resources.

6.2.1   Variations in National Income

Consider a social welfare function $W(x^1, \ldots, x^I)$ defined over states of the economy; Bergson (1938) has shown the conditions under which we can write it as $W(u^1(x^1), \ldots, u^I(x^I))$, where $u^1, \ldots, u^I$ are the utility functions of the agents in the economy.[12]

A social optimum is derived from the problem

Max $W(u^1(x^1), \ldots, u^I(x^I))$

subject to $\sum_{i=1}^{I} x^i = w.$

12. We shall often call $W(.)$ a Bergson-Samuelson social welfare function. See chapter 4 for a discussion of the difficulties in obtaining such a function. Milleron (1969) has shown under which conditions the choice of a social welfare function is equivalent to the choice of a distribution of income. Specifically, the individual utility functions must be homothetic.

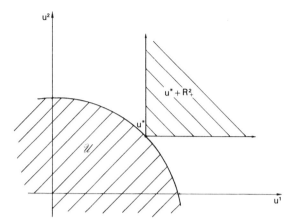

Figure 6.6

The marginal conditions are

$$\frac{\partial W}{\partial u^i}\frac{\partial u^i}{\partial x_l^i} = \frac{\partial W}{\partial u^{i'}}\frac{\partial u^{i'}}{\partial x_l^{i'}} \qquad \forall i, i'$$

$$l = 1, \dots, L,$$

that is, the marginal social utility of each good must be the same in all uses where $\partial W/\partial u^i$ is the weight (marginal) attributed to the marginal utility of agent i in the social welfare function.

This social welfare function is ordinal in the sense that an increasing transformation (identical) of all the utility functions and a redefinition of the welfare function leaves unchanged the ranking of social states. Nonetheless it is important to understand that the simultaneous choice of individual utility functions and of the function W determines the measure of social comparability of the utility levels of different agents. Even so, this concept of social utility is interesting because it allows us to associate to each optimal state a social welfare function representing the interpersonal choices of society implicit in the optimum.

When individual utility functions are concave (and therefore cardinal), the set of utility levels is a convex set (figure 6.6). To any optimal state u^* (on the upper-left-quadrant boundary of U), we can associate weights a_i (by a separation theorem)[13] so that u^* is attained by maximizing

13. $(u^* + R^2)$ and u^* are two convex sets that have the single point u^* in their intersection.

$$\sum_{i=1}^{I} a^i u^i(x^i),$$

which in turn becomes the implicit social welfare function associated with u^*.

Consider the vector of prices p associated with the Pareto-optimal solution to the maximization of the social welfare function as follows:

(I)
$$
\begin{cases}
\text{Max } W(u^1(x^1), \ldots, u^I(x^I)) \\
\text{subject to } \sum_{i=1}^{I} x^i = w.
\end{cases}
$$

Now p is proportional to the Lagrangian multipliers associated with the optimal solution to (I). If we imagine a change dw in the initial endowment vector, with its corresponding change in quantities consumed constrained by

$$\sum_{i=1}^{I} dx_l^i = dw_l \qquad l = 1, \ldots, L,$$

we obtain a variation in welfare of

$$dW = \sum_{i=1}^{I} \sum_{l=1}^{L} \frac{\partial W}{\partial u^i} \frac{\partial u^i}{\partial x_l^i} \, dx_l^i \propto$$

$$\sum_{i=1}^{I} \sum_{l=1}^{L} p_l \, dx_l^i = \sum_{l=1}^{L} p_l \left(\sum_{i=1}^{I} dx_l^i \right)$$

$$= \sum_{l=1}^{L} p_l \, dw_l.$$

Therefore, for a marginal change in initial endowments we have

$$dW \gtreqless 0 \Leftrightarrow \sum_{l=1}^{L} p_l \, dw_l \gtreqless 0.$$

Starting from a competitive equilibrium, the variation in national income evaluated at the initial prices provides a criterion for evaluating the change in social welfare if we consider that the observed competitive equilibrium corresponds to an optimal allocation of resources (from the perspective of this social welfare function). Then the distribution of dW between the agents can be ignored; in effect, a dollar for agent 1 is equivalent to a dollar for agent 2 since the distribution of income is optimal. Since the variation considered is a marginal one, the optimality of the distribution of income is unaffected.

6.2.2   The Compensation Principle

In order to avoid using a social welfare function, the following compensation principle[14] was developed:

If in state 2 a redistribution of goods can leave all the agents with a higher utility level than in state 1, state 2 is preferred to state 1.[15]

When this condition holds, the value of national income in terms of state 1 prices is higher in state 2.

Indeed, there exists a redistribution of goods such that

$$x'^i P^i x^{1i} \qquad i = 1, \ldots, I$$

with

$$\sum_{i=1}^{I} x'^i = \sum_{i=1}^{I} x^{2i}.$$

However, $x'^i P^i x^{1i}$ implies that $px'^i > px^{1i}$ since x^{1i} is the agent's best choice at prices p. Therefore

$$\sum_{i=1}^{I} px'^i = \sum_{i=1}^{I} px^{2i} > \sum_{i=1}^{I} px^{1i}.$$

Note that no redistribution of goods actually takes place; implicitly, we are assuming that society is indifferent between the allocation of a good to agent i or to agent i'. On the other hand, we must point out that the converse of the above proposition does not hold. A nonmarginal increase in national income does not necessarily imply the feasibility of such a compensation (see figure 6.7). Z is the set of vectors of initial endowments $\tilde{w}$ that make the allocations $(x^{21}, \ldots, x^{2I})$ that are preferred by all the agents to the initial state $(x^{11}, \ldots, x^{1I})$ feasible (that is, $\sum_{i=1}^{I} x^{2i} \leqslant \tilde{w}$), and p is the vector of prices associated with state 1.[16]

---

14. Hicks (1939).
15. This criterion does not induce a preordering on the social states because it is not transitive. See Arrow (1951) for a discussion of the criteria of Hicks, Kaldor, and Scitovsky with regard to social choice theory.
16. To prove that the budget line associated with p passes through w and is tangent to Z suppose the contrary and arrive at a contradiction.

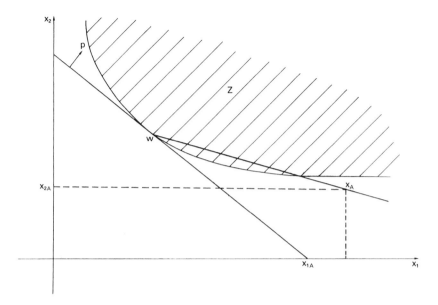

Figure 6.7

Let x^A be a vector of primary resources such that

$$\sum_{l=1}^{2} p_l x_l^A > \sum_{l=1}^{2} p_l w_l.$$

However, we can redistribute x^A in such a way as to increase the utility of each agent.

The converse of the proposition is true only in a neighborhood of $(x^{11}, \ldots, x^{1I})$; then

$$u^i(x^{2i}) - u^i(x^{1i}) \approx \sum_{l=1}^{L} u_l'^i(x^{1i})(x_l^{2i} - x_l^{1i})$$

$$\propto \sum_{l=1}^{L} p_l(x_l^{2i} - x_l^{1i}).$$

Assume that

$$\sum_{l=1}^{L} p_l \sum_{i=1}^{I} x_l^{2i} > \sum_{l=1}^{L} p_l \sum_{i=1}^{I} x_l^{1i}$$

and let

$$x''^i = x^{1i} + \frac{\sum\limits_{i=1}^{I} x^{2i} - \sum\limits_{i=1}^{I} x^{1i}}{I};$$

thus

$$u^i(x''^i) - u^i(x^{1i}) \propto \sum_{l=1}^{L} p_l \frac{\sum\limits_{i=1}^{I} x_l^{2i} - \sum\limits_{i=1}^{I} x_l^{1i}}{I} > 0 \quad \text{for} \quad i = 1, \ldots, I.$$

6.2.3   Aggregating the Surpluses

In cost-benefit analysis, a current practice is to sum the changes in the surpluses, calculated using ordinary demand functions, for the various agents concerned. The assumptions implicit in this method either

(i) the utility functions are additively separable and society considers the marginal social utility to be the same for each agent; or
(ii) the project is small and we are in the neighborhood of an optimal distribution of income.

Currently, the formula used most frequently is

$$\Delta S = -\sum_{i=1}^{I} x^i \cdot \Delta p - \frac{1}{2} \sum_{i=1}^{I} \sum_{l=1}^{L} \Delta p_l \Delta x_l^i$$

$$= -\left(\sum_{i=1}^{I} x^i\right) \cdot \Delta p - \frac{1}{2} \sum_{l=1}^{L} \Delta p_l \left(\sum_{i=1}^{I} \Delta x_l^i\right),$$

and this is valid only under these very restrictive conditions. Note that only aggregate information is needed here. This remark can be extended to the case of the linear Engel curves considered by Seade (1978).

   We continue to attribute the same weight to each of the agents. If they have parallel Engel curves, $\partial x/\partial R$ is the same vector for all agents. Using formula (4), we obtain

$$\sum_{i=1}^{I} C^i = \int_{p^1}^{p^2} \exp\left\{ -\int_{p^2}^{p} \frac{\partial x}{\partial R} \cdot dp' \right\} \left(\sum_{i=1}^{I} x^i \right) \cdot dp.$$

However, we should point out that even if $\sum_{i=1}^{I} C^i > 0$, we cannot be sure to find compensations that improve the situation of all agents (Boadway 1976).

Consider a classic example of measuring surplus that is valid when demand functions are quasi-linear. Assume an economy with two goods and let consumer i's utility function be

$$x_1^i + v^i(x_2^i) \qquad i = 1, \ldots, I.$$

Let w_1^i be the initial endowment of good 1 to consumer i and normalize the price of good 1 to 1. Therefore the aggregate demand function for good 2 is[17]

$$x_2 = \sum_{i=1}^{I} \left(\frac{dv^i}{dx_2^i}\right)^{-1}(p) = d_2(p).$$

Suppose that good 2 is produced using good 1 according to the technology $y_2 = g(y_1)$. The competitive supply for good 2 is therefore

$$y_2 = g\left(\left[\frac{dg}{dy_1}\right]^{-1}(1/p)\right),$$

where $p = C'(y_2)$, that is, where price equals marginal cost. The competitive equilibrium is determined by the intersection of the supply and demand curves (figure 6.8).

Let (p^*, y_2^*) be the market equilibrium for good 2 from which we can derive all the characteristics of equilibrium. The competitive equilibrium is Pareto optimal, in particular because the producer and the consumers face the same price for good 2 (the price in consumption equals the price in production). Now assume that the government needs a quantity T[18] of good 1. An initial solution consists of directly levying a tax of t^i units of good 1 on each agent i so that $T = \sum_{i=1}^{I} t^i$. If

$$(w_1^i - t^i) > \left(\frac{dv^i}{dx_2^i}\right)^{-1}(p^*),$$

the equilibrium price is unchanged. The consumers' loss in utility is exactly the amount T.

Another policy consists of taxing the consumption of good 2 at a rate t per unit. If p remains the price to the consumer, the price to the producer is then given by $\pi = p - t$ and supply is characterized by $\pi = p - t = C'(y_2)$, therefore $p = t + C'(y_2)$ (see figure 6.9).

---

17. We assume that the agents are at an interior maximum in their optimization problem.
18. Here we do not worry about the government's use of these resources.

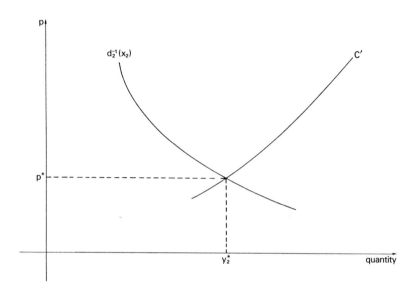

Figure 6.8

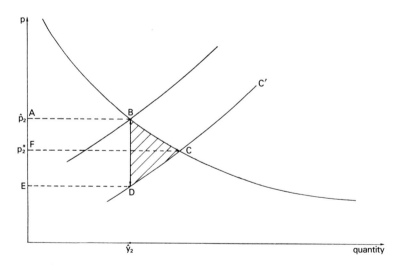

Figure 6.9

Let $(\hat{p}_2, \hat{y}_2)$ be the new equilibrium. For an identical collection of tax revenue, $t\hat{y}_2 = T$, the new equilibrium is socially inferior to the first policy prescription. When we move from one equilibrium to the other, the consumers lose FCBA and the producers lose FCDE, the sum of which exceeds T by BCD $\approx -\frac{1}{2}\Delta y_2 \cdot t$. Therefore BCD represents the loss due to the indirect method of taxation that, in causing the price to consumers to diverge from that to producers, leads to a Pareto-inefficient outcome.

Clearly, in the foregoing reasoning, distributional effects are neglected completely. We should point out that the argument in terms of surpluses has not contributed much to our understanding in addition to what we learned from a direct calculation of the difference between the values taken by $\sum_{i=1}^{I} u^i(x_1^i, x_2^i)$ in the two equilibria. It does, however, furnish a graphic illustration of the social loss.

6.2.4   The Contemporary Approach with Microeconomic Data

In the foregoing, we have maintained the assumption that only the Walrasian demand functions are observable. In fact, only a limited number of points on these functions are observable. The estimation of demand functions requires us to restrict ourselves to a limited class of demand functions and thus to a limited class of utility functions (if we assume that demand functions are derived from utility functions). Given an estimate of these utility functions, we can derive estimates of expenditure functions and of compensated demand functions leading to estimates of compensating or equivalent income variations.

Let $U(x, a)$ be a class of utility functions parametrized by the vector a. Let $V(p, R, a)$ and $C(p, u, a)$ be the indirect utility functions and the expenditure functions associated with this class. Define R^E as the income equivalent to the vector of parameters (p^1, R^1) that is, the income which allows us to attain the same level of utility as (p^1, R^1) for some other reference vector, say p^0. Specifically,

$$V(p^0, R^E, a) = V(p^1, R^1, a) = u.$$

By definition

$$R^E = C(p^0, u, a) = C(p^0, V(p^1, R^1, a), a) = r(p^0, p^1, R^1, a). \tag{5}$$

For example, for a Cobb-Douglas utility function with two goods, we have

$$R^E = \left[\frac{p_1^0}{p_1^1}\right]^{\alpha}\left[\frac{p_2^0}{p_2^1}\right]^{1-\alpha} R^1$$

$$a = (\alpha, 1 - \alpha).$$

For the linear expenditure functions characterized by

$$p_l x_l = p_l \gamma_l + \rho_l\left[R - \sum_{j=1}^{L} p_j \gamma_j\right] \qquad l = 1, \dots, L,$$

we have

$$R^E = \sum_{k=1}^{L} \gamma_k + \prod_{k=1}^{L}\left(\frac{p_k^0}{p_k^1}\right)^{\rho_k}\left[R - \sum_{j=1}^{L} p_j \gamma_j\right]$$

$$a = (\gamma_1, \dots, \gamma_L, \rho_1, \dots, \rho_L).$$

Estimating a system of demand equations for particular microeconomic parameters yields an estimate of a. Therefore from (5) we have an estimate of equivalent incomes for each consumer. Agents may differ according to income and may face different prices p^1. However, we must use a unique reference price vector p^0. For example, the effect of a fiscal reform taking us from environment $(p^0, (R^{0i}))$ to environment $(p^1, (R^{1i}))$ can be analyzed by comparing the vector of equivalent incomes $(R^{E1}, \dots, R^{EI})$ to the vector of initial incomes $(R^{01}, \dots, R^{0I})$. We can evaluate this vector of equivalent incomes with the help of $W(R^{E1}, \dots, R^{EI})$, a Bergson-Samuelson social welfare function. In fact, from (5) we see that, for p^0 fixed, the equivalent income $r(p^0, p^1, R^1, a)$ is an increasing transformation of the indirect utility function. Therefore we can define social welfare by choosing the particular cardinal representation given by equivalent income functions.

However, comparisons of social welfare made in this manner depend on the reference price, unless the utility functions of consumers are all identical and homothetic and the function W is homothetic. In this case we have, from the preface to this chapter,

$$V(p^1, R, a) = v(p^1, a)R$$

$$C(p^0, u, a) = c(p^0, a)u,$$

and therefore

$$r(p^0, p^1, R^1, a) = c(p^0, a)v(p^1, a)R^1.$$

Then, if $W = w \circ f$ with f homogeneous of degree 1 and w increasing, we have

$$W(R^{E1}, \ldots, R^{EI}) = w(c(p^0, a)v(p^1, a)f(R^{11}, \ldots, R^{1I})).$$

Therefore, the evaluation of the reform is independent of p^0.

For example, we may take

$$W(R^{E1}, \ldots, R^{EI}) = \sum_{i=1}^{I} \frac{(R^{Ei})^{1-\varepsilon}}{1 - \varepsilon},$$

where the value of ε lying between 0 and 1 expresses the collective decision maker's aversion to inequality. To obtain a more precise idea of redistributive effects, we can calculate the average gain (or average loss) of equivalent income by income class and then compute various indices of inequality (see King 1983).

6.3*   Derivation of Seade's Formula

By definition:

$$V(p^2, R^1 + C) = V(p^1, R^1)$$

$$V(p^2, R^1 + C) - V(p^2, R^1) = V(p^1, R^1) - V(p^2, R^1). \tag{6}$$

If $\lambda(p, R)$ is the marginal utility of income

$$\lambda(p, R) = \frac{\partial V}{\partial R}(p, R),$$

then Roy's identity yields

$$\frac{\partial V}{\partial p_l}(p, R) = -\lambda(p, R)x_l(p, R),$$

and (6) can be rewritten as

$$\int_{R^1}^{R^1+C} \frac{\partial V}{\partial R}(p^2, R)\, dR = \int_{p^2}^{p^1} \frac{\partial V}{\partial p}(p; R^1) \cdot dp \tag{7}$$

or

$$\int_{R^1}^{R^1+C} \lambda(p^2, R)\, dR = \int_{p^1}^{p^2} \lambda(p, R^1)x(p, R^1) \cdot dp. \tag{8}$$

If the marginal utility of income is independent of income, then

$$\int_{R^1}^{R^1+C} \lambda(p^2, R)\, dR = C\lambda(p^2).\tag{9}$$

On the other hand, the constancy of the marginal utility of income for a cardinal representation of preferences characterizes the utility functions for which Engel curves are linear (see preface to this chapter or Gorman 1953).

Finally,

$$\frac{\partial \lambda}{\partial p_l} = \frac{\partial}{\partial p_l}\left(\frac{\partial V}{\partial R}(p, R)\right)$$

$$= \frac{\partial}{\partial R}\left(\frac{\partial V}{\partial p_l}(p, R)\right),$$

and from Roy's identity this is

$$\frac{\partial \lambda}{\partial p_l} = -\frac{\partial}{\partial R}[\lambda(p, R)x_l(p, R)]$$

$$= -x_l(p, R)\frac{\partial \lambda}{\partial R}(p, R) - \lambda(p, R)\frac{\partial}{\partial R}x_l(p, R).$$

When $\lambda(p, R) = \lambda(p)$ is independent of income, the above simplifies to

$$\frac{\partial \lambda}{\partial p_l} = -\lambda(p)\frac{\partial}{\partial R}x_l(p, R) \qquad l = 1, \ldots, L.\tag{10}$$

By integrating (10), we obtain

$$\lambda(p) = \lambda(p^2)\exp\left\{-\int_{p^2}^{p}\frac{\partial x}{\partial R}(p', R^1)\, dp'\right\};$$

and (9) becomes

$$C = \int_{p^1}^{p^2}\frac{\lambda(p)}{\lambda(p^2)}x(p, R^1)\cdot dp$$

$$= \int_{p^1}^{p^2}\exp\left\{-\int_{p^2}^{p}\frac{\partial x}{\partial R}(p', R^1)\, dp'\right\}x(p, R^1)\cdot dp.$$

If the income elasticity of demand η varies slightly over the domain of price changes considered, then $\int_{p^2}^{p} \frac{\partial x}{\partial R}(p, R^1)\, dp$ can be approximated by $\frac{\eta}{R^1} \int_{p^2}^{p} x(p, R^1)\, dp$, from which it follows immediately by integration that

$$C = \frac{R^1}{\eta}\left[\exp\left\{\frac{\eta}{R^1} A\right\} - 1\right]$$

and if A/R^1 is small

$$C = A + \frac{\eta}{R^1} \cdot \frac{A^2}{2}$$

(Willig's approximation).

6.4*   Vartia's Algorithm

When demand functions satisfy the integrability conditions so that they can be treated as if they were derived from a utility function, it is clear that observing demand functions allows us to reconstruct utility functions. From these utility functions, we can derive the compensating income variations and the Hicksian demand functions. This approach is used in econometrics and discussed in section 6.4 with the help of parametric representations of utility functions. Vartia (1983) proposes several different algorithms that, starting from Walrasian demand functions, $x(p, R)$, yield the solution to the differential equation characterizing the compensating variation.

Suppose $p(1) = p^1$, $p(2) = p^2$ and take as given a differential curve $p(t)$ in the space of prices that allows us to go from p^1 to p^2. Let $R^1 = C(p^1, u^1)$ be the initial income and let $R(t)$ be the income that allows us to attain utility level u^1 in light of the prices $p(t)$, that is,

$$R(t) = C(p(t), u^1).$$

The compensating income variation in moving from p^1 to $p(t)$ is

$$C(t) = R(t) - R_1 = \int_{p^1}^{p(t)} \sum_{l=1}^{L} \frac{\partial C}{\partial p_l}(p, u^1)\, dp_l,$$

from which it follows that

$$\frac{dR(t)}{dt} = \sum_{l=1}^{L} \frac{\partial C}{\partial p_l}(p(t), u^1)\frac{dp_l(t)}{dt}.$$

However,

$$\frac{\partial C}{\partial p_l}(p, u^1) = \Psi_l(p, u^1) = x_l(p, R(t)) \qquad l = 1, \ldots, L;$$

therefore

$$\frac{dR(t)}{dt} = \sum_{l=1}^{L} x_1(p(t), R(t)) \frac{dp_l(t)}{dt}.$$

Vartia then gives several algorithms to integrate this nonlinear differential equation characterizing $R(t)$ with the initial condition $R(0) = R_0$. Once we have obtained $R(t)$, the Hicksian demand function is simply $x(p(t), R(t))$.

References

Arrow, K., 1951, *Social Choice and Individual Values*, Cowles Foundation.

Bergson, A., 1938, "A reformulation of certain aspects of welfare economics," *Quarterly Journal of Economics*, 521, 310–334.

Boadway, R., 1976, "The welfare foundation of cost benefit analysis," *Economic Journal*, 84, 926–939.

Dixit, A., and P. A. Weller 1979, "The three consumer's surpluses," *Economica*, 46, 125–135.

Gorman, W. M., 1953, "Community preference fields," *Econometrica*, 21, 63–80.

Hicks, J., 1939, "Foundations of welfare economics," *Economic Journal*, 49, 696–712.

King, M., 1983, "Welfare analysis of tax reforms using household data," *Journal of Public Economics*, 21, 183–214.

Milleron, J. C., 1969, "Distribution des revenus et utilité collective," *Annales de l'INSEE*, 2, 73–111.

Seade, J., 1978, "Consumer's surplus and linearity of Engel curves," *Economic Journal*, 88, 511–523.

Vartia, Y., 1983, "Efficient methods of measuring welfare change and compensated income in terms of ordinary demand functions," *Econometrica*, 51, 79–98.

Willig, R. D., 1976, "Consumer's surplus without apology," *American Economic Review*, 66, 589–597.

Recommended Reading

1. Milleron 1969 (relationship between the choice of an income distribution and the choice of a social welfare function).

2. Willig 1976 (approximations of compensating and equivalent variations).

3. Seade 1978 (linear Engel curves).

4. King 1983 (cost-benefit analysis of tax reforms with parametric representation of preferences).

7 Introduction to the Theory of the Second Best

In the preceding chapters, our approach has been the following. After identifying the sources of inefficiency, namely, externalities, public goods, increasing returns to scale, monopolistic behavior, etc., we characterized public policy prescriptions, for example, taxes and the creation of markets, designed to restore economic efficiency in the allocation of resources, that is, to achieve a first-best Pareto optimum. In characterizing these policies, we have endowed the government with a cornucopia of very powerful political economic instruments, such as personalized taxes and lump-sum transfers, that often surpass the informational capabilities or jurisdictions of the government or that neglect the necessary incentive requirements which any economic system encounters. What happens when we have certain constraints (institutional or incentive) that prevent the achievement of a first-best optimum and that require a definition of a second-best political optimum that takes into account the available political economic instruments?

Consider first the following general somewhat negative remarks:

(a) If a distortion exists in one sector (that is, there is some constraint that prevents the first-best optimal conditions from being satisfied in this sector), it is no longer generally desirable to apply the first-best optimality condition in the other sectors (see Malinvaud 1969, chapter IX, section 6).

(b) If n distortions (where $n \geqslant 2$) exist, we cannot claim that the competitive equilibrium with $n - 1$ distortions is preferable to the competitive equilibrium with n distortions (see Green and Sheshinski 1979).

(c) The problems of equity and efficiency can no longer be separated unless we use personalized lump-sum transfers as political economic instruments.[1]

(d) The results obtained in second-best analysis may contradict the economist's intuition developed in the first-best analysis.

However, the method of characterizing optimal policies is general, and we shall give several examples in order to illustrate the foregoing remarks in some very simple models. Then we shall give an example of the analysis of the second best in a more general model.

In all cases the problem can be summarized in a symbolic way as

---

1. See Guesnerie and Laffont (1978) for an example of second-best analysis with and without lump-sum transfers; see also section 7.5.

Max Social Welfare(e)

$e \in \mathscr{E}(t)$

$t \in \mathscr{T}$.

Social Welfare is a function of the state of the economic system e (that is, the equilibrium allocation). The constraints tell us that the state of the system is a function of the policy tools t ($e \in \mathscr{E}(t)$) and that these tools are themselves constrained ($t \in \mathscr{T}$) for institutional, moral, political, and other reasons.

We will observe below that this optimization problem is sometimes formalized in the space of quantities (primary space), sometimes in the space of prices and incomes (dual space).

7.1   Pricing Policy for a Firm Subject to a Budget Constraint

Consider an economy with three goods and a consumer for whom the utility function (strictly quasi-concave, increasing, and differentiable) is written as

$$U(x_1, x_2, x_3) = x_1 + v(x_2) + w(x_3).$$

The endowment in good 1 for this agent, w_1, is sufficiently large so that the utility maximum is not a corner solution. Goods 2 and 3 are produced by a public firm for which the cost function expressed in units of good 1 is strictly concave[2] and differentiable and written as

$$C(y_2, y_3),$$

where y_2 and y_3 are the outputs of goods 2 and 3.

The Pareto optimum is derived from the problem

$$\text{Max}\{x_1 + v(x_2) + w(x_3)\}$$

$$\text{subject to} \quad x_2 = y_2$$

$$x_3 = y_3 \tag{I}$$

$$x_1 = w_1 - C(y_2, y_3),$$

2. Therefore we have increasing returns.

for which the first-order conditions[3] are

$$v'(y_2^*) = \frac{\partial C}{\partial y_2}(y_2^*, y_3^*)$$

$$w'(y_3^*) = \frac{\partial C}{\partial y_3}(y_2^*, y_3^*).$$

By choosing prices so that

$$p_2^* = \frac{\partial C}{\partial y_2}(y_2^*, y_3^*)$$

$$p_3^* = \frac{\partial C}{\partial y_3}(y_2^*, y_3^*)$$

(with the price of good 1 normalized to 1), that is, by marginal cost pricing and by financing the losses of the public enterprise by lump-sum taxes on the consumers, a first-best optimum is achieved.

Denote the inverse demand functions by

$$p_2(y_2) = v'(y_2)$$

$$p_3(y_3) = w'(y_3).$$

Now assume that we impose a balanced budget constraint on the public enterprise so that

$$p_2(y_2)y_2 + p_3(y_3)y_3 - C(y_2, y_3) = 0.$$

Let λ be the Lagrangian multiplier associated with the budget constraint. The first-order conditions for solving (I) when the budget constraint is added are

$$p_2 - \frac{\partial C}{\partial y_2} + \lambda\left(p_2 + y_2\frac{dp_2}{dy_2} - \frac{\partial C}{\partial y_2}\right) = 0$$

$$p_3 - \frac{\partial C}{\partial y_3} + \lambda\left(p_3 + y_3\frac{dp_3}{dy_3} - \frac{\partial C}{\partial y_3}\right) = 0.$$

By denoting the price elasticities of demand for goods 2 and 3 as

---

3. Because of increasing returns, the first-order conditions are not sufficient. However, since they are necessary, the analysis is valid at the optimum in particular.

$$e_2 = -\frac{dy_2}{dp_2}\cdot\frac{p_2}{y_2} \qquad e_3 = -\frac{dy_3}{dp_3}\cdot\frac{p_3}{y_3},$$

these conditions can be rewritten as

$$\frac{p_2 - \partial C/\partial y_2}{p_2} = \frac{\lambda}{1+\lambda}\cdot\frac{1}{e_2}$$

$$\frac{p_3 - \partial C/\partial y_3}{p_3} = \frac{\lambda}{1+\lambda}\cdot\frac{1}{e_3}$$

We must no longer sell at marginal cost. Rather, optimal second-best pricing must make the relative gap between the price to the consumer and marginal cost proportional to the inverse of the price elasticity of the good with the coefficient of proportionality chosen to satisfy the budget constraint. This pricing policy is referred to as Ramsey-Boiteux pricing. If we interpret the gap between marginal cost and the optimal price as a tax, we can say that the goods for which demand is less elastic will be taxed more heavily. This result is rather intuitive inasmuch as the same gap between price and marginal cost produces a greater social loss when the elasticity of demand is larger (see figure 7.1).

Oftentimes the goods for which demand is less elastic are necessities, so that we can ask whether or not this pricing principle accords with social justice. Therefore it is appropriate to pursue the analysis in a model with several agents in order to treat the trade-off between equity and efficiency that arises (see the pioneering article by Boiteux 1956, who takes into account the cross-elasticities of demand, and see also problem 6).

7.2   The Two-Part Tariff and the Equity-Efficiency Trade-Off

In the previous section, we considered only linear pricing schedules. A two-part tariff corresponds to an expenditure of $A + px$ for a quantity x consumed. The amount A is a nonpersonalized fixed charge and p is the variable charge per unit. Clearly, a two-part tariff is a particular case of a general nonlinear pricing scheme (see figure 7.2).

If the government could use such an instrument in the problem of the preceding section, it could restore first-best efficiency by taking

$$C(y_2^*, y_3^*) - p_2^* y_2^* - p_3^* y_3^*$$

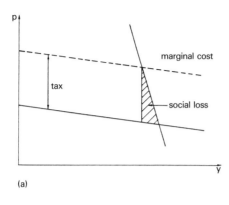

(a)

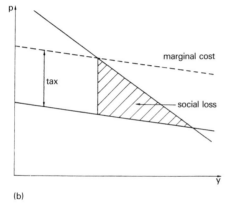

(b)

Figure 7.1
(a) Inelastic demand; (b) elastic demand.

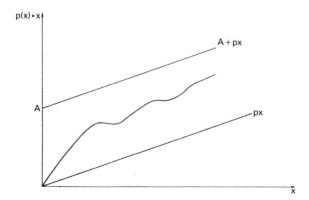

Figure 7.2

as the total fixed charge for both goods and by pricing at marginal cost. We will use the two-part tariff as a policy instrument to study the equity-efficiency tradeoff in the following two-good model.

All the consumers have the same utility function $U(x_1, x_2)$, which is strictly quasi-concave, increasing, and differentiable. Consumer i is endowed with income R^i, $i = 1, \ldots, I$. If the price of good 1 is normalized to 1, the demand function for good 2 for consumer i is obtained by solving the problem

Max $U(x_1, x_2)$

subject to $x_1 + px_2 = R^i - A,$

from which follows the individual demand function $x_2(p, R^i - A)$. Let $X_2(p, A)$ be the aggregate demand for good 2, that is $\sum_{i=1}^{I} x_2(p, R^i - A)$. We define

$$\frac{\partial X_2}{\partial R} \equiv \sum_{i=1}^{I} \frac{\partial x_2}{\partial R^i}(p, R^i - A)$$

and we observe that $\partial X_2/\partial R = -\partial X_2/\partial A$. If we require the budget to be balanced always, the nonpersonalized fixed charge and the unit price are related by

$IA + py = C(y),$

where C is the cost function for good 2 assumed to be differentiable and strictly concave.

We denote as $V(p, R^i - A) = U(R^i - A - px_2(p, R^i - A), x_2(p, R^i - A))$ the indirect utility function of consumer i and we consider the social welfare function given by

$$\sum_{i=1}^{I} \alpha^i V(p, R^i - A) \qquad \alpha^i \geqslant 0 \qquad \sum_{i=1}^{I} \alpha^i = 1.$$

Maximizing the social welfare function subject to the budget constraint is written as

$$\underset{(p, A)}{\text{Max}} \sum_{i=1}^{I} \alpha^i V(p, R^i - A)$$

subject to $IA + pX_2(p, A) - C(X_2(p, A)) = 0.$

Let λ be the Lagrangian multiplier associated with the budget constraint. The first-order conditions can be written as

$$\sum_{i=1}^{I} \alpha^i \frac{\partial V}{\partial p}(p, R^i - A) + \lambda \left[\left(p - \frac{dC}{dy} \right) \frac{\partial X_2}{\partial p}(p, A) + X_2(p, A) \right] = 0 \qquad (1)$$

$$-\sum_{i=1}^{I} \alpha^i \frac{\partial V}{\partial R}(p, R^i - A) + \lambda \left[I + \left(\frac{dC}{dy} - p \right) \frac{\partial X_2}{\partial R}(p, A) \right] = 0. \qquad (2)$$

By using Roy's identity $\partial V/\partial p = -x_2 \partial V/\partial R$, (1) yields

$$\left(p - \frac{dC}{dy} \right) \frac{\partial X_2}{\partial p} = \frac{1}{\lambda} \sum_{i=1}^{I} \alpha^i x_2(p, R^i - A) \frac{\partial V}{\partial R}(p, R^i - A) - X_2(p, A). \qquad (3)$$

From equation (2) we obtain

$$\lambda = \frac{\displaystyle\sum_{i=1}^{I} \alpha^i \frac{\partial V}{\partial R}(p, R^i - A)}{I + \left(\dfrac{dC}{dy} - p \right) \dfrac{\partial X_2}{\partial R}},$$

which can be approximated by

$$\frac{1}{I} \sum_{i=1}^{I} \alpha^i \frac{\partial V}{\partial R}(p, R^i - A)$$

under the assumption that the income effect is small. From (3), we obtain[4]

$$\frac{p - \dfrac{dC}{dy}}{p} \cdot \left(\frac{\partial X_2}{\partial p} \cdot \frac{p}{X_2} \right) = \frac{\text{Cov}\left(x_2(p, R^i - A), \alpha^i \dfrac{\partial V}{\partial R}(p, R^i - A) \right)}{\dfrac{1}{I} X_2(p, A) \cdot \dfrac{1}{I} \displaystyle\sum_{i=1}^{I} \alpha^i \dfrac{\partial V}{\partial R}(p, R^i - A)}.$$

Once again we see that the gap between price and marginal cost must be inversely related to the elasticity of the good, here adjusted by the term on the right.

For a normal good, $\partial X_2/\partial p \cdot p/X_2 < 0$. For a social utility function that favors low-income agents, we have

$$\text{Cov}\left(x_2(p, R^i - A), \alpha^i \frac{\partial V}{\partial R}(p, R^i - A) \right) < 0.$$

4. Cov indicates covariance.

Since the richer an agent is in good 1, the more of good 2 he consumes and the less social weight we wish to give him after adjusting for his marginal utility of income. Therefore in this case where $p > dC/dy$ we must price above marginal cost. The uniformity of the fixed charge bodes ill from the perspective of equity because it is borne equally by all. Therefore it is preferable to price above marginal cost and lower the fixed charge necessary to balance the budget. Explicitly, we accept the loss in efficiency from abandoning the first-order conditions for a first-best optimum in the interest of distributive justice (see Feldstein 1972).

7.3   Externalities and Uniform Taxes

In chapter 1 we saw that personalized taxes allow us to restore Pareto efficiency in economies with externalities. However, the informational and administrative complexity of personalized taxes leads us to consider the consequences of uniform taxes. Consider an exchange economy with two goods, where the utility function of consumer i is

$$U^i(x_1^i, x_2^i, x_2^{-i}) = x_1^i + v^i(x_2^i, x_2^{-i}) \qquad i = 1, \dots, I$$

with

$$x_2^{-i} = (x_2^1, \dots, x_2^{i-1}, x_2^{i+1}, \dots, x_2^I).$$

In order to simplify the analysis, assume that

$$\frac{\partial^2 v^i}{\partial x_2^i \partial x_2^j} = 0 \quad \text{and} \quad \frac{\partial v^i}{\partial x_2^j} \leqslant 0 \qquad \forall j \neq i \qquad \forall i = 1, \dots, I. \tag{4}$$

Let R^i be the income of consumer i when the price of good 1 is normalized to 1 and the price of good 2 is p.[5] Let t^i be the personalized tax that agent i must pay for each unit of good 2 he consumes. His demand function is derived from the problem

Max $U^i(x_1^i, x_2^i, x_2^{-i})$

such that $(p + t^i)x_2^i + x_1^i = R^i$.

Ignoring corner solutions, we obtain

5. We assume that good 2 is produced from good 1 using a linear technology that supports price p.

$$x_2^i = x_2^i(p + t^i),$$

a function that does not depend on income due to the separability of the utility function and that does not depend on the demand for other goods due to assumption (4).

The first-best optima corresponding to the utilitarian criterion are solutions to[6]

$$\underset{(t^i)}{\text{Max}} \left\{ \sum_{i=1}^{I} x_1^i + \sum_{i=1}^{I} v^i(x_2^i(p + t^i), (x_2^j(p + t^j))) \right\}$$

such that $p \sum_{i=1}^{I} x_2^i(p + t^i) + \sum_{i=1}^{I} x_1^i = \sum_{i=1}^{I} R^i,$

from which the first-order conditions are

$$\sum_{j=1}^{I} \frac{\partial v^j}{\partial x_2^i} \cdot \frac{\partial x_2^i}{\partial p} = p \frac{\partial x_2^i}{\partial p} \qquad i = 1, \dots, I.$$

From the first-order conditions for maximizing the utility of consumer i, we have

$$\frac{\partial v^i}{\partial x_2^i} = p + t^i,$$

from which it follows that

$$t^i = -\sum_{j \ne i} \frac{\partial v^j}{\partial x_2^i} \qquad i = 1, \dots, I.$$

If we impose the constraint $t^i = t$, $i = 1, \dots, I$, the second-best optima corresponding to the utilitarian criterion are solutions to

$$\underset{t}{\text{Max}} \left\{ \sum_{i=1}^{I} x_1^i + \sum_{i=1}^{I} v^i(x_2^i(p + t), (x_2^j(p + t))) \right\}$$

such that $p \sum_{i=1}^{I} x_2^i(p + t) + \sum_{i=1}^{I} x_1^i = \sum_{i=1}^{I} R^i.$

It follows that

6.   We   define $v^i(x_2^i(p + t^i), (x_2^j(p + t^j))) \equiv v^i(x_2^i(p + t^i), x_2^1(p + t^1), \dots, x_2^{i-1}(p + t^{i-1}),$ $x_2^{i+1}(p + t^{i+1}), \dots, x_2^I(p + t^I)).$

$$t = \frac{\sum\limits_{i=1}^{I} \left(-\frac{\partial x_2^i}{\partial p} \right) \left(-\sum\limits_{j \neq i} \frac{\partial v^j}{\partial x_2^i} \right)}{\sum\limits_{i=1}^{I} \left(-\frac{\partial x_2^i}{\partial p} \right)}.$$

Thus the optimal uniform tax emerges as a convex combination of personalized taxes with weights equal to $\dfrac{\partial x_2^i}{\partial p} \Big/ \sum\limits_{i=1}^{I} \dfrac{\partial x_2^i}{\partial p}$. In particular, when we have a negative externality so that $\partial v^j / \partial x_2^i < 0$, $\forall i, \forall j \neq i$, we must still tax the generators of this externality despite the uniformity of taxes. When assumption (4) is suppressed, the uniformity constraint can lead to a counter-intuitive result, subsidizing the consumption of good 2 (Diamond 1973). Moreover in the context of the second best, it is appropriate in general to tax the other goods. (Balcer 1980).

7.4   Incentive Constraint

The institutional constraints imposed in the above examples of second-best analysis are somewhat artificial because we have not provided a fundamental explanation for them. Quite often, their origin lies in informational considerations. Consequently, would it not be better to impose these informational constraints directly and then optimize the social criteria subject to these fundamental constraints? By borrowing the differential approach used in chapter 5, we give an example of such an analysis.[7] Consider a monopolist whose cost function is

$$C(q, \theta) = c_0 + \theta q, c_0 > 0 \quad \text{if} \quad q > 0$$

$$C(0, \theta) = 0,$$

where θ is a parameter unknown by the center, $\theta \in [0, 1]$. From the revelation principle, we know that any regulatory policy is isomorphic to a direct revelation mechanism. Ignoring expenditures, the total value to the consumers of a quantity q of the good produced by the monopolist is

$$V(q) = \int_0^q P(t) \, dt,$$

7. See Baron and Myerson (1982).

where $P(.)$ is the inverse demand function, which is assumed to be decreasing. Therefore consumer surplus is $V(q) - qP(q)$.

A social state is characterized by a quantity produced q and a lump-sum transfer t to the producer. If the mechanism $(q(\theta), t(\theta))$ is revealing, the solution of the problem

$$\text{Max}_{\tilde{\theta}} \{q(\tilde{\theta})P(q(\tilde{\theta})) - c_0 - q(\tilde{\theta})\theta + t(\tilde{\theta})\}$$

is obtained for $\tilde{\theta} = \theta$, from which follows the first-order condition that we can transform into an identity (see chapter 5):

$$\frac{d}{d\theta}(q(\theta)P(q(\theta))) - \theta\frac{dq}{d\theta}(\theta) + \frac{dt}{d\theta}(\theta) = 0.$$

We then have

$$t(\theta) = -\int_{\theta}^{1}\left\{\tau\frac{dq}{d\tau}(\tau) - \frac{d}{d\tau}(q(\tau)P(q(\tau)))\right\}d\tau + K$$

$$= \theta q(\theta) + \int_{\theta}^{1} q(\tau)\,d\tau - q(\theta)P(q(\theta)) + K. \tag{5}$$

The local second-order condition is written $dq/d\theta \leqslant 0$ and we can easily show that for a transfer defined by (5), this is a sufficient condition.

To induce a low-cost firm to reveal its cost, it is necessary that the output requested decrease with the announced marginal cost parameter and that the firm be compensated by an appropriate transfer. The profit of the firm is then

$$\Pi(\theta) = K + \int_{\theta}^{1} q(\tau)\,d\tau - c_0 \tag{6}$$

and

$$\frac{d\Pi}{d\theta} = -q(\theta) \leqslant 0.$$

To insure that the firm does not go out of business, profit must always be positive. Since $\Pi(.)$ is decreasing in θ, it is sufficient to impose the condition $\Pi(1) \geqslant 0$ or $K \geqslant c_0$.

The optimal revelation mechanism is that which maximizes the objective function of the center subject to the incentive constraints given by (5),

$dq/d\theta \leqslant 0$, and $\Pi(1) \geqslant 0$. As the objective function we take the weighted average of consumer surplus and monopoly profit and we assume that the center has a prior uniform distribution over θ. It chooses the mechanism that maximizes the expected value of social welfare subject to the incentive constraints, that is,

$$\text{Max} \int_0^1 [V(q(\theta)) - q(\theta)P(q(\theta)) - t(\theta)] \, d\theta + \alpha \int_0^1 \Pi(\theta) \, d\theta,$$

where α represents the weight attributed to the profit of the monopolist. By using (5), the center's problem can be rewritten as:

$$\text{Max} \int_0^1 (V(q(\theta)) - (2 - \alpha)\theta q(\theta) - c_0) \, d\theta - (1 - \alpha)\Pi(1)$$

$$\Pi(1) \geqslant 0 \tag{7}$$

$$\frac{dq}{d\theta}(\theta) \leqslant 0, \tag{8}$$

for which the solution is

$$\Pi(1) = 0, \qquad \frac{dV}{dq}(q) = (2 - \alpha)\theta.$$

We then have $q(\theta) = (\partial V/\partial q)^{-1}[(2 - \alpha)\theta]$, a function that is indeed decreasing.

The mechanism obtained can be interpreted as a rule of modified marginal cost pricing given by

$$P(\theta) = \tilde{c}_m(\theta) = (2 - \alpha)\theta$$

and a transfer

$$t(\theta) = \theta q(\theta) - q(\theta)P(q(\theta)) + \int_\theta^1 q(\tau) \, d\tau + c_0.$$

This must be compared to the optimal pricing rule with complete information composed of marginal cost pricing given by

$$p^*(\theta) = \theta$$

and a transfer equal to the fixed cost c_0 when $\alpha \leqslant 1$.

The social welfare obtained with incomplete information is less than that obtained with complete information because an incentive price for the monopolist leads to a divergence from the first-best rule of price equal to marginal cost. Incomplete information creates a rent for the monopolist because the center wants to make sure that the output is produced regardless of the productivity of the firm. Here this rent is costly to the center because the weight attributed to the profit of the monopolist is less than 1. To countervail this loss, the center reduces output from the first-best level requiring a selling price above marginal cost so as to equate supply and demand.

7.5   Introduction to a General Approach

Before concluding this chapter and this book, I will give a more general example of second-best analysis and derive the rule:

When the center can make lump-sum transfers to the consumers at will, the social value of the goods coincides with the consumer prices.

Consider an economy with I consumers, J producers, and L goods. Suppose that all the agents behave competitively except for producer 1 who deviates by not maximizing his profit at the given prices.

Let $p \in R^L$ be the vector of producer prices and $\pi \in R^L$ be the vector of consumer prices, so that

$$\pi = p + t,$$

where $t \in R^L$ is the vector of taxes. Let $x^i(\pi, R^i)$, $i = 1, \ldots, I$, be the competitive demand functions of the consumers who have disposable incomes of $(R^1, \ldots, R^I)$. Let $V^i(\pi, R^i)$ be the indirect utility function of consumer i, $i = 1, \ldots, I$. Let $y^j(p)$, $j = 2, \ldots, J$, be the competitive supply functions of the $J - 1$ competitive firms, and let $\eta^1(p)$ be the supply function of the deviant firm. Finally, let $f(y^g)$ be the production function of a public firm and let w be the vector of endowed primary resources.

By making all the necessary convexity and differentiability assumptions, the second-best optima are characterized by the first-order conditions of the problem

$$\underset{(p, \pi, R, y^g)}{\text{Max}} \sum_{i=1}^{I} \alpha^i V^i(\pi, R^i)$$

$$-\sum_{i=1}^{I} x^i(\pi, R^i) + \sum_{j=2}^{J} y^j(p) + \eta^1(p) + y^g + w \geqslant 0 \tag{9}$$

$$f(y^g) \geqslant 0. \tag{10}$$

Maximization takes place with respect to the vectors of prices, incomes, and outputs of the public firm subject to the constraints of supply equal to demand on all markets and to the technical constraints of the public firm.

Let ρ_l, $l = 1, \ldots, I$, and μ be the Lagrangian multipliers associated with constraints (9) and (10) respectively. First-order conditions for this problem can be written as

$$\sum_{i=1}^{I} \alpha^i \frac{\partial V^i}{\partial \pi_k} - \sum_{l=1}^{L} \rho_l \left(\sum_{i=1}^{I} \frac{\partial x_l^i}{\partial \pi_k} \right) = 0 \qquad k = 1, \ldots, L \tag{11}$$

$$\sum_{l=1}^{L} \rho_l \left[\sum_{j=2}^{J} \frac{\partial y_l^j}{\partial p_k} + \frac{\partial \eta_l^1}{\partial p_k} \right] = 0 \qquad k = 1, \ldots, L \tag{12}$$

$$\rho_l + \mu \frac{\partial f}{\partial y_l^g} = 0 \qquad l = 1, \ldots, L \tag{13}$$

$$\alpha^i \frac{\partial V^i}{\partial R^i} - \sum_{l=1}^{L} \rho_l \frac{\partial x_l^i}{\partial R^i} = 0 \qquad i = 1, \ldots, I. \tag{14}$$

Multiplying (14) by x_k^i for all i and adding this to (11), we have

$$\sum_{i=1}^{I} \alpha^i \left[\frac{\partial V^i}{\partial \pi_k} + x_k^i \frac{\partial V^i}{\partial R^i} \right] - \sum_{l=1}^{L} \rho_l \sum_{i=1}^{I} \left(\frac{\partial x_l^i}{\partial \pi_k} + x_k^i \frac{\partial x_l^i}{\partial R^i} \right) = 0. \tag{15}$$

From Roy's identity, $\dfrac{\partial V^i}{\partial \pi_k} + x_k^i \dfrac{\partial V^i}{\partial R^i} = 0$ and (15) can be reduced to

$$\sum_{l=1}^{L} \rho_l \sum_{i=1}^{I} \left(\frac{\partial x_l^i}{\partial \pi_k} + x_k^i \frac{\partial x_l^i}{\partial R^i} \right) = 0. \tag{16}$$

We know that the compensated demand functions are homogeneous of degree zero with respect to prices (see preface to chapter 6). Then, from the Slutsky equations,

$$\frac{\partial x_l^i}{\partial \pi_k} + x_k^i \frac{\partial x_l^i}{\partial R^i} = \frac{\partial x_l^i}{\partial \pi_k} \bigg|_{U=cte};$$

therefore

$$\sum_{k=1}^{L} \pi_k \sum_{i=1}^{I} \left(\frac{\partial x_l^i}{\partial \pi_k} + x_k^i \frac{\partial x_l^i}{\partial R^i} \right) = 0. \tag{17}$$

Under regularity assumptions the symmetric matrix $\left(\dfrac{\partial x_l^i}{\partial \pi_k} + x_k^i \dfrac{\partial x_l^i}{\partial R^i} \right)$ has rank $(L - 1)$, and (16) and (17) imply

$$\rho_l = k\pi_l \qquad l = 1, \ldots, L.$$

The social values of the goods, that is, the values of the Lagrangian multipliers associated with the scarcity constraints, are therefore proportional to the consumer prices. A normalization of consumer prices can be chosen so as to have $\rho_l = \pi_l, l = 1, \ldots, L$. On the other hand, (13) implies

$$\frac{\rho_l}{\rho_k} = \frac{\partial f / \partial y_l^g}{\partial f / \partial y_k^g} \quad \text{for any } k, l = 1, \ldots, L.$$

Consequently, prices supporting decentralization of the activity of the public firm coincide with consumer prices.

Consider the more specific case when the deviating firm is the sole producer of good 1, a final consumption good, and this firm minimizes its cost function given by

$$C(y_1^1, p_{-1}) \quad \text{where} \quad p_{-1} = (p_2, \ldots, p_L).$$

Let $\xi(y_1^1, p_{-1})$ be the function that determines the inputs for a level of output given by y_1^1. This function is homogeneous of degree zero in p_{-1}. Let $\eta_1^1(p)$ be the supply of good 1. Let λ be the multiplier associated with the additional constraint given by

$$y_1^1 = \eta_1^1(p).$$

The first-order conditions are analogous to those given above. Equation (12) can be decomposed into

$$\sum_{l=2}^{L} \rho_l \left(\sum_{j=2}^{J} \frac{\partial y_l^j}{\partial p_k} + \frac{\partial \xi_l}{\partial p_k} \right) + \lambda \frac{\partial \eta_1^1}{\partial p_k} = 0 \qquad k = 2, \ldots, L \tag{18}$$

$$\lambda \frac{\partial \eta_1^1}{\partial p_1} = 0, \tag{19}$$

and maximization with respect to y_1^1 yields

$$\rho_1 + \sum_{l=2}^{L} \rho_l \frac{\partial \xi_l}{\partial y_1^1} + \lambda = 0. \tag{20}$$

In general, (19) implies $\lambda = 0$. (18) with homogeneity of degree 0 of $y^j(.)$, $j = 2, \ldots, J$, and of $\xi(.)$ and symmetry of $\left(\sum_{j=2}^{J} \frac{\partial y_l^j}{\partial p_k} + \frac{\partial \xi_l}{\partial p_k} \right)$ implies

$$p_l = k' \rho_l \qquad l = 2, \ldots, L.$$

By normalizing production prices so that $k' = 1$, (20) yields

$$\pi_1 = -\sum_{l=2}^{L} p_l \frac{\partial \xi_l}{\partial y_1^1} = \frac{\partial C}{\partial y_1^1}(y_1^1, p_{-1}).$$

Therefore, the consumer price is equal to marginal cost and the deviant producer behaves like a competitive producer faced with a vector of prices given by $(\pi_1, p_2, \ldots, p_L)$ since he both minimizes his costs and equates his marginal cost to π_1. At the optimum, only one good, good 1, is taxed with the rate given by $t_1 = \pi_1 - p_1$. Since the constraint $y_1^1 = \eta_1^1(p)$ has a zero multiplier, first-best efficiency is also restored. In effect, all the agents appear as if they are behaving competitively with respect to the unique vector of prices given by

$$(\pi_1, p_2, \ldots, p_L) = (\pi_1, \pi_2, \ldots, \pi_L).$$

7.6*   Discount Rate for Public Investment

In the model of section 7.5, we have seen that the prices used by public firms must be consumer prices and not producer prices. In an intertemporal model, several rates of interest exist; for example, the subjective rate of interest of the consumers, which is analogous to consumer prices, and the net technical rate of interest, which is analogous to producer prices. In the absence of distortions, the interest rate is equal to both the subjective interest rate and the technical interest rate in a competitive equilibrium. Therefore the discount rate to be used by public firms is this unique interest rate. With distortions, the optimal second-best discount rate is a complex combination of the different rates, as we shall see in the example below.

Consider an economy with one good, one consumer, and two periods, which is taken to be an abstraction for an economy with a large number of identical consumers. Let $U_1(x_1) + U_2(x_2)$ be the intertemporal utility function of the consumer. He can either use his endowment w in the first period for consumption x_1 or lend it at the interest rate r. The private firms borrow a quantity i from him and produce output $f(i)$ in the second period. However, the government imposes a sales tax t per unit of output sold so that the profits of the private firms are

$$\Pi_i = (1 - t)f(i) - (1 + r)i.$$

Using these revenues $tf(i)$, the government finances the production of a public good at level k that, to simplify the notation, enters additively into the utility function in the second period. The balanced-budget constraint is

$$k = tf(i). \tag{21}$$

The public firms borrow an amount g at rate r and produce $h(g)$ of the good in the second period. Their profit $\Pi_g = h(g) - (1 + r)g$ is distributed to the consumer. The supply-equals-demand constraints can be written as

$$x_1 = w - g - i$$

$$x_2 = (1 + r)(g + i) + T,$$

where

$$T = \Pi_i + \Pi_g + k.$$

Optimizing behavior for the consumer leads to

$$U'_1 - (1 + r)U'_2 = 0. \tag{22}$$

Optimizing behavior for the private firm leads to

$$(1 - t)f'(i) = 1 + r. \tag{23}$$

Therefore, after substituting the supply-equals-demand constraints, the second-best optimum is characterized by

$$\underset{(k,g,r,i)}{\text{Max}} \ \{U_1(w - g - i) + U_2(f(i) + h(g))\}$$

subject to (21), (22), and (23).

Notice that

$$\frac{\partial x_1}{\partial r} = \frac{U'_2}{U''_1 + (1 + r)^2 U''_2}; \quad \frac{\partial i}{\partial r} = \frac{1}{(1 - t)f''(i)}$$

are the derivatives of the demand for consumption in the first period and the demand for investment obtained by differentiating (22) and (23). By substituting (21) and (23) into the objective function and into (22), the problem is reduced to one with a single constraint. A simple calculation then shows that

$$1 + \rho = h'(g) \doteq \frac{(1 + r)\dfrac{\partial x_1}{\partial r} + \dfrac{(1 + r)}{1 - t}\dfrac{\partial i}{\partial r}}{\dfrac{\partial i}{\partial r} + \dfrac{\partial x_1}{\partial r}}.$$

The optimal second-best discount rate ρ emerges as a weighted average of the subjective interest rate $U_1'/U_2' - 1 = r$ and of the technical interest rate (or net marginal productivity)

$$f'(i) - 1 = \frac{r + t}{1 - t}$$

with weights equal to $\partial x_1/\partial r$ and $\partial i/\partial r$ respectively. (See Sandmo and Drèze 1971 and Marchand and Pestieau 1984).

7.7*   Optimal Indirect Taxation

The optimal pricing problem for a public firm subject to a budget constraint, called the Ramsey-Boiteux problem (see section 7.1), is almost identical to the problem of optimal indirect taxation designed to generate a revenue for financing a public good. Here we treat this problem by taking into account income effects. Let $f(z, y) = 0$ be the implicit production function describing the production of an output level y of the public good using a vector of inputs z. Using the same notation as in section 7.5, we normalize the prices so that $\Pi_1 = p_1 = 1$ and we choose units so that $\partial f/\partial z_1 = 1$ at the optimum. Thus we can equate producer prices to the vector $(\partial f/\partial z_k)$.

First consider the case of a single consumer. Let y be the quantity of the public good financed by indirect taxes. Let $(x_i(\Pi, R, y))$ be his demand functions for private goods given y and let $V(\Pi, R, y)$ be his indirect utility function. The vector of optimal taxes is the solution to

$$\operatorname*{Max}_{\Pi} V(\Pi, R, y)$$

subject to $f(z, y) = 0$ (24)

$$z = w - x(\Pi, R, y).$$ (25)

After substituting (25) into (24), we write the first-order conditions of maximization over Π, R with λ the Lagrangian multiplier as

$$\frac{\partial V}{\partial \Pi_l} - \lambda \sum_{k=1}^{L} \frac{\partial f}{\partial z_k} \cdot \frac{\partial x_k}{\partial \Pi_l} = 0 \tag{26}$$

$$\frac{\partial V}{\partial R} = \lambda \sum_{k=1}^{L} \frac{\partial f}{\partial z_k} \cdot \frac{\partial x_k}{\partial R}. \tag{26'}$$

However, by definition,

$$\frac{\partial f}{\partial z_k} = p_k = \Pi_k - t_k;$$

by Roy's identity,

$$\frac{\partial V}{\partial \Pi_l} = -x_l \frac{\partial V}{\partial R};$$

and by the budget constraint,[8]

$$\sum_{k=1}^{L} \Pi_k \frac{\partial x_k}{\partial \Pi_l} = -x_l.$$

Therefore (26) becomes

$$-x_l \frac{\partial V}{\partial R} + \lambda x_l + \lambda \sum_{k=1}^{L} t_k \frac{\partial x_k}{\partial \Pi_l} = 0.$$

Finally, by using the Slutsky equations, we have

$$\left[\lambda - \left(\frac{\partial V}{\partial R} + \lambda \sum_{k=1}^{L} t_k \frac{\partial x_k}{\partial R} \right) \right] x_l = -\lambda \sum_{k=1}^{L} t_k \left(\frac{\partial x_k}{\partial \Pi_l} \right)_{u=Cte}.$$

Let

$$\gamma = \frac{\partial V}{\partial R} + \lambda \sum_{k=1}^{L} t_k \frac{\partial x_k}{\partial R}$$

be the aggregate social marginal utility of income made up of the direct marginal utility of the consumer and the indirect utility resulting from an increase in taxes. By using the symmetry property of the Slutsky matrix,

8. Note that the derivatives are taken with y constant, that is, with a constant government budget: $\sum_k t_k x_k =$ constant. The budgetary constraint of the consumer can be written as $\sum_k p_k x_k + \sum_k t_k x_k = R$, which implies, with the above remark, that $\sum_k p_k \partial x_k / \partial R = 1$. From (26'), $\partial V / \partial R = \lambda$.

we have

$$-\frac{\sum_{k=1}^{L} t_k \left(\dfrac{\partial x_l}{\partial \Pi_k}\right)_{u=Cte}}{x_l} = \frac{\lambda - \gamma}{\lambda} \qquad l = 1, \ldots, L. \tag{27}$$

In the neighborhood of optimal taxes, the relative reduction in compensated demand resulting from a proportional marginal increase in taxes must be the same for each good. In particular, it must be equal to $(\lambda - \gamma)/\lambda$. But λ is the opportunity cost of public funds, that is, the cost to the government of obtaining one additional dollar by using optimal taxes, and γ is the marginal social utility of this dollar. Therefore $(\lambda - \gamma)/\lambda$ is the relative additional charge due to indirect taxation (in France, the Planning Commission recommended using a value for λ of 1.5 in 1986).

Diamond (1975) generalizes this analysis to the case of many agents and he includes a uniform lump-sum tax. The problem then becomes quite similar to optimal pricing with a two-part tariff (see section 7.2). If we let α^i be the weight of consumer i in the social utility function, the problem can be written as

$$\text{Max } \sum_{i=1}^{I} \alpha^i V^i(\Pi, T, y)$$

subject to $f(z, y) = 0$

$$z = w - \sum_{i=1}^{I} x^i(\Pi, T, y) \equiv w - X(\Pi, T, y),$$

where x^i and V^i are expressed here in terms of the lump-sum transfer and the remaining income is assumed to be a function of prices. By using analysis similar to that used above, we can obtain the analogue of (27), that is,

$$-\sum_{k=1}^{L} t_k \left(\frac{\partial X_l}{\partial \Pi_k}\right)_{u=Cte} = \left(\frac{\lambda - \bar{\gamma}_l}{\lambda}\right) X_l \tag{28}$$

with

$$\bar{\gamma}_l = \sum_{i=1}^{I} \left(\frac{x_l^i}{X_l}\right) \gamma^i,$$

where

$$\gamma^i = \alpha^i \frac{\partial V^i}{\partial T} + \lambda \sum_{k=1}^{L} t_k \frac{\partial x_k^i}{\partial T}. \tag{29}$$

Optimizing with respect to the lump-sum transfer yields

$$\sum_{i=1}^{I} \alpha^i \frac{\partial V^i}{\partial T} + \lambda \sum_{k=1}^{L} p_k \frac{\partial X_k}{\partial T} = 0$$

or

$$\sum_{i=1}^{I} \alpha^i \frac{\partial V^i}{\partial T} = \lambda \left(I - \sum_{k=1}^{L} t_k \frac{\partial X_k}{\partial T} \right). \tag{30}$$

Using (29) and noticing that $\bar{\gamma} = \sum_{i=1}^{I} \frac{\gamma^i}{I} = \lambda$, we can write (28) as

$$\frac{\sum_{k=1}^{L} t_k \left(\frac{\partial X_l}{\partial \Pi_k} \right)_{u=Cte}}{X_l} = \frac{\text{Cov}(\gamma^i, x_l^i)}{\bar{\gamma} E x_l},$$

which is called the many-person Ramsey formula.

Our preceding rule has to be modified. At the optimum, the relative reduction in compensated demand resulting from a proportional marginal increase in taxes must be smaller for goods consumed by persons whose income has a higher marginal social utility. Neglecting the cross-substitution effects yields

$$\frac{t_l}{\Pi_l} = -\frac{\text{Cov}(\gamma^i, x_l^i)}{e_l^C \cdot \bar{\gamma} \cdot E x_l},$$

where e_l^C is the compensated price elasticity for good l. Therefore, the government must tax at a lower rate and eventually subsidize the goods consumed in larger proportions by persons with low incomes if we wish to give these persons a larger weight in the social welfare function (see sections 7.1, 7.2). Notice that by using the concept of compensated demand elasticity, we no longer need to make approximate statements by ignoring aggregate income effects as we did in section 7.2.

7.8*   Rationing, Free Goods, and Welfare

The rationing of certain commodities and the provision of free goods are obviously deleterious to efficiency in an economy satisfying the assumptions of the basic microeconomic model. To introduce them would create distortions. However, if distortions already exist, their introduction may be beneficial.

For example, consider an economy with three goods, a system of indirect taxes, and one in which all consumers have the same utility function

$$x_1^i + v(x_2^i) + w(x_3^i) \qquad i = 1, \ldots, I.$$

At equilibrium,

$$v'(x_2^i) = \Pi_2 = p_2 + t_2$$

$$w'(x_3^i) = \Pi_3 = p_3 + t_3.$$

Suppose that we have a small decrease dx_2 in the consumption of good 2 by consumer i. His welfare loss is given by $v'(x_2^i) \, dx_2 = \Pi_2 \, dx_2$. The decrease in cost is $p_2 \, dx_2$. Therefore, social gain occurs if good 2 had been subsidized ($t_2 < 0$). Analogously, if good 2 had been taxed ($t_2 > 0$), to achieve a social gain it would have been necessary to consider a small increase in the consumption of good 2 (See Guesnerie and Roberts 1984 for an in-depth study of this problem of the second best).

In this book, the fundamentals of public economics have been cast in the Walrasian framework, that is, we assumed that prices were flexible enough to equate supply and demand in all markets. If, on the contrary, prices are rigid and rationing occurs, public policy prescriptions must be modified accordingly. Consider an example of cost-benefit analysis applied to a public good. Suppose that each consumer i, $i = 1, \ldots, I$ has the utility function $x_1^i + v(x_2^i) + w(y)$, where y is a public good. The price of good 1 is normalized to 1 and the price of good 2 is fixed at a level $\bar{p}$ such that the demand from consumers is greater than supply:

$$\sum_{i=1}^{I} x_2^i(\bar{p}) > \sum_{i=1}^{I} w_2^i.$$

The public good is produced using good 2 and the question is: What prices should the public enterprise use? In the absence of rationing, it should use the market price $\bar{p}$ to evaluate its input and equate the marginal utility of the public good $Iw'(y)$ to its marginal cost. Call r the uniform quantity of good 2 rationed to each consumer in the equilibrium with rationing. Denote by $C(y)$ the cost of the public good in units of good 2. The second-best optimum is derived from the problem

$$\underset{(r,y)}{\text{Max}} \sum_{i=1}^{I} [w_1^i + v(r) + w(y)]$$

$$\text{subject to} \quad Ir + C(y) = \sum_{i=1}^{I} w_2^i,$$

where r is the uniform ration of good 2 to the consumers. From the foregoing discussion it immediately follows that

$$Iw'(y) = \frac{dv}{dx_2^i}(r)C'(y) > \bar{p}C'(y).$$

Since good 2 is rationed, the market price must not be used to calculate the marginal cost of good 2, but rather a larger price $(dv/dx_2^i > \bar{p})$ is in order. On the other hand, if the input were in excess supply (for example, labor when it is not fully employed), it would be necessary to use a price lower than the market price in cost computations.

From this example, one might be led to reconsider the entire theory of public economics for an economy with rigid disequilibrium prices (see, for example, Marchand, Mintz, and Pestieau 1985). However, we should proceed carefully for two reasons. First, we seem to be mixing up short- and long-term problems. It is unreasonable to revise the tax code every quarter according to short-term fluctuations. Second, we are uncomfortable with a disequilibrium theory that lacks a fundamental explanation (perhaps informational) of price rigidities. For example, why not simply use taxes to alter prices?

References

Balcer, Y., 1980, "Taxation of externalities: direct vs. indirect," *Journal of Public Economics*, 13, 121–129.

Baron, D., and R. Myerson 1982, "Regulating a monopolist with unknown costs," *Econometrica*, 50, 911–930.

Boiteux, M., "Sur le question des monopoles astreints à l'équilibre budgétaire," *Econometrica*, 24, 22–40.

Diamond, P., 1973, "Consumption externalities and imperfect corrective pricing," *Bell Journal of Economics and Management Science*, 52, 6.538.

Diamond, P., 1975, "A many-person Ramsey tax rule," *Journal of Public Economics*, 4, 335–242.

Diamond, P., and J. Mirrlees 1971, "Optimal taxation and public production," *American Economic Review*, 61, 8–27 and 261–278.

Feldstein, M., 1972, "Equity and efficiency in public sector pricing: the optimal two-part tariff," *Quarterly Journal of Economics*, 86, 175–187.

Green, J., and E. Sheshinski 1979, "Competitive inefficiencies in the presence of constrained transactions, *Journal of Economic Theory*, 10, 343.

Guesnerie, R., 1974, "Un formalisme général pour les problèmes de second rang. Son application à la détermination des règles de calcul économique public sous une hypothèse simple de fiscalité," *Cahiers du Séminaire d'Econométrie*.

Guesnerie, R., and J.-J. Laffont 1978, "Taxing price markers," *Journal of Economic Theory*, 19, 423–455.

Guesnerie, R., and K. Roberts 1984, "Effective policy tools and quantity controls," *Econometrica*, 52, 59–86.

Malinvaud, E., 1969, *Leçons de théorie microéconomique*, Dunod, Paris.

Marchand, M., and P. Pestieau 1984, "Discount rates and shadow prices for public investments," *Journal of Public Economics*, 24, 153–169.

Marchand, M., J. Mintz, and P. Pestieau 1985, "Public production and shadow pricing in a model of disequilibrium in labor and capital markets," *Journal of Economic Theory*, 2, 237–250.

Sandmo, A., and J. Drèze 1971, "Discount rates for public investment in closed and open economies," *Economica*, 38, 395–412.

Recommended Reading

1. Boiteux 1956 (a seminal paper).

2. Guesnerie 1974 (a general framework for second-best analysis).

3. Diamond and Mirrlees 1971; Guesnerie and Laffont 1978 (examples of second-best analysis in general equilibrium).

4. Baron and Myerson 1972 (second-best analysis with an explicit incentive constraint).

WORKED PROBLEMS

Problem 1
Externalities and Optimal Taxation

Statement of the Problem

Consider an economy with two goods and I consumers. Each consumer is given four units of good 1 as an initial endowment. Good 2 is produced using good 1 according to the technology

$$y_2 = \sqrt{z_1} \qquad z_1 \geq 0 \qquad y_2 \geq 0.$$

The production of good 2 generates a negative externality affecting the consumers' preferences so that the utility function of consumer i is written as

$$U^i(x_1^i, x_2^i, y_2) = x_1^i + \text{Log } x_2^i - \tfrac{1}{2} \text{Log } y_2 \qquad i = 1, \ldots, I.$$

Assume that consumer i considers the externality y_2 as parameter, that is, he neglects the impact of his own consumption of good 2 on the production of good 2.

1. Assuming that each consumer receives one Ith of the profits of the firm producing good 2 from good 1, determine the competitive equilibrium in this private property economy.

2. Explain why the competitive equilibrium is not Pareto optimal. Characterize all the Pareto optima in which each consumer consumes a positive amount of good 1. What is the Pareto optimum corresponding to maximization according to the Rawls criterion (maximin)? Calculate the per capita utility loss in the competitive equilibrium using this Pareto optimum as a benchmark.

3. Go back to the initial situation in the first question. What is the tax per unit of output that must be imposed on the producer of good 2 to restore Pareto efficiency? (The government's budget is balanced with the help of lump-sum transfers on the consumers). What is the utility level achieved by a typical consumer if the lump-sum transfer is the same for all consumers?

4. In light of the difficulties encountered in the solution to question 3, we decide to nationalize the firm and to impose a zero profit condition on it. Show that this policy is even more detrimental than the laissez-faire situation of the first question. Explain why this policy is detrimental.

5. After nationalization and the imposition of a balanced-budget constraint, we decide to tax the consumption of good 2 under the assumption that we

can distribute these revenues by lump-sum transfers to the consumers. What is the optimal tax? Why do we now obtain a Pareto optimum? Explain why the amount of taxes collected here is greater than the sum collected in question 3.

6. Now suppose that the firm producing good 2 behaves like a monopolist and sets its price by applying a markup over marginal cost m (price equals marginal cost plus m). Supposing that the consumers always behave competitively and that profits are redistributed equally, graph the equilibrium utility level for a typical consumer as a function of m. What do you observe?

Solution

1. Normalize the price of good 1 at 1 and let p be the price of good 2. The firm maximizes its profit subject to its production function, that is,

Max $py_2 - z_1$

subject to $y_2 = \sqrt{z_1}$,

which yields the supply function $y_2(p) = p/2$ and profits $\Pi(p) = p^2/4$. Since the profits are distributed equally among the consumers, the optimization problem for a typical consumer is

$$\text{Max} \left\{ x_1^i + \text{Log } x_2^i - \frac{1}{2} \text{Log } y_2 \right\}$$

subject to $x_1^i + px_2^i \leqslant 4 + \dfrac{\Pi(p)}{I}$,

which yields the demand functions

$$x_2^i = \frac{1}{p} \qquad x_1^i = 3 + \frac{p^2}{4I}.$$

To obtain the relative price in equilibrium, it is sufficient to equate supply and demand for good 2 in the following way:

$$\frac{I}{p} = \frac{p}{2},$$

from which

$$p^{ec} = \sqrt{2I}$$

and

$$y_2^{ec} = \sqrt{\frac{I}{2}}, \quad \Pi(p^{ec}) = \frac{I}{2}$$

$$x_2^i = \frac{1}{\sqrt{2I}}, \quad x_1^i = \frac{7}{2} \quad i = 1, \ldots, I.$$

The utility level achieved by a typical consumer is

$$U_{ec}^i = \frac{7}{2} - \frac{1}{4} \text{Log } 2I^3.$$

The utility level decreases with the number of agents because of both the decreasing returns and the negative externality generated in the production of the necessary good, good 2.

2. The competitive equilibrium is not a Pareto optimum because the producer does not take into account the negative externality which he imposes on the consumers. The Pareto optima are characterized by solutions to the problem

$$\text{Max } \sum_{i=1}^{I} \alpha^i U^i(x_1^i, x_2^i, y_2); \qquad \alpha^i \geqslant 0, i = 1, \ldots, I$$

subject to $\quad \sum_{i=1}^{I} x_2^i \leqslant y_2 \qquad\qquad\qquad\qquad\qquad (\lambda)$

$$\sum_{i=1}^{I} x_1^i + y_2^2 \leqslant 4I. \qquad\qquad\qquad (\mu)$$

The Lagrangian is written as:

$$\mathcal{L} = \sum_{i=1}^{I} \alpha^i U^i + \lambda \left(y_2 - \sum_{i=1}^{I} x_2^i \right) + \mu \left(4I - \sum_{i=1}^{I} x_1^i - y_2^2 \right),$$

which yields first-order conditions of the form

$$\frac{\partial \mathcal{L}}{\partial x_1^i} = \alpha^i - \mu \leqslant 0 \quad (=0 \text{ if } x_1^i > 0) \qquad i = 1, \ldots, I.$$

Since we are looking for optima in which all the consumers consume a positive amount of good 1, we must have

$\alpha^i = \mu \quad \forall i \qquad i = 1, \ldots, I,$

which we may take to be equal to 1 without any loss of generality. Following in this manner, we have

$$\frac{\partial \mathcal{L}}{\partial x_2^i} = \frac{1}{x_2^i} - \lambda = 0 \quad \text{(since } x_2^i \neq 0 \text{ at an interior optimum)} \tag{1}$$

$$\frac{\partial \mathcal{L}}{\partial y_2} = \frac{-I}{2y_2} + \lambda - 2y_2 = 0 \tag{2}$$

(2) yields

$$\lambda = 2y_2 + \frac{I}{2y_2}$$

and (1) implies

$$\sum_{i=1}^{I} x_2^i = \frac{I}{\lambda}.$$

The equality of supply and demand for good 2 yields $y_2 = I/\lambda$ from which it follows that $y_2 = \sqrt{I}/2$. Therefore, the Pareto optima with strictly positive quantities consumed of good 1 by all agents are characterized by

$$y_2 = \frac{\sqrt{I}}{2}$$

$$x_2^i = \frac{1}{2\sqrt{I}} \qquad i = 1, \ldots, I$$

$$\sum_{i=1}^{I} x_1^i = \frac{15}{4} I.$$

Here the Rawlsian criterion is equivalent to equalizing the utility levels of all the agents, from which it follows that

$$y_2 = \frac{\sqrt{I}}{2} \qquad x_2^i = \frac{1}{2\sqrt{I}} \qquad x_1^i = \frac{15}{4},$$

and the utility level associated with this is

$$U_0^i = 3.40 - \frac{3}{4} \text{Log } I \qquad i = 1, \ldots, I,$$

from which the per capita social loss due to the noninternalization of the externalities in the competitive equilibrium is

$$\Delta = 0.25 - \frac{1}{4} \text{Log } 2 = 0.074.$$

3. To achieve a Pareto optimum, it is necessary to encourage the producer to produce $\sqrt{I}/2$. Let t be the tax per unit of output imposed on the producer. He solves the problem $\text{Max}(p - t)y_2 - y_2^2$, which yields the supply function

$$y_2(p - t) = \frac{p - t}{2}.$$

Here $p - t$ is the producer's price, and p is the consumer's price. Since the demand of each consumer is independent of income, we always have an aggregate demand of I/p for good 2.

The equilibrium consumer price associated with tax t_{et} yielding output at a level $\sqrt{I}/2$ is therefore

$$p_{et} = 2\sqrt{I}$$

and

$$t_{et} = p_{et} - 2y_2 = \sqrt{I}.$$

From the foregoing, the tax revenue collected is $t_{et}y_2 = I/2$ and, to balance the government's budget, we must distribute in lump-sum transfers an amount equal to $I/2$, that is, $1/2$ to each agent if we wish to use egalitarian transfers. The amount of profit is $I/4$ and the income of a typical consumer is $R^i = 19/4$, from which it follows that

$$x_1^i = \frac{15}{4} \qquad x_2^i = \frac{1}{2\sqrt{I}},$$

and these are the quantities consumed in an egalitarian optimum.

4. Nationalize the firm and impose a zero profit condition on it, that is,

$$py_2 = y_2^2 \quad \text{or} \quad p = y_2.$$

To satisfy the aggregate demand of I/p, the firm must produce $y_2 = \sqrt{I}$ and sell it at a price $p_n = \sqrt{I}$. Because of decreasing returns, the competitive firm earned positive profit. If we impose on the firm the conditions that it both meet demand and make zero profits, it will produce still more and thus aggravate the effects of the externalities. The budget constraint for agent i is $x_1^i + px_2^i = 4$, which yields $x_1^i = 3$, and the utility level associated with this is $3 - \frac{3}{4} \operatorname{Log} I$, yielding a per capita loss of $0.5 - 1/4 \operatorname{Log} 2 = 0.324$ compared to the laissez-faire competitive equilibrium.

5. Let $p - t$ be the producer's price; the balanced-budget condition for the firm yields $y_2 = p - t$, and the equilibrium of supply and demand implies

$$p - t = \frac{I}{p} \quad \text{or} \quad t = p - \frac{I}{p}.$$

The utility level of the typical consumer is

$$3 + \operatorname{Log} \frac{I}{p} - \frac{1}{2} \operatorname{Log} y_2 - \frac{t}{I} y_2, \tag{3}$$

where the last term represents the lump-sum transfer (assumed to be egalitarian as above). Therefore (3) can be rewritten as

$$4 - \frac{1}{2} \operatorname{Log} I - \frac{1}{2} \operatorname{Log} p - \frac{I}{p^2},$$

from which it follows that the price p^* maximizing the utility of a typical agent is

$$p^* = 2\sqrt{I} \qquad t^* = \frac{3}{2}\sqrt{I} \qquad y^* = \frac{\sqrt{I}}{2}.$$

The tax revenues collected equal $(3/4)I$ compared to $I/2$ in question 3 because behavior deviates more from the optimum in this question.

6. The cost function is $c(y_2) = y_2^2$ so that pricing according to marginal cost plus a markup m leads to a consumer price of

$$p = 2y_2 + m.$$

On the other hand, to satisfy aggregate demand it is necessary that

$$y_2 = \frac{I}{p},$$

from which it follows that the relation between the markup and the consumer price must be

$$m = p - \frac{2I}{p}.$$

To each level of markup m there corresponds a utility level for the typical consumer that we shall calculate.

Profit is given by $I - (I^2/p^2)$, with

$$U^i = 4 - \frac{I}{p^2} + \text{Log}\,\frac{1}{p} - \frac{1}{2}\,\text{Log}\,\frac{I}{p}$$

$$= 5 - \text{Log}\sqrt{I} - \frac{1}{2}\,\text{Log}\,p - \frac{I}{p^2}.$$

The optimal price for good 2 is $p = 2\sqrt{I}$ and p can be considered to vary between $\sqrt{I/2}$ and $+\infty$ (p and the markup are related by the equation $m = p - (2I/p)$). We graph U^i as a function of p (figure P1.1) or as a function of the markup (figure P1.2).

The equilibrium for the monopolist using markup pricing is preferred to the competitive equilibrium for an entire range of markups because the

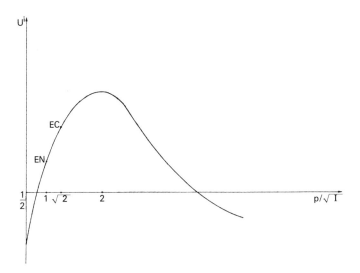

Figure P1.1

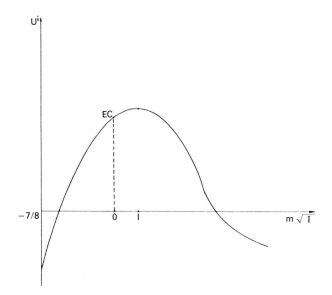

Figure P1.2

markup leads to a decrease in the output of the good generating negative externalities. There even exists a markup level $\sqrt{I}$ that restores optimality. This level is equivalent to the optimal tax found in question 3 because the markup added to marginal cost plays the same role as a tax on a competitive firm (one that minimizes its costs and therefore equates its production price to its marginal cost).

Problem 2
Financing Public Goods and the Theory of the Second Best

Statement of the Problem

Consider an economy with I consumers and three goods. Two of the goods are private (goods 1 and 2) and one is a pure public good (good 3). Consumer i, $i = 1, \ldots, I$ has the utility function

$$U^i(x_1^i, x_2^i, x_3) = x_1^i + 2 \operatorname{Log} x_2^i + \operatorname{Log} x_3,$$

where x_1^i (resp. x_2^i) indicates the quantity of good 1 consumed (resp. of good 2 consumed), and where x_3 indicates the quantity of the public good consumed. The latter is the same for all consumers because it is a pure public good that everyone must use.

Good 1 is the only good available in the economy as a primary resource. Let w_1^i (with $w_1^i > 2$) be the initial endowment of good 1 to consumer i. Good 2 is produced using good 1 according to the technology

$$y_2^1 = \sqrt{y_1^1}, \qquad y_1^1 \geqslant 0 \qquad y_2^1 \geqslant 0,$$

where y_1^1 is the input of good 1 and y_2^1 is the output of good 2. Good 3 (the public good) is produced using good 1 according to the technology

$$y_3^2 = y_1^2 \qquad y_1^2 \geqslant 0 \qquad y_3^2 \geqslant 0,$$

where y_1^2 is the input of good 1 and y_3^2 is the output of good 3.

1. The Pareto optima in which each of the I consumers consumes a strictly positive quantity of good 1 can be obtained by maximizing the objective function $\sum_{i=1}^{I} U^i(x_1^i, x_2^i, x_3)$, subject to the technological constraints and the scarcity constraints (that is, the supply-demand equilibrium for each of the three goods). Calculate these optima. Verify that the output of the public good is the same in each one.

2. Assume that each consumer is entitled to a share of one Ith of the firms' profits. With that in mind, the government can achieve any one of the optima calculated in question 1 as a competitive equilibrium in the market for private goods; to accomplish this, the government

(i) sets the level of output of the public good;
(ii) establishes prices for the private goods and
(iii) imposes lump-sum transfers on the consumers.

Calculate the prices established. Show that the sum of the lump-sum transfers is equal to the cost of financing the public good.

3. Now assume that it is impossible to use lump-sum transfers as we did in the second question. Then we decide to tax good 2 to finance the production of the public good (that is, if p_2 is the production price of good 2, $\pi_2 = p_2 + t$ is the consumption price of the same good). Calculate the tax t on good 2 that is sufficient to finance the quantity of the public good determined in question 1.

4. Explain how this tax generates a social loss, that is, prevents the achievement of a Pareto optimum. Calculate the social loss (that is, the variation in $\sum_{i=1}^{I} U^i$ from question 1 to question 3). Recalculate this loss using the concept of surplus. In the space (y_2^1, π_2), graph the social loss.

5. Given that the method of financing the public good is taxing good 2, explain why the second-best optimum requires an output of the public good that is different from the one obtained in question 1. Write the optimization problem that yields the second-best output of the public good. Calculate this output and the corresponding social loss. From this, derive the social benefit obtained by second-best optimization compared with this situation in question 4.

Solution

1. We are interested only in the Pareto optima for which the quantities consumed of good 1 by each consumer are strictly positive, that is $x_1^i > 0$, $i = 1, \ldots, I$. The set of feasible allocations is characterized by the following inequalities:

$$(\mathrm{I}) \quad \begin{cases} \displaystyle\sum_{i=1}^{I} x_1^i \leqslant \sum_{i=1}^{I} w_1^i - y_1^1 - y_1^2 \\[2ex] \displaystyle\sum_{i=1}^{I} x_2^i \leqslant y_2^1 \\[2ex] x_3 \leqslant y_3^2 \\[1ex] y_2^1 \leqslant \sqrt{y_1^1} \\[1ex] y_3^2 \leqslant y_1^2 \\[1ex] y_1^1 \geqslant 0 \quad y_2^1 \geqslant 0 \quad y_1^2 \geqslant 0 \quad y_3^2 \geqslant 0 \\[1ex] x_1^i > 0 \quad i = 1, \ldots, I; \quad x_2^i \geqslant 0 \quad i = 1, \ldots, I. \end{cases}$$

The strictly increasing utility functions and the logarithmic form excluding zero quantities consumed of goods 2 and 3 in an interior Pareto optimum leads us to simplify (I) to

$$(\text{II}) \quad \begin{cases} \displaystyle\sum_{i=1}^{I} x_1^i = \sum_{i=1}^{I} w_1^i - (y_2^1)^2 - y_3^2 \\[2ex] \displaystyle\sum_{i=1}^{I} x_2^i = y_2^1 \\[2ex] x_3 = y_3^2 \\[1ex] x_1^i > 0 \qquad i = 1, \dots, I. \end{cases}$$

The set of feasible allocations is convex. Therefore, the Pareto optima $x_1^i > 0, i = 1, \dots, I$) are obtained by solving the problem

$$(\text{III}) \quad \text{Max} \left(\sum_{i=1}^{I} x_1^i + 2 \text{ Log } x_2^i + \text{Log } x_3 \right)$$

subject to

$$\sum_{i=1}^{I} x_1^i = \sum_{i=1}^{I} w_1^i - (y_2^1)^2 - y_3^2 \tag{1}$$

$$\sum_{i=1}^{I} x_2^i = y_2^1 \tag{2}$$

$$x_3 = y_3^2. \tag{3}$$

Indeed to use different weights for different consumers would lead to an allocation of all of good 1 to the agent (or to the agents) with largest weight because of the linearity of the utility functions in the quantity of good 1 consumed.

Let p_1, p_2, and p_3 be the Lagrangian multipliers associated with constraints (1), (2), and (3) respectively. The first-order conditions (which are also sufficient due to the concavity of the utility functions) of the maximization problem (III) are written as

$$p_1 = 1$$

$$\frac{2}{x_2^i} = p_2 \qquad i = 1, \dots, I$$

$$\frac{I}{x_3} = p_3$$

$2y_2^1 p_1 = p_2$

$p_1 = p_3,$

from which it immediately follows that

$y_3^2 = x_3 = I$

$y_2^1 = \sqrt{I}; \qquad x_2^i = \frac{1}{\sqrt{I}} \quad i = 1, \ldots, I; \qquad p_2 = 2\sqrt{I}$

$\sum_{i=1}^{I} x_1^i = \sum_{i=1}^{I} w_1^i - 2I; \qquad p_1 = p_3 = 1.$

The allocations of (x_1^i) differ according to the Pareto optimum considered with $x_1^i > 0$, $i = 1, \ldots, I$. Social welfare equal to the sum of individual utilities is $\sum_{i=1}^{I} w_1^i - 2I$.

2. Let $\{(x_1^{*i}), (x_2^{*i}), x_3^*, y_2^{*1}, y_3^{*2}\}$ be any Pareto optimum (with $x_1^{*i} > 0$, $i = 1, \ldots, I$). If the government chooses an output level for the public good $y_3^{*2} = x_3^* = I$, and prices for the private good proportional to the Lagrangian multipliers in problem (III), that is, $p_1^* = 1$ and $p_2^* = 2\sqrt{I}$, the optimum is decentralizable by a competitive economy if the incomes of the consumers $i = 1, \ldots, I$ are chosen to satisfy

$R^{*i} = p_1^* x_1^{*i} + p_2^* x_2^{*i} = x_1^{*i} + 2.$

In effect, the producer of good 2 maximizes his profits by solving the problem:

$\text{Max}(2\sqrt{I} y_2^1 - y_1^1)$

subject to $\quad y_2^1 = \sqrt{y_1^1}; \qquad y_2^1 \geq 0; \qquad y_1^1 \geq 0,$

From which it follows that

$y_1^1 = I; \qquad y_2^1 = \sqrt{I} = y_2^{*1}.$

Consumer i maximizes his utility given income R^{*i} and the government's policy x_3^*, by solving the problem

$\text{Max}(x_1^i + 2 \text{ Log } x_2^i + \text{Log } x_3^*)$

subject to $\quad x_1^i + 2\sqrt{I} x_2^i = R^{*i},$

from which it follows that

$$x_2^i = \frac{1}{\sqrt{I}} = x_2^{*i} \qquad x_1^i = R^{*i} - 2 = x_1^{*i}.$$

This is an example of the decentralization theorem for a convex economy with private goods. Once the output of the public good, y_3^{*2}, and the input of good 1 necessary to produce it, y_1^{*2}, are chosen, we are left with an economy that has only private goods. Moreover, the optimality of the allocation considered implies Pareto optimality for the allocation of private goods when y_3^{*2} and y_1^{*2} are fixed.

In a private property economy, consumer i is endowed with his initial primary resources w_1^i and a share (chosen equally for each consumer) in the profits of the firm producing good 2, that is,

$$w_1^i + \frac{1}{I}(p_2^* y_2^{*1} - y_1^{*1}) = w_1^i + 1.$$

So that he has an income level R^{*i} that supports decentralization of the considered Pareto optimum, we must impose a lump-sum transfer of T^{*i} such that

$$R^{*i} = w_1^i + 1 - T^{*i},$$

that is,

$$T^{*i} = w_1^i - x_1^{*i} - 1.$$

Since these transfers are calculated so as to allow a consumer to be able to purchase his allocation of private goods (x_1^{*i}, x_2^{*i}) by spending all his income, the sum of the lump-sum transfers must exactly finance the output of the public good. Effectively, we have

$$\sum_{i=1}^{I} T^{*i} = \sum_{i=1}^{I} w_1^i - \sum_{i=1}^{I} x_1^{*i} - I = I.$$

3. Now consider a case in which lump-sum transfers are infeasible, so that we appeal to an indirect tax on the quantity consumed of good 2 to finance the output level, $y_3^{*2} = I$, of the public good determined in the first question. Let t be the tax rate so that the consumption price becomes $\pi_2 = p_2 + t$. If the price of good 1 remains normalized at $p_1 = 1$, the demand for good 2 is determined by solving the problem

$\text{Max}(x_1^i + 2 \text{ Log } x_2^i + \text{Log } x_3^*)$

subject to $\quad x_1^i + (p_2 + t)x_2^i = R^i.$

Thus $x_2^i = 2/(p_2 + t)$ is independent of income because of the quasi-linearity of the utility function in x_1^i. Therefore, the aggregate demand for 2 is $x_2 = 2I/(p_2 + t)$, an amount that must be equal to output level y_2^1.

In a competitive equilibrium, the production price of good 2, p_2, is always equal to marginal cost, that is, $2y_2^1$ (since the cost function is given by $(y_2^1)^2$). The tax t and the quantity of good 2 compatible with profit-maximizing behavior of the firm producing good 2 and utility-maximizing behavior by each consumer are therefore related by

$$y_2^1 = \frac{2I}{2y_2^1 + t},$$

or

$$y_2^1(t) = \frac{-t + \sqrt{t^2 + 16I}}{4}.$$

The tax that finances I units of the public good is defined by

$$I = t^* y_2^1(t^*) = \frac{-t^{*2} + t^*\sqrt{t^{*2} + 16I}}{4},$$

which yields $t^* = \sqrt{2I}.$

4. Now the output of good 2 is

$$y_2^1 = \sqrt{\frac{I}{2}}.$$

Therefore, the profit of the firm producing good 2 is $I/2$, a sum to be shared equally among all the consumers. Consequently, consumer i's maximization problem is written as

$\text{Max}(x_1^i + 2 \text{ Log } x_2^i + \text{Log } x_3^*)$

subject to $\quad x_1^i + (\sqrt{2I} + \sqrt{2I})x_2^i = w_1^i + \dfrac{1}{2},$

which yields

$$x_2^i = \sqrt{\frac{1}{2I}} \qquad x_1^i = w_1^i - \frac{3}{2}.$$

Therefore the level of social welfare achieved is

$$\sum_{i=1}^{I} w_1^i - \frac{3I}{2} + 2I \, \text{Log} \, \frac{1}{\sqrt{2I}} + I \, \text{Log} \, I = \sum_{i=1}^{I} w_1^i - \left(\frac{3}{2} + \text{Log} \, 2 \right) I,$$

which represents a per capita social loss equal to $\text{Log} \, 2 - 1/2 = 0.19$.

The tax on good 2 generates a social loss because the marginal rate of substitution of consumer i between goods 1 and 2, which is $p_2^* + t^* = 2\sqrt{2I}$, is different from the marginal rate of transformation between these two goods, which is $p_2^* = \sqrt{2I}$. Thus a necessary condition for Pareto optimality no longer holds. Another approach consists in calculating the social loss directly by using the concept of surplus,

$$\int_{\sqrt{I/2}}^{\sqrt{I}} \left(\frac{2I}{y} - 2y \right) dy = \left(\text{Log} \, 2 - \frac{1}{2} \right) I.$$

This analysis is summarized in figure P2.1.

5. Since financing the public good creates a social loss, it is preferable to produce a smaller quantity of the public good than I, the desirable quantity

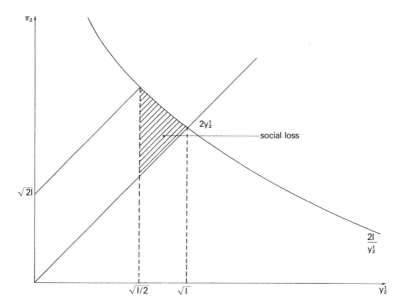

Figure P2.1

to produce when financing did not involve a social loss (because of lump-sum transfers as in question 2). When the quantity of the public good that we wish to finance with a tax on good 2 is x_3, we must have $t y_2^1 = x_3$. On the other hand, the demand for y_2^1 with a tax rate t is $y_2^1 = 2I/(p_2 + t)$. Finally, competitive behavior on the part of the producer requires $p_2 = 2 y_2^1$, which yields

$$2(y_2^1)^2 + x_3 = 2I,$$

or

$$y_2^1(x_3) = \sqrt{I - \frac{x_3}{2}}.$$

This specifies the relationship between the consumption of the public good and the competitive supply of good 2 when the public good is financed by a tax on good 2. To obtain the optimal second-best allocation, we can maximize the utility generated by the public good net of the social loss that accrues from this method of financing. The problem becomes

$$\underset{x_3}{\text{Max}} \left(I \operatorname{Log} x_3 - x_3 - \int_{\sqrt{I - (x_3/2)}}^{\sqrt{I}} \left(\frac{2I}{y} - 2y \right) dy \right),$$

or, equivalently, to maximize the social utility represented by the sum of individual utilities.

$$\underset{x_3}{\text{Max}} \left(\sum_{i=1}^{I} w_1^i - x_3 - (y_2^1(x_3))^2 + 2I \operatorname{Log} \frac{y_2^1(x_3)}{I} + I \operatorname{Log} x_3 \right).$$

These two procedures are equivalent because the surplus exactly measures the social loss due to the quasi-linearity of the utility functions; moreover, the maximands differ only by a constant of integration.

The first-order conditions for this maximization problem are written as

$$\frac{I}{x_3} - 1 - \frac{I}{I - (x_3/2)} \cdot \frac{1}{2} + \frac{1}{2} = 0,$$

or as

$$2I^2 - 3I x_3 + \frac{(x_3)^2}{2} = 0,$$

or

$$x_3 = (3 \pm \sqrt{5})I.$$

Since $I - (x_3/2) > 0$, that is $x_3 < 2I$, we have $x_3 = (3 - \sqrt{5})I$. Therefore the social loss is

$$\Delta = (I \operatorname{Log} I - I) - (I \operatorname{Log} x_3 - x_3) + \int_{\sqrt{((-1+\sqrt{5})/2)I}}^{\sqrt{I}} d(I \operatorname{Log} y^2 - y^2)$$

$$= I \operatorname{Log} I - I - I \operatorname{Log} I(3 - \sqrt{5}) + I(3 - \sqrt{5}) + I \operatorname{Log} I$$

$$- I \operatorname{Log} I\left(\frac{-1 + \sqrt{5}}{2}\right) - I + I\left(\frac{-1 + \sqrt{5}}{2}\right).$$

Therefore the per capita social loss is $\Delta/I = 0.13$. We calculate the per capita gain from second-best optimization (going from question 4 to question 5) as $0.19 - 0.13 = 0.06$.

Problem 3
Revelation of Preferences for Public Goods and Observability of Quantities of Private Goods Consumed

Statement of the Problem

Consider an economy with I consumers, two private goods and a pure public good. The utility function of consumer i is given by

$$U^i(x_1^i, x_2^i, y) = x_1^i + \theta^i(y + \sqrt{x_2^i}),$$

where $x_1^i(x_2^i)$ indicates the quantity consumed of good 1 (good 2) by consumer i and where y is the quantity consumed of the public good. $\theta^i \in R_+$ is a taste parameter known only to consumer i. The values θ^i can be assumed to be the result of independent draws from an unknown distribution with finite mean and variance. The endowment of good 1 to consumer i is w_1^i, $i = 1, \ldots, I$.

Good 2 is produced using good 1 according to the technology

$$y_2 = -y_1 \qquad y_1 \leqslant 0,$$

where y_1 is the input of good 1 and y_2 is the output of good 2. The public good is also produced using good 1; the cost function expressed in units of good 1 associated with this production process is

$$I \cdot (y^2/2).$$

Bankruptcy issues are ignored.

1. What is the Pareto-optimal level of the public good when all the consumers consume strictly positive amounts of good 1?

2. Assume that the cost of producing the public good is shared equally among all the consumers and that good 2 is produced by competitive firms. We shall retain this framework until question 6. Determine the indirect utility function of consumer i, $V^i(\theta^i, y)$, as a function of θ^i and of y. Then consider the game in which each agent announces a taste parameter $\tilde{\theta}^i$, knowing that the collective decision maker will choose a level of output for the public good according to the decision rule

$$y = \frac{\sum_{i=1}^{I} \tilde{\theta}^i}{I}. \tag{1}$$

By assuming, for simplicity, that each agent can announce one response $\tilde{\theta}^i$ in R, show that the game does not have a Nash equilibrium in general.

3. Characterize the mechanisms with side payments measured in good 1 that allow the collective decision maker to elicit the true responses $\tilde{\theta}^i =$

θ^i, as dominant strategies. Show that mechanisms leading to dominant strategy equilibria exist.

4. Instead of using the mechanisms of question 3, suppose that the collective decision maker estimates θ^i based on his observation of the quantity consumed of good 2 and chooses the corresponding level of output of the public good according to formula (1). Knowing this decision rule, the agents behave strategically and change their consumption of good 2. Calculate the social loss that results from this behavior and show that it tends to zero when I tends to infinity.

5. Calculate the tax on the quantity consumed of good 2 that eliminates the deviant behavior on the market for good 2 derived in question 4. Compare this with the result derived in question 3.

6. Now we try to make the burden of financing the public good depend on the preferences of the agents by using the weights

$$\delta^i = \frac{\theta^i}{\sum_{k=1}^{I} \theta^k}.$$

Treat questions 3 and 4 in this way. Show that the asymptotic results, when I tends to infinity, are different.

Solution

1. The level of output of the public good corresponding to a Pareto optimum in which all agents consume a strictly positive amount of good 1 is the solution to the following problem (see solution to problem I):

$$\text{Max} \sum_{i=1}^{I} [x_1^i + \theta^i(y + \sqrt{x_2^i})]$$

subject to
$$\sum_{i=1}^{I} x_1^i = \sum_{i=1}^{I} w_1^i - \frac{Iy^2}{2} - \sum_{i=1}^{I} x_2^i$$

$$x_1^i \geqslant 0 \qquad x_2^i \geqslant 0 \qquad i = 1, \ldots, I$$

$$y \geqslant 0,$$

which yields $y = \sum_{i=1}^{I} \theta^i/I$.

2. Normalize the price of good 1 equal to 1. Since the production technology for good 2 using good 1 is linear with a coefficient of 1, the price of good

2 is also 1. Agent i chooses his quantities to consume of goods 2 and 1 subject to his budget constraint by solving the following problem:

$$\underset{(x_1^i, x_2^i)}{\text{Max}} \; [x_1^i + \theta^i(y + \sqrt{x_2^i})]$$

subject to $\quad x_1^i + x_2^i = w_1^i - \dfrac{y^2}{2}$

$$x_1^i \geqslant 0 \qquad x_2^i \geqslant 0,$$

since $y^2/2$ is the cost imputed to agent 1 for financing the public good at a level y. The optimal choices are

$$x_2^i = \left(\frac{\theta^i}{2}\right)^2 \qquad x_1^i = w_1^i - \frac{y^2}{2} - \left(\frac{\theta^i}{2}\right)^2.$$

Therefore the indirect utility function of agent i is

$$V^i(\theta^i, y) = w_1^i - \frac{y^2}{2} + \theta^i y + \frac{(\theta^i)^2}{4}.$$

On the basis of the responses $\tilde{\theta}^i$, which may be different from the true parameters $\tilde{\theta}^i$, the collective decision maker chooses the quantity of the public good to maximize the utilitarian criterion

$$\text{Max} \sum_{i=1}^{I} V^i(\tilde{\theta}^i, y),$$

which yields

$$y = \frac{1}{I} \sum_{i=1}^{I} \tilde{\theta}^i.$$

We shall ignore the fact that y could be negative (because a priori the $\tilde{\theta}^i$ may have any sign). The problem could be treated more rigorously by taking into account this sign constraint. Now we study the possibility of a Nash equilibrium in this game of responses.

Let $\tilde{\theta}^k, k \neq i$ be the responses of the other agents; agent i's best response is determined by the program

$$\underset{\tilde{\theta}^i}{\text{Max}} \; V^i(\tilde{\theta}^i, \theta^i, y)$$

subject to $\quad y = \dfrac{[\tilde{\theta}^i + \sum_{k \neq i} \tilde{\theta}^k]}{I},$

or

$$\underset{\tilde{\theta}^i}{\text{Max}} \left[w_1^i - \frac{1}{2} \left[\frac{\tilde{\theta}^i + \sum_{k \neq i} \tilde{\theta}^k}{I} \right]^2 + \theta^i \left[\frac{\tilde{\theta}^i + \sum_{k \neq i} \tilde{\theta}^k}{I} \right] + \frac{(\theta^i)^2}{4} \right]$$

for which the solution is

$$\tilde{\theta}^i = I \left[\theta^i - \frac{\sum_{k \neq i} \tilde{\theta}^k}{I} \right] \qquad i = 1, \ldots, I, \tag{1}$$

or

$$\theta^i = \frac{1}{I} \sum_{k=1}^{I} \tilde{\theta}^k. \tag{2}$$

Since (2) must hold for all the agents, a Nash equilibrium exists only if the agents have identical tastes.

If we take into account sign constraints, Nash equilibria exist but they correspond to a quantity of public good very different from the optimal quantity. Thus, in both cases, it seems that agents' manipulation of this mechanism leads to an unsatisfactory allocation. The decision maker must design a more sophisticated mechanism if he wants to secure a better choice for the public good.

3. We shall compute side payments in good 1 which lead each agent to announce his true parameter θ^i as a dominant strategy of the game. Let $t^i(\tilde{\theta}^i, \tilde{\theta}^{-i})$ be the transfer in good 1 received by agent i if he announces $\tilde{\theta}^i$ and if the other agents announce $\tilde{\theta}^{-i} = (\tilde{\theta}^1, \ldots, \tilde{\theta}^{i-1}, \tilde{\theta}^{i+1}, \ldots, \tilde{\theta}^I)$. On the other hand, agent i knows that the decision maker uses his response according to rule (1) of the statement of the problem. Therefore, his best response is a solution to the problem

$$\underset{\tilde{\theta}^i}{\text{Max}} \left[w_1^i - \frac{1}{2} \left[\frac{\tilde{\theta}^i + \sum_{k \neq i} \tilde{\theta}^k}{I} \right]^2 + \theta^i \left[\frac{\tilde{\theta}^i + \sum_{k \neq i} \tilde{\theta}^k}{I} \right] + \frac{(\theta^i)^2}{4} + t^i(\tilde{\theta}^i, \tilde{\theta}^{-i}) \right]$$

for which, the first-order necessary condition is

$$\frac{\partial t^i}{\partial \theta^i}(\tilde{\theta}^i, \tilde{\theta}^{-i}) = \frac{-\theta^i}{I} + \frac{(\tilde{\theta}^i + \sum_{k \neq i} \tilde{\theta}^k)}{I^2}. \tag{3}$$

A necessary condition for telling the truth to be a dominant strategy is that it must be the solution to (3) regardless of the responses of the other agents. Moreover, we want the agent to tell the truth whatever the truth may be; so that we have the following identity (by suppressing the $\sim$):

$$\frac{\partial t^i}{\partial \theta^i}(\theta^i, \theta^{-i}) \equiv \theta^i \left[\frac{1}{I^2} - \frac{1}{I} \right] + \frac{\sum_{k \neq i} \theta^k}{I^2}.$$

By integrating, we derive

$$t^i(\theta^i, \theta^{-i}) = \theta^i \frac{\sum_{k \neq i} \theta^k}{I^2} - \frac{(\theta^i)^2}{2} \left(\frac{I-1}{I^2} \right) + h^i(\theta^{-i}), \tag{4}$$

where $h^i(.)$ is any function of responses from the other agents that represents the constant of integration. When the transfer is defined by (4), it is easy to show that consumer i's problem is concave in $\tilde{\theta}^i$ because

$$\frac{\partial^2 U^i}{\partial \tilde{\theta}^{i2}} = -\frac{1}{I},$$

so that $\tilde{\theta}^i = \theta^i$ is truly a global maximum.

The balanced-budget condition is written as

$$\sum_{i=1}^{I} t^i(\theta) \equiv 0, \quad \text{for any } \theta,$$

or

$$\sum_{i=1}^{I} \theta^i \left(\frac{\sum_{k \neq i} \theta^k}{I^2} \right) - \sum_{i=1}^{I} \frac{(I-1)}{2I^2}(\theta^i)^2 + \sum_{i=1}^{I} h^i(\theta^{-i}) \equiv 0, \quad \text{for any } \theta,$$

or

$$\frac{1}{I^2} \left(\sum_{k=1}^{I} \theta^k \right)^2 - \frac{(I+1)}{2I^2} \sum_{k=1}^{I} (\theta^k)^2 + \sum_{i=1}^{I} h^i(\theta^{-i}) \equiv 0, \quad \text{for any } \theta. \tag{5}$$

To demonstrate the existence of equilibrium mechanisms, we restrict ourselves to looking for symmetric quadratic functions $h^i(.)$, that is,

$$h^i(\theta^1, \ldots, \theta^{i-1}, \theta^{i+1}, \ldots, \theta^I) = \alpha \sum_{k \neq i} (\theta^k)^2 + \beta \sum_{\substack{k \neq i \\ h \neq i \\ h \neq k}} \theta^k \theta^h.$$

The symmetry assumption according to which α and β are independent of i is analogous to the anonymity assumption in social choice theory. By setting (5) equal to zero, we derive

$$\alpha = \frac{1}{2I^2} \qquad \beta = -\frac{1}{I^2(I-2)}.$$

Therefore the following transfers elicit true responses and insure a balanced budget:

$$t^i(\theta^i, \theta^{-i}) = \theta^i \frac{\sum_{j \neq i} \theta^j}{I^2} - \frac{(\theta^i)^2}{2}\left(\frac{I-1}{I^2}\right) + \frac{1}{2I^2}\sum_{k \neq i}(\theta^k)^2 - \frac{1}{I^2(I-2)}\sum_{\substack{h \neq i \\ k \neq i \\ h \neq k}}\theta^k\theta^h.$$

The possibility of obtaining a balanced budget here is quite special since it follows from the indirect utility functions $V^i(.)$ being quadratic in y (see Green and Laffont 1979, cited in chapter 5).

4. Now suppose that the collective decision maker uses the following strategy. He observes the quantity consumed of good 2 and he knows that the agent chooses an optimal amount of good 2 such that $x_2^i = (\theta^i/2)^2$. From observing $\tilde{x}_2^i$, he estimates the taste parameter to be $\tilde{\theta}^i = 2\sqrt{\tilde{x}_2^i}$ and chooses a quantity of the public good accordingly, so that

$$y = \frac{\sum_{i=1}^I \tilde{\theta}^i}{I} = \frac{2}{I}\sum_{i=1}^I \sqrt{\tilde{x}_2^i}.$$

However, agent i knows the relationship between his quantity consumed of good 2 and the output of the public good. Behaving strategically, he determines his best choice for good 2 by solving the problem

$$\text{Max}_{x_2^i} \left\{ w_1^i - \frac{2}{I^2}\left(\sqrt{\tilde{x}_2^i} + \sum_{k \neq i}\sqrt{\tilde{x}_2^k}\right)^2 - \tilde{x}_2^i \right.$$

$$\left. + \theta^i\left[\sqrt{\tilde{x}_2^i} + \frac{2}{I}\left(\sum_{k \neq i}\sqrt{\tilde{x}_2^k} + \sqrt{\tilde{x}_2^i}\right)\right]\right\},$$

where the (x_2^j) are the quantities consumed of good 2 by the other agents. Again ignoring sign and bankrupcy constraints, the Nash equilibrium is characterized by the first-order conditions for this maximization problem given by

$$\sqrt{\tilde{x}_2^i} + \frac{2}{I^2}\sum_{k=1}^I \sqrt{\tilde{x}_2^k} = \theta^i\left(\frac{2+I}{2I}\right) \qquad i = 1, \dots, I. \tag{6}$$

Summing (6) over i, we have

$$\sum_{k=1}^{I} \sqrt{\tilde{x}_2^k} = \frac{\sum_{k=1}^{I} \theta^k}{2},$$

from which, substituting in (6), we have

$$\tilde{x}_2^i = \left[\theta^i \left(\frac{2+I}{2I} \right) - \frac{1}{I^2} \sum_{k=1}^{I} \theta^k \right]^2, \tag{7}$$

a quantity that is different from true consumption when θ^i differs from the mean of the tastes because

$$\sqrt{\tilde{x}_2^i} = \frac{\theta^i}{2} + \frac{1}{I} \left(\theta^i - \frac{1}{I} \sum_{k=1}^{I} \theta^k \right).$$

Here the quantity chosen of the public good, $y = \sum_{i=1}^{I} \theta^i / I$, is Pareto optimal (a result that is not generalizable); but nonetheless strategic behavior leads to a social loss due to the distortions in the quantities consumed of good 2. The variation in utility compared to the optimum from question 1 due to this distortion is equal to, for agent i,

$$\Delta U^i = \frac{1}{I^2} \left[\theta^i - \frac{\sum_{k=1}^{I} \theta^k}{I} \right]^2.$$

Each agent loses because of manipulation, and the social loss according to the utilitarian criterion is

$$\Delta U = \frac{1}{I^2} \sum_{i=1}^{I} \left[\theta^i - \frac{\sum_{k=1}^{I} \theta^k}{I} \right]^2.$$

If we assume that the θ^i are drawn independently from a probability distribution with mean μ and finite variance σ^2, since

$$\frac{1}{I} \sum_{i=1}^{I} \left(\theta^i - \frac{\sum_{k=1}^{I} \theta^k}{I} \right)^2$$

is the sample variance, $I \Delta U$ tends toward σ^2 and the social loss tends toward zero when I tends toward infinity. In fact, when I tends toward infinity, the impact of agent I's distortion on the quantity produced of the public good tends toward zero, whereas the cost of a distortion in his quantity consumed the consumption of good 2 remains bounded below for him. Therefore his distortion tends toward zero, and, moreover, at a sufficiently rapid speed here, so that the social loss tends toward zero. The possibility of observing the quantity consumed of good 2 thus greatly limits the seriousness of the incentive problem.

5. To counteract this strategic behavior, the decision maker can levy taxes on the consumption of good 2 to induce each agent to consume the amount $\hat{x}_2^i = (\theta^i/2)^2, i = 1, \ldots, I$. Consider the taxes t^i as functions of the quantities consumed of good 2, (x_2^i). A necessary condition for $\hat{x}_2^i$ to be the best consumption choice of good 2 for agent i, regardless of the other agents' consumption choices, is determined by solving the problem

$$\text{Max}_{x_2^i} \left\{ w_1^i - \frac{2}{I^2} \left(\sqrt{x_2^i} + \sum_{k \neq i} \sqrt{x_2^k} \right)^2 - x_2^i \right.$$

$$\left. + \theta^i \left(\sqrt{x_2^i} + \frac{2}{I} \sum_{k \neq i} \sqrt{x_2^k} + \frac{2}{I} \sqrt{x_2^i} \right) + t^i(x_2^i, x_2^{-i}) \right\}$$

for each (x_2^k), which yields the first-order condition

$$\sqrt{\hat{x}_2^i} \frac{\partial t^i}{\partial x_2^i}(\hat{x}_2^i, x_2^{-i}) = \frac{2}{I^2} \left(\sqrt{\hat{x}_2^i} + \sum_{k \neq i} \sqrt{\hat{x}_2^k} \right) + \sqrt{\hat{x}_2^i} - \theta^i \left(\frac{2+I}{2I} \right).$$

This condition must hold for every $\theta^i = 2\sqrt{\hat{x}_2^i}$ and for all (x_2^k), from which it follows that

$$\frac{\partial t^i}{\partial x_2^i}(x_2^i, x_2^{-i}) \equiv -\frac{2}{I^2}(I - 1) + \frac{2\sum_{k \neq i} \sqrt{x_2^k}}{I^2 \sqrt{x_2^i}},$$

and by integration

$$t^i(x_2^i, x_2^{-i}) = \frac{4}{I^2} \left(\sum_{k \neq i} \sqrt{x_2^k} \right) \sqrt{x_2^i} - \frac{2(I - 1)}{I^2} x_2^i + h(x_2^{-i}).$$

It is interesting to note that this tax can be rewritten as

$$t^i = -\frac{2(I + 1)}{I^2} x_2^i + \frac{2y}{I} \sqrt{x_2^i} + h(x_2^{-i}).$$

This is a nonlinear tax on the consumption of good 2 for which the coefficient of the nonlinear part depends on the quantity of the public good. On the other hand, since $\theta^i = 2\sqrt{x_2^i}$, the tax can be rewritten as

$$t^i = \left(\sum_{k \neq i} \theta^k \right) \frac{\theta^i}{I^2} - \frac{(I - 1)}{2I^2} (\theta^i)^2 + \tilde{h}(\theta^{-i}),$$

which is truly the type of transfer payment obtained in question 3 to elicit truthful revelation.

Given the definition of the mechanism, inducing the agents to consume $\hat{x}_2^i = (\theta^i/2)^2$ is equivalent to inducing them to announce $\tilde{\theta}^i = \theta^i$, from which the foregoing result follows. Even though it is possible to observe an activity variable of the consumer, we do not enlarge the class of mechanisms that support the maximization of the utilitarian criteria because this variable is manipulable. However, it is important to remember that with a large number of agents, observing the quantities consumed of good 2 leads to a choice that is a considerable improvement over the decision based on the collective decision maker's expectations.

6. The share of the cost of the public good is now $\dfrac{I\theta^i}{\sum_{k=1}^{I} \theta^j} \cdot \dfrac{y^2}{2}$ instead of $y^2/2$. The transfers that elicit truthful revelation are now

$$t^i(\theta^i, \theta^{-i}) = \frac{\sum_{k \neq i} \theta^k}{2I} \cdot \theta^i + h^i(\theta^{-i}).$$

If

$$h^i(\theta^{-i}) = -\frac{1}{2I(I-2)} \sum_{\substack{k \neq i \\ h \neq i \\ h \neq k}} \theta^h \theta^k,$$

the budget is even balanced.

In a manner analogous to that in question 4, the strategic choice of consumption for good 2 can be characterized by

$$\sqrt{x_2^i} = \frac{1}{2}\left(\frac{2+I}{1+I}\right)\theta^i - \frac{1}{2}\frac{(I+2)}{(I+1)(1+2I)} \sum_{k=1}^{I} \theta^k,$$

from which the quantity of public good produced is

$$y^d = \left(\frac{I+2}{1+2I}\right) \cdot y^*,$$

where $y^* = \sum_{i=1}^{I} \theta^i/I$ is the Pareto-optimal output of the public good.

The social loss resulting from this strategic behavior now has two components: first, the output of the public good is not Pareto optimal, and second, the quantities consumed of good 2 are distorted. Let $\delta(i)$ be the proportion of cost $Iy^2/2$ imputed ex post to agent i, so that

$$\delta(i) = \frac{[(1 + 2I)\theta^i - \sum_{k=1}^{I} \theta^k]}{(1 + I)\sum_{k=1}^{I} \theta^k}.$$

The variation in utility for agent i is

$$\Delta U^i = -\tfrac{1}{2}[(y^*)^2 - I\delta(i)(y^d)^2] - [x_2^{*i} - x_2^{di}]$$

$$+ \theta^i[\sqrt{x_2^{*i}} - \sqrt{x_2^{di}}] + \theta^i[y^* - y^d],$$

and since $\sum_{i=1}^{I} \delta(i) = 1$, we have

$$\Delta U = \sum_{i=1}^{I} [\sqrt{x_2^{*i}} - \sqrt{x_2^{di}}][\theta^i - (\sqrt{x_2^{*i}} + \sqrt{x_2^{di}})]$$

$$+ (y^* - y^d)\left[\sum_{i=1}^{I} \theta^i - \frac{1}{2}(y^* + y^d)\right]$$

$$= \frac{I}{4(1 + I)^2}[\sigma^2(I) + \mu(I)^2] + A(I)\mu(I)^2 I^2,$$

where $\sigma^2(I)$ indicates the sample variance of the distribution of θ^i and $\mu(I)$ is the sample mean, so that

$$A(I) = -\frac{(I + 2)}{2(I + 1)^2(1 + 2I)} + \frac{(I + 2)^2 I}{4(1 + I)^2(1 + 2I)^2} + \frac{(I - 1)^2}{2I(1 + 2I)^2},$$

which yields

$$\frac{\Delta U}{I} \to \frac{3}{16}\mu^2 \quad \text{when} \quad I \to \infty.$$

Therefore, the social loss does not tend to zero as it did in question 3. Furthermore, the loss computed is only an average social loss. The losses suffered by the various agents differ greatly among agents. We have seen that there are two distortions, the distortion on the quantities consumed of good 2 that has a negative effect on all agents and the distortion on the choice of the public good reducing its output. The latter has a positive effect on those who don't like the public good very much and a negative effect on those who like it a lot. Since

$$\lim_{I \to \infty} \Delta U^i = \frac{3}{4}\theta^i\mu - \frac{9}{16}\mu^2$$

the agents for whom $\theta^i < \tfrac{3}{4}\mu$ benefit from manipulation (in the limit).

Problem 4
Optimal Redistributive Taxation

Statement of the Problem

The utility of each agent depends on his consumption of good x according to the function

$$u(x) = \text{Log } x.$$

The agent's income R depends on his talent n (which is an unobservable variable) and his level of education e according to the multiplicative formula

$$R = ne.$$

The cost (measured in units of the consumption good) of acquiring education e is

$$g(e) = \frac{e^{1+\lambda}}{1+\lambda} \qquad \lambda > 0.$$

In the absence of an income tax, the consumption behavior of an agent with talent n who has attained an education level e is given by

$$c(n, e) = ne - g(e).$$

In this problem, we assume that each agent chooses an optimal level of education. There exist a large number of agents whose talents are represented by the continuous distribution

$$f(n) = \delta \underline{n}^{\delta} \frac{1}{n^{1+\delta}} \qquad \delta > 1 \qquad \underline{n} > 0$$

$$n > \underline{n}$$

$$\lambda\delta - \lambda - 1 > 0.$$

1. The government wants to redistribute income for equity reasons. Assuming that the government uses the Rawlsian (maximin) criterion and that the variable n is observable, what is the optimal income tax as a function of n, denoted $I(n)$?

2. Now recognize the informational impossibility of using talent as the basis for income taxation. Consider the optimal (according to the Rawlsian criterion) linear tax based on income $R = ne$, that is,

$$I(R) = -\alpha + (1 - \beta)R.$$

Derive α and β. Derive the effective consumption level of an agent with talent n. Deduce from this the social loss according to the Rawlsian criterion created by the impossibility of taxing characteristics (n) directly.

3. When $\lambda = 1$, study the classes of taxes that are incentive compatible when the level of education is observable. For this purpose, we can characterize the mechanisms $[e(n), I(n)]$ that reveal the true characteristics as dominant strategies. We obtain the best revelation mechanism according to the Rawlsian criterion; we interpret it as a tax on education and we compare it to the income tax in the complete information case and to the best linear income tax in the incomplete information case.

Solution

1. After taxing income, consumption is equal to

$$C(n, e) = ne - g(e) - I(n).$$

Maximizing the utility of consumption, which is equivalent to maximizing $C(n, e)$, leads to $n = g'(e)$, which yields the optimal level of education $e = n^{1/\lambda}$ and the consumption level

$$C(n) = \frac{\lambda}{1 + \lambda} n^{(1+\lambda)/\lambda} - I(n).$$

The Rawlsian (maximin) criterion leads to equalizing all consumption levels. However, average net revenue is given by

$$\frac{\lambda}{1 + \lambda} \int_{\underline{n}}^{\infty} n^{(1+\lambda)/\lambda} f(n) \, dn = \frac{\lambda \delta \underline{n}^{\delta}}{1 + \lambda} \cdot \frac{\lambda}{\lambda \delta - 1 - \lambda} n^{(1+\lambda-\lambda\delta)/\lambda}$$

$$= \frac{\lambda}{1 + \lambda} \cdot \frac{\lambda \delta}{\lambda \delta - 1 - \lambda} \underline{n}^{(1+\lambda)/\lambda},$$

from which the optimal tax is

$$I(n) = -\frac{\lambda}{1 + \lambda} \cdot \frac{\lambda \delta}{\lambda \delta - 1 - \lambda} \cdot \underline{n}^{(1+\lambda)/\lambda} + \frac{\lambda}{1 + \lambda} n^{(1+\lambda)/\lambda}$$

$$= \frac{\lambda}{1 + \lambda} n^{(1+\lambda)/\lambda} \left[1 - \frac{\lambda \delta}{\lambda \delta - 1 - \lambda} \cdot \left(\frac{\underline{n}}{n} \right)^{(1+\lambda)/\lambda} \right].$$

This tax structure corresponds to an implicit rate of personalized net income taxation given by

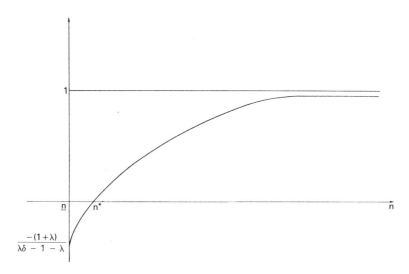

Figure P4.1

$$1 - \frac{\lambda\delta}{\lambda\delta - 1 - \lambda}\left(\frac{n}{\underline{n}}\right)^{(1+\lambda)/\lambda}.$$

From figure P4.1, we see that the optimal tax rate is negative up to a critical level of talent given by

$$n^* = \underline{n}\left(\frac{\lambda\delta}{\lambda\delta - 1 - \lambda}\right)^{\lambda/(1+\lambda)},$$

and positive above this level with the tax rate tending toward 100% as n tends toward infinity.

2. With the linear tax, consumption can be written as

$$C(n, e) = ne - g(e) + \alpha - (1 - \beta)R = \alpha + \beta ne - g(e).$$

Then the optimal level of education is

$$e = (\beta n)^{1/\lambda},$$

and the consumption level associated with this is

$$C(n) = \alpha + \frac{\lambda}{1 + \lambda}(\beta n)^{(1+\lambda)/\lambda}.$$

Since we are redistributing income, the budget constraint of the government can be written as

$$\alpha = (1 - \beta) \int_{\underline{n}}^{\infty} y(n)f(n)\, dn$$

$$= (1 - \beta) \int_{\underline{n}}^{\infty} \beta^{1/\lambda} n^{(1+\lambda)/\lambda} \delta \underline{n}^{\delta} n^{-1-\delta}\, dn$$

or

$$\alpha = \frac{(1 - \beta)\lambda\delta\beta^{1/\lambda}}{\lambda\delta - 1 - \lambda} \underline{n}^{(1+\lambda)/\lambda}$$

by assuming that $\lambda\delta - 1 - \lambda > 0$.

Since consumption increases with n, maximizing the consumption of the least favored individual corresponds to maximizing $C(\underline{n})$, that is, maximizing

$$(1 - \beta)\beta^{1/\lambda}\frac{\lambda\delta}{\lambda\delta - 1 - \lambda}\underline{n}^{(1+\lambda)/\lambda} + \frac{\lambda}{1 + \lambda}\beta^{(1+\lambda)/\lambda}\underline{n}^{(1+\lambda)/\lambda},$$

the first-order condition for which is

$$\left(\frac{1}{\lambda}\beta^{(1-\lambda)/\lambda} - \frac{1+\lambda}{\lambda}\beta^{1/\lambda}\right)\frac{\lambda\delta}{\lambda\delta - 1 - \lambda}\underline{n}^{(1+\lambda)/\lambda} + \beta^{1/\lambda}\underline{n}^{(1+\lambda)/\lambda} = 0$$

or

$$\left(\frac{1}{\lambda}\beta^{-1} - \frac{1+\lambda}{\lambda}\right)\frac{\lambda\delta}{\lambda\delta - 1 - \lambda} + 1 = 0$$

$$\beta^* = \frac{\delta}{1 + \lambda + \delta}.$$

Then the consumption level of an agent with talent n is given by

$$C^*(n) = \frac{(1 + \lambda)}{(1 + \lambda + \delta)}\left(\frac{\delta}{1 + \lambda + \delta}\right)^{1/\lambda}\frac{\lambda\delta}{\lambda\delta - 1 - \lambda}\underline{n}^{(1+\lambda)/\lambda}$$

$$+ \frac{\lambda}{1 + \lambda}\left(\frac{\delta}{1 + \lambda + \delta}\right)^{(1+\lambda)/\lambda}\underline{n}^{(1+\lambda)/\lambda}$$

The social loss (according to the Rawlsian criterion) is given by (see figure P4.2):

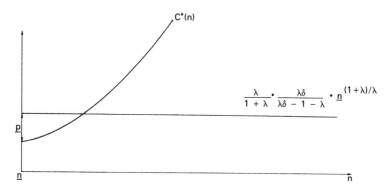

Figure P4.2

$$P = -\left[\frac{\lambda(1+\lambda)}{\lambda\delta - 1 - \lambda} + \frac{\lambda}{1+\lambda}\right] \underline{n}^{(1+\lambda)/\lambda}\left(\frac{\delta}{1+\lambda+\delta}\right)^{(1+\lambda)/\lambda}$$

$$+ \frac{\lambda}{1+\lambda} \cdot \frac{\lambda\delta}{\lambda\delta - 1 - \lambda}\underline{n}^{(1+\lambda)/\lambda}.$$

Social loss increases with the variance of talents and decreases with the cost elasticity of education as the following examples illustrate.

$\underline{n} = 1$	$\lambda = 1$	$\delta =$	3	$P = 0.60$
		$\delta =$	10	$P = 0.10$
		$\delta =$	100	$P = 0.01$
	$\lambda = 10$	$\delta =$	3	$P = 0.21$

In the case $\underline{n} = 10$, $\delta = 3$, $\lambda = 1$, the social loss in utility is $\Delta_R = 0.9$.

The same exercise can be performed with the utilitarian criterion; in this case, however, the marginal rate of optimal taxation $1 - \beta^*$ cannot be explicitly calculated. Numerical calculations show that the marginal rate of taxation is smaller when the social criterion is the utilitarian criterion rather than the Rawlsian criterion, as the following table illustrates.

Marginal rate of taxation:

		Utilitarian Criterion	Rawlsian Criterion
$\delta = 2.5$	$\lambda = 0.75$	0.34	0.41
	$\lambda = 1.00$	0.35	0.44
	$\lambda = 1.25$	0.34	0.43

$\delta = 3$ $\lambda = 0.60$ 0.29   0.34
               $\lambda = 0.75$ 0.27   0.36
               $\lambda = 1.00$ 0.27   0.40

In the case $n = 10$, $\delta = 3$, $\lambda = 1$, the social loss in utility is $\Delta_u = 0.19$. The utilitarian criterion yields smaller taxes and less redistribution than the Rawlsian criterion and consequently less distortion. Note, however, that Δ_R and Δ_u are measured by different social welfare functions.

3. When the level of education is observable, the revelation principle assures us that any regulatory mechanism is equivalent to a revelation mechanism in which the agent must announce his level of talent and then the mechanism defines a level of education $e(\tilde{n})$ and a tax levy $I(\tilde{n})$. The agent will announce the true level n if n is a solution to the problem

$$\text{Max } ne(\tilde{n}) - g(e(\tilde{n})) - I(\tilde{n}),$$
$$\tilde{n}$$

the first-order condition for which is

$$\left[n - \frac{dg}{de}(e(n)) \right] \frac{de}{dn}(n) - \frac{dI}{dn} = 0$$

$$I(n) = \int_{\underline{n}}^{n} \left[t - \frac{dg}{de}(e(t)) \right] \frac{de}{dt}(t)\, dt + K \tag{1}$$

The local second-order condition is $de/dn \geqslant 0$, and along with (1) these conditions are sufficient because

$$[ne(n) - g(e(n)) - I(n)] - [ne(\tilde{n}) - g(e(\tilde{n})) - I(\tilde{n})]$$

$$= (\tilde{n} - n)e(\tilde{n}) + \int_{\tilde{n}}^{n} e(t)\, dt,$$

a sum that is positive due to the weak monotonicity of $e(.)$.

The taxes and education levels in the mechanisms that induce the agents to tell the truth are therefore characterized by

$$\frac{de}{dn}(n) \geqslant 0$$

$$I(n) = \int_{\underline{n}}^{n} \left[t - \frac{dg}{de}(e(t)) \right] \frac{de}{dt}(t)\, dt + K,$$

with

$$K = -\int_{\underline{n}}^{\infty} \left(\int_{\underline{n}}^{n} \left[t - \frac{dg}{de}(e(t)) \right] \frac{de}{dt}(t)\, dt \right) f(n)\, dn,$$

since we are using redistributive taxes. Subject to these constraints, the utility level increases with n because $du/dn = e(n)$.

Maximizing according to the Rawlsian criterion must involve maximizing the net income of agent n subject to the constraint that $(de/dn)(n) \geqslant 0$. We have

$$\int_{\underline{n}}^{n} \left\{ t - \frac{dg}{de}(e(t)) \right\} \frac{de}{dt}(t)\, dt = ne(n) - \underline{n}\,e(\underline{n}) - g(e(n)) + g(e(\underline{n})) - \int_{\underline{n}}^{n} e(t)\, dt;$$

therefore

$$-K = g(e(\underline{n})) - \underline{n}\,e(\underline{n}) + \int_{\underline{n}}^{\infty} [ne(n) - g(e(n))]f(n)\, dn - \int_{\underline{n}}^{\infty} \int_{\underline{n}}^{n} e(t)\, dt\, f(n)\, dn$$

$$= g(e(\underline{n})) - \underline{n}\,e(\underline{n}) + \int_{\underline{n}}^{\infty} \left[ne(n) - g(e(n)) - \int_{\underline{n}}^{n} e(t)\, dt \right] f(n)\, dn,$$

where the net revenue of agent $\underline{n}$ is given by

$$\int_{\underline{n}}^{\infty} \left[ne(n) - g(e(n)) - \int_{\underline{n}}^{n} e(t)\, dt \right] f(n)\, dn.$$

Denote $\psi(n) = \int_{\underline{n}}^{n} e(t)\, dt$ and $\dot{\psi}(n) = e(n)$. The maximization problem can be written as

$$\underset{\psi(.)}{\text{Max}} \int_{\underline{n}}^{\infty} [n\dot{\psi}(n) - g(\dot{\psi}(n)) - \psi(n)]f(n)\, dn \quad \text{with} \quad \begin{array}{l} \psi(\underline{n}) = 0 \\ \dot{\psi}(n) \geqslant 0 \\ \ddot{\psi}(n) \geqslant 0 \end{array}$$

or $\quad \underset{\psi(.)}{\text{Max}} \int_{\underline{n}}^{\infty} F(\psi, \dot{\psi}, n)\, dn \qquad \text{with} \quad \begin{array}{l} \psi(\underline{n}) = 0 \\ \dot{\psi}(n) \geqslant 0 \\ \ddot{\psi}(n) \geqslant 0. \end{array}$

The Euler condition

$$\frac{d}{dn} \frac{\partial F}{\partial \dot{\psi}} = \frac{\partial F}{\partial \psi}$$

can be written as

$$\ddot{\psi} - \frac{(1 + \delta)}{n}\dot{\psi} + (\delta - 1) = 0,$$

yielding a general solution given by

$$e(n) = \left(\frac{\delta - 1}{\delta}\right)n + kn^{1+\delta}.$$

The right-hand endpoint condition ($\lim_{n \to \infty} \partial F/\partial \dot{\psi} = 0$) is written as

$$\lim_{n \to \infty} \left(\frac{1}{\delta}n - kn^{1+\delta}\right)f(n) = 0,$$

which yields $k = 0$.

Since F is concave in $(\psi, \dot{\psi})$, these necessary conditions are also sufficient and the unique solution is given by

$$e(n) = \frac{\delta - 1}{\delta} \cdot n.$$

Agent $\underline{n}$'s net income is then

$$R(\underline{n}) = \int_{\underline{n}}^{\infty}\left[ne(n) - \frac{e(n)^2}{2} - \int_{\underline{n}}^{n} e(t)\,dt\right]f(n)\,dn = \frac{(\delta - 1)^2}{2\delta(\delta - 2)}\underline{n}^2,$$

an amount that is smaller than both the income in the optimal solution with complete information,

$$\frac{\delta}{2(\delta - 2)}\underline{n}^2,$$

and also the income under the optimal linear tax,

$$\frac{\delta^2}{2(2 + \delta)(\delta - 2)}\underline{n}^2.$$

The tax on agent n is given by

$$I(n) = \int_{\underline{n}}^{n} [t - e(t)]\frac{de}{dt}(t)\,dt + K$$

$$= \frac{(\delta - 1)}{2\delta^2}(n^2 - \underline{n}^2) - \frac{(\delta - 1)}{(\delta - 2)\delta^2}\underline{n}^2,$$

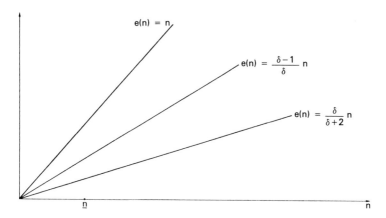

Figure P4.3

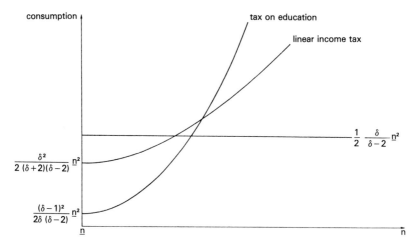

Figure P4.4

or, as a function of the education level, by

$$\frac{e^2}{2(\delta - 1)} - \frac{(\delta - 1)}{2\delta(\delta - 2)}\underline{n}^2.$$

His net income is

$$\frac{(\delta - 1)}{2\delta}\underline{n}^2 + \frac{(\delta - 1)}{2\delta(\delta - 2)}\underline{n}^2$$

or

$$\frac{(\delta - 1)^2}{2\delta(\delta - 2)}\underline{n}^2 + \frac{(\delta - 1)}{2\delta}(n^2 - \underline{n}^2),$$

a sum that we can compare with net income under the optimal linear tax,

$$\frac{\delta^2}{2(\delta + 2)(\delta - 2)}\underline{n}^2 + \frac{\delta^2}{2(\delta + 2)^2}(n^2 - \underline{n}^2).$$

According to the maximin criterion, the optimal linear income tax is preferable to the optimal nonlinear tax on education. The profiles of education and consumption levels are graphed in figures P4.3 and P4.4, respectively.

Problem 5
The Control of an Oligopolistic Industry

Statement of the Problem

Consider an economy with two goods and one representative competitive consumer.[1] The consumer is endowed initially with good 1 in the amount $w_1 > 4 \operatorname{Log} 4$. This good will be the numéraire. The utility function of the consumer is written as

$$4 \operatorname{Log}(1 + x_2) + x_1,$$

where $x_1 \geqslant 0$ indicates his consumption of good 1, and $x_2 \geqslant 0$ indicates his consumption of good 2.

The consumer is endowed with none of good 2 initially. Good 2 is produced in an industry made up of firms, each one having a fixed cost measured in good 1 of $\alpha > 0$, and a unitary constant marginal cost measured in good 1.

The price of good 1 is normalized to 1 and the price of good 2 is denoted p.

1. Preliminary Questions—
(a) How can the industry be organized so as to achieve a Pareto optimum?
(b) Determine the Pareto optimum.
(c) Derive the demand function for good 2, $x_2(p)$, as well as the inverse demand function $p(x_2)$.

2. A Monopolistic Industrial Structure—Assume that a single firm produces good 2. This firm behaves as a monopolist maximizing its profit. To close the model, assume that profit of the firm is distributed to the consumer, who treats this profit as a parameter, that is, he does not consider the relationship between his behavior and the monopolist's profit which he receives. Determine the monopolist's equilibrium. Why is the obtained allocation not Pareto optimal? Derive the subsidy per unit of good 2 sold, τ, that makes the monopolist produce at a Pareto optimum. What do you think of a policy that regulates a monopolist by subsidization? What assumptions in the model lead to this solution?

3. An Oligopolistic Industry—Consider an industry made up of n firms. Cost as a function of the level of output y for any firm is written as

$$C(y) = \alpha + y, \quad \alpha > 0 \quad \text{if} \quad y > 0$$
$$0 \qquad\qquad \text{if} \quad y = 0.$$

1. This consumer represents a large number of small consumers.

Let y^j be the output of firm j. Aggregate output is therefore $\sum_{j=1}^{n} y^j$, and, if $p(.)$ is the inverse demand function derived in question 1, the market price for good 2 is $p(\sum_{j=1}^{n} y^j)$.

A *Cournot equilibrium with n producing firms* is an n-tuple $y^{*1} > 0, \ldots,$ $y^{*n} > 0$ such that

(i) $p\left(\sum_{j=1}^{n} y^{*j} \right) y^{*i} - C(y^{*i}) \geq 0 \qquad i = 1, \ldots, n;$

(ii) for $i = 1, \ldots, n,$

$$p\left(\sum_{j \neq i}^{n} y^{*j} + y^{*i} \right) y^{*i} - C(y^{*i}) \geq p\left(\sum_{j \neq i}^{n} y^{*j} + y^i \right) - C(y^i)$$

$$\text{for all } y^i \geq 0.$$

(i) indicates that each firm must make nonnegative profits; (ii) indicates that, for all i, the output of firm i, y^{*i}, is its best strategy given the output levels of the other firms $y^{*j}, j \neq i$.

A *symmetric equilibrium with n producing firms* is a Cournot equilibrium with n firms where

$$y^{*1} = y^{*2} = \cdots = y^{*n} > 0.$$

For this entire problem we are interested only in symmetric equilibria. First of all, we determine the aggregate output for an oligopolistic industry with n firms. We consider an arbitrary firm i. Let Y be the output of the other firms. Derive the reaction function for firm i, that is, the optimal strategy of firm i as a function of Y, $y(Y)$. Figure P5.1 indicates the shape of the reaction function.

Explain how a symmetric Cournot equilibrium with n producing firms is obtained at the intersection of the segment AB of the reaction function and the straight line given by

$$y = \frac{1}{n-1} Y$$

in figure P5.1. From this, compute a critical number n^* so that a symmetric Cournot equilibrium exists with n producing firms when n is less than or equal to n^*. Consider the case $n = 2$. Determine the optimal subsidy for good 2 that leads the duopolists to produce the Pareto-optimal level of good 2 obtained in question 1. Is the allocation thus obtained a Pareto optimum?

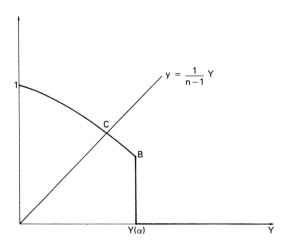

$$y = \frac{1}{n-1}\,Y$$

Figure P5.1

4. An Oligopolistic Industry with Free Entry—In the preceding question, the number of firms was considered to be exogenous. Now we make this number endogenous by assuming free entry. A *Cournot equilibrium with free entry* is a number of firms n and an n-tuple of outputs $y^{*1} > 0, \ldots,$ $y^{*\bar{n}} > 0$ such that $y^{*1}, \ldots, y^{*\bar{n}}$ is a Cournot equilibrium with $\bar{n}$ producing firms. Furthermore,

(iii) $\quad p\left(\sum_{j=1}^{\bar{n}} y^{*j} + y \right) y - C(y) < 0 \qquad$ for all $\quad y > 0.$

(iii) indicates that any additional firm planning to enter the industry will incur losses regardless of its output level so long as it expects the firms currently in the industry to continue to produce their current output levels (y^{*j}).

(a) Derive a symmetric Cournot equilibrium with free entry.
(b) Examine the limit of this equilibrium when α tends toward zero. Discuss this result.

Solution

1. (a) Since marginal cost is constant, we must have only a single producer to minimize fixed costs.

　(b) A necessary condition for Pareto optimality is the equality of the marginal rate of substitution between goods 2 and 1 with the marginal rate of transformation between goods 2 and 1. Consequently, we have

$$\frac{4}{1 + x_2} = 1,$$

or

$$x_2^* = 3.$$

The output level of good 2 is Pareto optimal if and only if the net utility derived from consuming three units of good 2 is greater than the fixed cost, that is, if $4 \operatorname{Log} 4 - 3 \geqslant \alpha$; then $x_1 = w_1 - 3 - \alpha$.

On the contrary, if $\alpha > 4 \operatorname{Log} 4 - 3$, the Pareto optimum requires zero output for good 2.

(c) The demand function for good 2, $x_2(p)$, is derived from the maximization problem

$$\operatorname*{Max}_{x_1 \geqslant 0, x_2 \geqslant 0} \{4 \operatorname{Log}(1 + x_2) + x_1\} \tag{1}$$

such that $px_2 + x_2 = w_1$.

Since $w_1 > 4$, the optimum solution is an interior maximum characterized by the first-order condition for (1) given by

$$\frac{4}{1 + x_2} = p,$$

or

$$x_2(p) = \frac{4}{p} - 1 \qquad \text{if} \quad 0 < p \leqslant 4$$

$$= 0 \qquad \text{if} \qquad p > 4.$$

2. Let $p(x_2) = 4/(1 + x_2)$ be the inverse demand function. The monopolist maximizes profit, which is a concave function of x_2. He consequently solves

$$\operatorname*{Max}_{x_2 > 0} \{p(x_2)x_2 - x_2 - \alpha\},$$

which yields $x_2^m = 1$.

If this output corresponds to a positive profit level, that is, if $1 - \alpha \geqslant 0$ the monopoly output is indeed $x_2^m = 1$. If $\alpha > 1$, the monopolist does not produce anything.

In all cases where the Pareto optimum requires a strictly positive output of good 2 (that is, $\alpha \leqslant 4 \, \mathrm{Log} \, 4 - 3$), the monopolist's output is insufficient. Effectively, he reduces his output in order to benefit from a higher price. He equates marginal revenue, not price, to marginal cost.

Let τ be the subsidy per unit of output received by the monopolist. Then he solves the problem

$$\underset{y > 0}{\mathrm{Max}} \, \{(p(y) + \tau)y - y - \alpha\},$$

which yields

$$y = \frac{2}{\sqrt{1 - \tau}} - 1.$$

Therefore, choosing $\tau = 3/4$ leads to a Pareto-optimal output of good 2.

It is necessary to subsidize the monopolist to induce him to produce more than he would if he equated marginal revenue to marginal cost. Beyond problems of observability, which can make this solution difficult to achieve in practice, our intuition makes us uncomfortable with the distributive aspects of this policy. Indeed, we probably presume that the shareholders in a monopoly are rich, and therefore, that we increase the income of the rich when we increase the monopolist's profit. Such a difficulty does not arise in our simple economy since there is only a single consumer. However, we note that if the government can tax the profits of the monopolist at a rate up to 100%, any negative distributive effects from subsidization can be eliminated. Therefore, it is the impossibility of taxing at a 100% rate (the justification for which lies in the negative incentive effects that such a rate would have on output) that would lead to a modification in the policy of subsidization for equity reasons.

3. Let $\pi(y, Y)$ be the profit of any firm when its output is $y > 0$ and the output of all the other firms is Y. Consequently, we have

$$\pi(y, Y) = \frac{4y}{(1 + Y + y)} - y - \alpha.$$

Therefore the profit-maximizing output level is

$$
\begin{aligned}
y(Y) &= 2(1 + Y)^{1/2} - (1 + Y) \quad \text{if} \quad \pi(y, Y) \geqslant 0 \\
&\qquad\qquad\qquad\qquad\qquad\quad \text{and} \quad y(Y) > 0 \\
&= 0 \qquad\qquad\qquad\qquad\quad\; \text{otherwise.}
\end{aligned}
$$

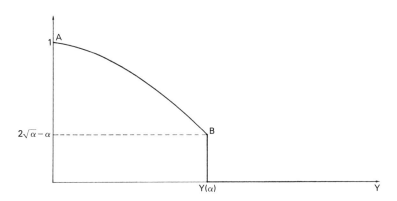

Figure P5.2

If $\pi(y, Y) = 0$, the firm is indifferent between producing output level y or shutting down (see figure P5.2).

Let $Y(\alpha) = 3 - 4\sqrt{\alpha} + \alpha$ be the value of output of the other firms such that this firm chooses to shut down. For $Y(\alpha)$, the nonzero level of output that yields zero profit is given by $y(Y(\alpha)) = 2\sqrt{\alpha} - \alpha$. Consider the straight line $y = [1/(n - 1)]Y$. If this line lies above B (that is, for n sufficiently small), it intersects AB, like C in figure P5.1. Let $(\hat{Y}, \hat{y})$ be the intersection of the two curves; $(\hat{y}, \ldots, \hat{y})$ (n times) makes up a Cournot equilibrium with n producing firms. In fact, for $\hat{Y} = (n - 1)\hat{y}$, the optimal reaction of any firm is simply $\hat{y}$.

If $n = 1$, the intersection point is A and we are again at the monopoly equilibrium that exists when $\alpha < 1$. As n increases, we find a critical value n^* so that for $n = n^* + 1$, the straight line $y = [1/(n - 1)]Y$ passes below AB. There can be no symmetric Cournot equilibrium with n producing firms when $n \geqslant n^* + 1$. To be sure, this critical value n^* depends on the value of α. The smaller α, the larger n^*, since the ordinate for B is $2\sqrt{\alpha} - \alpha$.

Consider a value of n for which we have an intersection between AB and $y = [1/(n - 1)]Y$ (that is, $n \leqslant n^*$). Aggregate output is $[n/(n - 1)]Y$, where Y is defined by

$$\frac{Y}{n - 1} = -(Y + 1) + 2(1 + Y)^{1/2},$$

so that

$$Y = \frac{n-1}{n^2}(n - 2 + 2\sqrt{n^2 - n + 1}).$$

If $n = 2$, aggregate output is $\sqrt{3}$. For this equilibrium to be feasible, the fixed cost must be sufficiently small; or, more precisely,

$$3 - 4\sqrt{\alpha} + \alpha > \frac{1}{2}\sqrt{3},$$

which yields $\alpha < 0.46$.

The output obtained in this manner is not Pareto optimal. We calculate the unit subsidy that supports the Pareto-optimal quantity of good 2, exactly 3 units. When the subsidy is τ per unit of output, the typical firm maximizes

$$\frac{4y}{1 + Y + y} - (1 - \tau)y,$$

which yields

$$y = -(1 + Y) + 2\left(\frac{1 + Y}{1 - \tau}\right)^{1/2}.$$

Therefore the equilibrium is characterized by

$$\frac{1}{n - 1}Y = -(1 + Y) + 2\left(\frac{1 + Y}{1 - \tau}\right)^{1/2}.$$

For $n = 2$, the level of Y corresponding to a Pareto optimum is $3/2$. It follows therefore that $\tau = 3/8$. However, the allocation obtained is not Pareto optimal because we pay the fixed cost twice instead of once.

4. (a) A symmetric Cournot equilibrium with free entry is associated with a critical number of firms n^* that is determined by the largest value of n for which $y = [1/(n - 1)]Y$ intersects AB. Effectively, we have both a Cournot equilibrium and free entry because, due to the downward sloping nature of AB and the definition of n^*, the straight line with equation $y = (1/n^*)Y$ does not intersect AB: $(1/n^*)Y(\alpha) < [1/(n^* - 1)]Y^*$. Thus $[n^*/(n^* - 1)]Y^* > Y(\alpha)$, that is, for the aggregate output corresponding to n^*, no additional firm wishes to enter (see figure P5.3).

Analytically, n^* is determined by

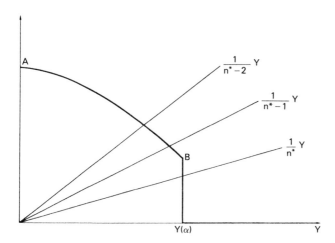

Figure P5.3

$$\frac{1}{n^* - 1} Y(\alpha) > y(Y(\alpha)) > \frac{1}{n^*} Y(\alpha),$$

or

$$\frac{3 - 4\sqrt{\alpha} + \alpha}{2\sqrt{\alpha} - \alpha} + 1 > n^* > \frac{3 - 4\sqrt{\alpha} + \alpha}{2\sqrt{\alpha} - \alpha}.$$

(b) Aggregate output in the symmetric Cournot equilibrium with free entry is

$$\frac{1}{n^*}(n^* - 2 + 2\sqrt{n^{*2} - n^* + 1}).$$

When α tends toward zero, n^* tends toward infinity and aggregate output tends toward 3. Therefore, output is Pareto optimal. Since there are a large number of firms we have a wasteful replication of fixed costs. However, n^* times α tends toward zero with α, that is, this inefficiency is asymptotically negligible. Therefore, we can say that the Cournot equilibrium with free entry approximates a Pareto optimum when fixed costs are small with respect to the size of the market.

Problem 6
Peak-Load Pricing

Statement of the Problem

Consider an economy with three goods. Good 1 is telephone use during the day, good 2 is telephone use during the night, and good 3 is an aggregation of all other goods and is taken to be the numéraire. Let

$$U(x_1, x_2, x_3) = \alpha \, \text{Log} \, x_1 + \beta \, \text{Log} \, x_2 + x_3$$

$$\alpha > 0, \quad \beta > 0$$

be the utility function of a typical consumer where x_1 is daytime telephone usage, x_2 is nighttime telephone usage, and x_3 is the consumption of the numéraire. There is a continuum of consumers who differ only by their initial endowments in the numéraire, denoted by income w. Let $f(w)$ be a uniform density function over the interval $[\underline{w}, \overline{w}]$ characterizing the distribution of income. As a normalization, we choose $\overline{w} - \underline{w} = 1$.

Suppose that the consumer must pay an initial hook-up charge A and then a unit price p during the day and a unit price q during the night for telephone service.

The optimization problem of a consumer with income w is written

$$\text{Max } \alpha \, \text{Log} \, x_1 + \beta \, \text{Log} \, x_2 + x_3$$

subject to $\quad px_1 + qx_2 + x_3 = w - A.$

1. Derive the individual demand functions for telephone usage and the aggregate functions $X_1(p)$ and $X_2(q)$. Suppose that $\underline{w}$ is sufficiently large so that the question of whether or not a consumer is interested in any telephone service at all never arises.

Telephone production entails an investment in capacity of K for which the marginal cost is constant at d. K must satisfy

$$K \geqslant X_1 \qquad K \geqslant X_2.$$

Furthermore, the marginal maintenance cost is b for telephone usage both at night and during the day. Assume that the firm producing telephone service is bound by a zero profit constraint.

2. Explain why this constraint can be written as

$$A + (p - b - d)X_1(p) + (q - b)X_2(q) = 0,$$

when we assume that the day period is the peak period.

3. Write the indirect utility function for a consumer with income w, that is, $V(p, q, w - A)$. Derive the optimal pricing schedule (p^*, q^*, A^*) for a utilitarian planner constrained to balance the budget. Discuss this result.

4. Return to the problem with a general differentiable and concave utility function $U(x_1, x_2, x_3)$. Let $x_1(p, q, w - A)$ and $x_2(p, q, w - A)$ be the individual demand functions. Write the maximization exercise for a utilitarian planner constrained to balance the budget analogous to the one in question 3 but for the general case. Write the first-order conditions for this problem.

We neglect the aggregate cross substitution effects characterized as

$$E\frac{\partial x_1}{\partial q} + Ex_2 E\frac{\partial x_1}{\partial w} \quad \text{and} \quad E\frac{\partial x_2}{\partial p} + Ex_1 E\frac{\partial x_2}{\partial w}.$$

Let

$$e_1^C = \frac{-p}{Ex_1}\left\{E\frac{\partial x_1}{\partial p} + Ex_1 E\frac{\partial x_1}{\partial w}\right\}$$

be the compensated elasticity of demand for good 1 with respect to p where the notation E indicates the expectation with respect to the uniform distribution. Similarly,

$$e_2^C = \frac{-q}{Ex_2}\left\{E\frac{\partial x_2}{\partial q} + Ex_2 E\frac{\partial x_2}{\partial w}\right\}.$$

By using Roy's identity, show that

$$\frac{\frac{(p - b - \beta)}{p}(-e_1^C)}{\frac{q - b}{q}(-e_2^C)} = \frac{\text{Cov}\left(\frac{\partial V}{\partial w}, x_1\right)\Big/Ex_1}{\text{Cov}\left(\frac{\partial V}{\partial w}, x_2\right)\Big/Ex_2}.$$

Discussion   What happens if the goods are normal and if the rich consume relatively more of good 2?

Solution

1. The consumer who has an income of w solves the problem

$\text{Max}\{\alpha \log x_1 + \beta \log x_2 + x_3\}$

subject to $px_1 + qx_2 + x_3 = w - A,$

which yields

$$x_1 = \frac{\alpha}{p} \qquad x_2 = \frac{\beta}{q}.$$

Therefore

$$X_1(p) = \frac{\alpha}{p} \qquad X_2(q) = \frac{\beta}{q}.$$

2. The firms' revenues are

$A + pX_1(p) + qX_2(q);$

the firms's costs are

$bX_1(p) + bX_2(q) + dK.$

Since the peak period is period 1, $K = X_1(p)$. This yields a budget constraint of $A + (p - b - d)X_1(p) + (q - b)X_2(q) = 0.$

3. $V(p, q, w - A) = \alpha \, \text{Log} \, \dfrac{\alpha}{p} + \beta \, \text{Log} \, \dfrac{\beta}{q} + w - A - \alpha - \beta;$

$$\text{Max} \int_{\underline{w}}^{\overline{w}} V(p, q, w - A) \, dw$$

subject to $A + (p - b - d)X_1(p) + (q - b)X_2(q) = 0$

$$\Leftrightarrow \underset{(p,q)}{\text{Max}} \left\{ -\alpha \, \text{Log} \, p - \beta \, \text{Log} \, q + (p - b - d)\frac{\alpha}{p} + (q - b)\frac{\beta}{q} \right\}$$

from which it follows that

$p = b + d, \quad q = b, \quad \text{and} \quad A = 0.$

Here we find the Boiteux-Steiner conditions. The off-peak period price is equal to the marginal maintenance cost. The peak period price is equal to the sum of the marginal maintenance cost and the marginal cost of capacity.

4. Let

$$V(p, q, w - A)$$
$$= U(x_1(p, q, w - A), x_2(p, q, w - A), w - A - px_1(p, q, w - A)$$
$$- qx_2(p, q, w - A)).$$

The problem for the utilitarian planner is

$$\text{Max} \int_{\underline{w}}^{\overline{w}} V(p, q, w - A)\, dw.$$

subject to $A + (p - b - d)Ex_1(p, q, w - A)$
$$+ (q - b)Ex_2(p, q, w - A) = 0$$

The first-order conditions are

$$E\frac{\partial V}{\partial p} + \lambda(p - b - d)E\frac{\partial x_1}{\partial p} + \lambda(q - b)E\frac{\partial x_2}{\partial p} + \lambda Ex_1 = 0 \tag{1}$$

$$E\frac{\partial V}{\partial q} + \lambda(q - b)E\frac{\partial x_2}{\partial q} + \lambda(p - b - d)E\frac{\partial x_1}{\partial q} + \lambda Ex_2 = 0 \tag{2}$$

$$E\frac{\partial V}{\partial w} + \lambda\left\{(p - b - d)E\frac{\partial x_1}{\partial w} + (q - b)E\frac{\partial x_2}{\partial w} - 1\right\} = 0. \tag{3}$$

From Roy's identity,

$$\frac{\partial V}{\partial p} = -x_1\frac{\partial V}{\partial w}; \quad \frac{\partial V}{\partial q} = -x_2\frac{\partial V}{\partial w}.$$

Multiplying (3) by Ex_1 and adding this to (1), we have

$$\text{Cov}\left(\frac{\partial V}{\partial w}, x_1\right) = \lambda(p - b - d)\left[E\frac{\partial x_1}{\partial p} + Ex_2 E\frac{\partial x_1}{\partial w}\right]$$

$$+ \lambda(q - b)\left[E\frac{\partial x_2}{\partial p} + Ex_1 E\frac{\partial x_2}{\partial w}\right]. \tag{4}$$

Multiplying (3) by Ex_2 and adding this to (2), we have:

$$\text{Cov}\left(\frac{\partial V}{\partial w}, x_2\right) = \lambda(p - b - d)\left[E\frac{\partial x_1}{\partial q} + Ex_2 E\frac{\partial x_1}{\partial w}\right]$$

$$+ (q - b)\left[E\frac{\partial x_2}{\partial q} + Ex_2 E\frac{\partial x_2}{\partial w}\right]. \tag{5}$$

Since we neglect the aggregate cross-substitution effects, we have immediately from (4) and (5)

$$\frac{\dfrac{p - b - d}{p} \cdot e_1^C}{\dfrac{q - b}{q} \cdot e_2^C} = \frac{\dfrac{\text{Cov}\left(\frac{\partial V}{\partial w}, x_1\right)}{Ex_1}}{\dfrac{\text{Cov}\left(\frac{\partial V}{\partial w}, x_2\right)}{Ex_2}} = \frac{\text{Cov}\left(\frac{\partial V}{\partial w}, \frac{x_1}{Ex_1}\right)}{\text{Cov}\left(\frac{\partial V}{\partial w}, \frac{x_2}{Ex_2}\right)}.$$

If the rich consume relatively more of good 2, we have

$$0 > \text{Cov}\left(\frac{\partial V}{\partial w}, \frac{x_1}{Ex_1}\right) > \text{Cov}\left(\frac{\partial V}{\partial w}, \frac{x_2}{Ex_2}\right),$$

which yields

$$\frac{\dfrac{p - b - d}{p}}{\dfrac{q - b}{q}} < \frac{1/e_1^C}{1/e_2^C}.$$

If the two goods are consumed in the same proportions by all the agents, the ratio of the divergence from marginal cost of the Boiteux-Steiner prices is uniquely related to the ratio of the compensated elasticities. This result is consistent with the traditional one in which the smaller the elasticity of a good, the larger the divergence between price and marginal cost. Furthermore, with the utilitarian criterion, we treat less favorably the good consumed in relatively higher quantities by the rich.

Problem 7
Optimal Taxation of a Discriminating Monopolist with Incomplete Information

Statement of the Problem

Consider a monopolist faced with a continuum of consumers in the interval $[0, 1]$. Each consumer is characterized by a thrice-continuously-differentiable utility function given by $u(q, \theta) + x$, where x is the quantity consumed of good 1 (taken to be the numéraire) and q is the quantity consumed of good 2, a good produced by the monopolist. The parameter $\theta \in [\underline{\theta}, \bar{\theta}]$ specifies his tastes (known only to him) for good 2. Assume that $\partial^2 u / \partial q^2 < 0$ and $\partial u / \partial \theta > 0$.

The distribution of tastes is characterized by a uniform distribution over the interval $[\underline{\theta}, \bar{\theta}]$ and we assume that $\bar{\theta} - \underline{\theta} = 1$. The consumers are endowed with a sizeable amount of good 1, $\bar{x}$, so that their behavior is always characterized by their first-order conditions. The monopolist has a linear cost function given by $C(q) = cq$. Moreover, we make the following assumptions

$$\frac{\partial^2 u}{\partial q \partial \theta} > 0 \qquad \text{(CS+)}$$

$$\frac{\partial^3 u}{\partial \theta \partial q^2} \geqslant 0 \qquad \text{(S)}$$

$$\frac{\partial^3 u}{\partial \theta^2 \partial q} \leqslant 0. \qquad \text{(NB)}$$

1. Denote by $q^*(\theta)$, $\theta \in [\underline{\theta}, \bar{\theta}]$ the consumption profile that corresponds to an interior Pareto-optimal allocation. Show that $q^*(.)$ is an increasing function of its argument.

2. Let $(q(\theta), t(\theta))$ be a differentiable revelation mechanism that induces consumer θ to reveal his true characteristic. More precisely, if he announces θ, he receives a quantity $q(\theta)$ of good 2 and must pay an amount $t(\theta)$ of good 1. Moreover, assume that the monopolist must guarantee to each consumer a positive increment in utility given by

$$u(q(\theta), \theta) - t(\theta) \geqslant 0 \quad \forall \theta \in [\underline{\theta}, \bar{\theta}]. \qquad \text{(I)}$$

Characterize the revelation mechanisms (first- and second-order conditions) subject to the constraint (I).

3. Write the optimization program for the monopolist who maximizes expected profits and who is required to supply his product to all the

consumers. Show that the optimal profile $\bar{q}(\theta)$ for the monopolist is an increasing function. Interpret the optimal revelation mechanism as a nonlinear pricing schedule.

4. The government tries to regulate this monopolist by imposing a linear tax τ on the quantity consumed of good 2. Derive the optimal profile $q(\theta, \tau)$ for the monopolist when the tax is τ. Assume that the government maximizes a weighted average of the consumers' utilities (with weight equal to 1), the monopolist's profits (with weight δ) and taxes (with weight λ) where $\delta \geqslant \lambda$. Then determine the optimal tax τ^* assuming an interior maximum. Discuss these results (in particular, the result when $\lambda = \delta = 1$).

Hint: A reader who has difficulty with this general framework can first solve the particular case where

$$u(q, \theta) = \theta q - \tfrac{1}{2}q^2.$$

Solution

1. Since the utility functions are quasi-linear, the consumption profile $q^*(\theta)$ that corresponds to an interior Pareto-optimal allocation is obtained by maximizing the sum of the utilities as follows:

$$\text{Max} \int_{\underline{\theta}}^{\bar{\theta}} [u(q(\theta), \theta) + x(\theta)]\, d\theta$$

subject to $\int_{\underline{\theta}}^{\bar{\theta}} x(\theta)\, d\theta = \bar{x} - c \int_{\underline{\theta}}^{\bar{\theta}} q(\theta)\, d\theta,$

which yields

$$\frac{\partial u}{\partial q}(q^*(\theta), \theta) = c \quad \forall \theta \in [\underline{\theta}, \bar{\theta}]. \tag{1}$$

By differentiating (1), we obtain

$$\frac{dq^*}{d\theta} = \frac{-\partial^2 u/\partial q \partial \theta}{\partial^2 u/\partial q^2} > 0;$$

the sign follows from the strict concavity of u in q and assumption (CS+).

2. Faced with the revelation mechanism $(q(.), t(.))$, the consumer with tastes $\hat{\theta}$ announces the θ that maximizes $u(q(\theta), \hat{\theta}) - t(\theta) + \bar{x}$, which yields the first-order necessary condition

$$\frac{\partial u}{\partial q}(q(\theta), \theta)\frac{dq}{d\theta}(\theta) - \frac{dt}{d\theta}(\theta) = 0 \tag{2}$$

and the second-order necessary condition

$$\frac{\partial^2 u}{\partial q \partial \theta}\frac{dq}{d\theta} \geq 0,$$

which, from (CS+), becomes

$$\frac{dq}{d\theta} \geq 0. \tag{3}$$

Now we show that (2) and (3) are also sufficient conditions. It must be the case that

$$u(q(\theta), \theta) - t(\theta) - u(q(\theta'), \theta) + t(\theta') \geq 0 \quad \text{for any} \quad \theta, \theta'. \tag{4}$$

Using (2), (4) becomes

$$u(q(\theta), \theta) - u(q(\theta'), \theta) + \int_\theta^{\theta'} \frac{\partial u}{\partial q}(q(s), s)\frac{\partial q}{\partial \theta}(s)\, ds \geq 0. \tag{5}$$

However,

$$\frac{\partial u}{\partial q}\frac{\partial q}{\partial \theta} = \frac{d}{d\theta}(u(q, \theta)) - \frac{\partial u}{\partial \theta}(q(\theta), \theta),$$

from which (5) is rewritten as

$$u(q(\theta'), \theta') - u(q(\theta'), \theta) - \int_\theta^{\theta'} \frac{\partial u}{\partial \theta}(q(s), s)\, ds$$

$$= \int_\theta^{\theta'} \left[\frac{\partial u}{\partial \theta}(q(\theta'), s) - \frac{\partial u}{\partial \theta}(q(s), s) \right] ds$$

$$= \int_\theta^{\theta'} \left(\int_{q(s)}^{q(\theta')} \frac{\partial^2 u}{\partial q \partial \theta}(\tilde{q}, s)\, d\tilde{q} \right) ds \geq 0 \quad \text{from (CS+) and (3).} \tag{6}$$

The incentive-compatible revelation mechanisms insuring a nonzero gain in utility for all consumers are therefore characterized by (2), (3), and

$$u(q(\theta), \theta) - t(\theta) \geq 0 \quad \forall \theta \in [\underline{\theta}, \bar{\theta}]. \tag{7}$$

From (2), we have

$$t(\theta) = u(q(\theta), \theta) - u(q(\underline{\theta}), \theta) - \int_{\underline{\theta}}^{\theta} \frac{\partial u}{\partial \theta}(q(s), s)\, ds + K;$$

then (7) becomes

$$u(q(\underline{\theta}), \underline{\theta}) + \int_{\underline{\theta}}^{\theta} \frac{\partial u}{\partial \theta}(q(s), s)\, ds - K \geqslant 0 \quad \forall \theta \in [\underline{\theta}, \bar{\theta}]. \tag{8}$$

3. The monopolist maximizes his profit subject to the incentive and individual rationality constraints, that is,

$$\text{Max} \int_{\underline{\theta}}^{\bar{\theta}} [t(\theta) - cq(\theta)]\, d\theta$$

subject to (2), (3), and (8).

Denote by $U(\theta)$ the gain in utility for a consumer with tastes θ. From $\partial u / \partial \theta > 0$ and (2), it follows that

$$dU / d\theta > 0.$$

The condition of a positive utility gain will be satisfied for all consumers if it is satisfied for the consumer with tastes $\underline{\theta}$. Since the monopolist wishes to maximize t, he chooses K so that $U(\underline{\theta}) = 0$, which in turn yields $K = u(q(\underline{\theta}), \underline{\theta})$.

The optimization problem for the monopolist then reduces to

$$\text{Max} \int_{\underline{\theta}}^{\bar{\theta}} [t(\theta) - cq(\theta)]\, d\theta$$

subject to $t(\theta) = u(q(\theta), \theta) - \int_{\underline{\theta}}^{\theta} \frac{\partial u}{\partial \theta}(q(s), s)\, ds$ \hfill (9)

$$\frac{dq}{d\theta}(\theta) \geqslant 0.$$

By substituting (9) into the maximand and subsequently integrating by parts, we have

$$\text{Max} \int_{\underline{\theta}}^{\bar{\theta}} \left\{ u(q(\theta), \theta) - cq(\theta) - (\bar{\theta} - \theta)\frac{\partial u}{\partial \theta}(q(\theta), \theta) \right\} d\theta$$

subject to $\dfrac{dq}{d\theta} \geqslant 0.$

For the time being, we ignore the constraint. Since the integrand is concave in q, the optimal solution $\bar{q}(\theta)$ is characterized by the Euler equation

$$\frac{\partial u}{\partial q}(q, \theta) - c - (\bar{\theta} - \theta)\frac{\partial^2 u}{\partial q \partial \theta} = 0. \tag{10}$$

By differentiating (10), we obtain

$$\frac{d\bar{q}}{d\theta} = -\frac{2\dfrac{\partial^2 U}{\partial q \partial \theta} - (\bar{\theta} - \theta)\dfrac{\partial^3 u}{\partial \theta^2 \partial q}}{\dfrac{\partial^2 u}{\partial q^2} - (\bar{\theta} - \theta)\dfrac{\partial^3 u}{\partial \theta \partial q^2}} > 0 \quad \text{from (CS+), (S), and (NB).}$$

Therefore it was legitimate to neglect the constraint $dq/d\theta \geqslant 0$.

The appropriate transfer is obtained by substituting $\bar{q}$ into (9), which yields the nonlinear unit price (by denoting as $\bar{\theta}(q)$ the inverse function of $\bar{q}(\theta)$):

$$p(q) = \frac{t(\bar{\theta}(q))}{q} = \frac{u(q, \bar{\theta}(q))}{q} - \frac{1}{q}\int_{\theta}^{\bar{\theta}(q)}\frac{\partial u}{\partial \theta}(q(s), s)\,ds.$$

4. We assume that the government can impose a tax τ per unit of the good sold by the monopolist. Then we may treat the monopolist's selling cost as if it were $c + \tau$ instead of c. Aside from this, the analysis of the preceding question is unchanged. If we let $\bar{q}(\theta, \tau)$ be the optimal consumption profile for the monopolist with the tax taken as given, $\bar{q}(\theta, \tau)$ is characterized by an equation analogous to (10):

$$\frac{\partial u}{\partial q}(q, \theta) - (c + \tau) - (\bar{\theta} - \theta)\frac{\partial^2 u}{\partial \theta \partial q}(q, \theta) = 0. \tag{11}$$

Notice that $\dfrac{\partial \bar{q}}{\partial \theta}(\theta, \tau) > 0$ and $\dfrac{\partial \bar{q}}{\partial \tau}(\theta, \tau) < 0$. The increase in utility for consumer θ is written as

$$U(\theta, \tau) = \int_{\theta}^{\theta}\frac{\partial u}{\partial \theta}(\bar{q}(s, \tau), s)\,ds. \tag{12}$$

The profit accruing to the monopolist from this transaction with consumer θ is

$$\pi(\theta, \tau) = u(\bar{q}(\theta, \tau), \theta) - (c + \tau)\bar{q}(\theta, \tau) - \int_{\theta}^{\theta}\frac{\partial u}{\partial \theta}(\bar{q}(s, t), s)\,ds. \tag{13}$$

The tax revenue obtained by the government from consumer θ is $\tau q(\theta, \tau)$. The government chooses τ to solve the problem

$$\text{Max} \int_{\underline{\theta}}^{\bar{\theta}} [U(\theta, \tau) + \delta\pi(\theta, \tau) + \lambda\tau q(\theta, \tau)] \, d\theta. \tag{14}$$

By substituting (12) and (13) into (14) and integrating by parts, the maximand becomes

$$\int_{\underline{\theta}}^{\bar{\theta}} \left\{ (1 - \delta)(\bar{\theta} - \theta)\frac{\partial u}{\partial \theta}(\bar{q}(\theta, \tau), \theta) + \delta[u(\bar{q}(\theta, \tau), \theta) - (c + \tau)\bar{q}(\theta, \tau)] \right.$$

$$\left. + \lambda\tau\bar{q}(\theta, \tau) \right\} d\theta.$$

The first-order condition for this problem is

$$E\left\{ (1 - \delta)(\bar{\theta} - \theta)\frac{\partial^2 u}{\partial q \partial \theta} \cdot \frac{\partial \bar{q}}{\partial \tau} \right\} + \delta E\left\{ \left(\frac{\partial u}{\partial q} - (c + \tau) \right)\frac{\partial \bar{q}}{\partial \tau} - \bar{q} \right\}$$

$$+ \lambda E\left\{ \bar{q} + \tau\frac{\partial \bar{q}}{\partial \tau} \right\} = 0.$$

By using the definition of $\bar{q}$ and (11), we obtain

$$\tau^* = \frac{(\delta - \lambda)E\bar{q} - E\left\{ (\bar{\theta} - \theta)\frac{\partial^2 u}{\partial q \partial \theta} \cdot \frac{\partial \bar{q}}{\partial \tau} \right\}}{\lambda E \partial \bar{q}/\partial \tau} < 0.$$

We have $d\tau^*/d\delta < 0$, $d\tau^*/d\lambda > 0$. If $\lambda = \delta = 1$, then

$$\tau^* = -\frac{E(\bar{\theta} - \theta)\frac{\partial^2 u}{\partial q \partial \theta} \cdot \frac{\partial \bar{q}}{\partial \tau}}{E \partial \bar{q}/\partial \tau}.$$

In the case of complete information, the monopolist would be able to discriminate perfectly among the consumers and extract all the consumer surplus. In the case of asymmetric information, the consumers retain a portion of the surplus, an amount that increases with θ. To limit this surplus retained by the consumers, which reduces his profit from its potential amount, the monopolist tends to decrease the level of production (a strategy that has no first-order cost in the neighborhood of the perfect information optimum). To countervail this tendency, the government must subsidize output. See figure P7.1 for a graphical presentation of the optimal consumption profiles.

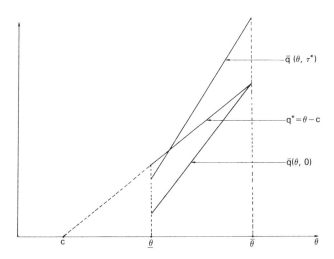

Figure P7.1

The solution for the example where $\lambda = \delta = 1$ and $u(q, \theta) = \theta q - \frac{1}{2}q^2$ is

$$\tau^* = -(E\theta - \underline{\theta}) = -\frac{(\bar{\theta} - \underline{\theta})}{2}$$

$$\bar{q}(\theta, \tau) = (2\theta - \bar{\theta}) - c - \tau^*$$

$$= 2\theta - c - \left(\frac{\bar{\theta} + \underline{\theta}}{2}\right).$$

Supplementary Readings Laffont, J.-J., 1985, "Optimal taxation of a non linear pricing monopolist," *GREMAQ*, 8521; Maskin, E., and J. Riley 1984, "Monopoly with incomplete information," *Rand Journal of Economics*, 15, 171–196; Spence, M., 1977, "Nonlinear prices and welfare," *Journal of Public Economics*, 8, 1–18.

Problem 8
Externalities, Incomplete Information, and Quotas

Statement of the Problem

Consider an economy with two goods and a continuum of consumers. The consumers differ only by a characteristic θ indicating their preferences. Consumer θ's utility function is given by

$$x_1 + (\alpha + \theta)x_2 - \frac{x_2^2}{2} - k\theta \int_1^2 sx_2(s)\,ds,$$

where the last term represents a negative externality ($k > 0$) due to the quantities consumed of good 2 by the other consumers. The characteristic θ is distributed uniformly over the interval $[1, 2]$. Each consumer is endowed with good 1, in an amount w_1, that is sufficiently large so that the constraint $x_1 \geq 0$ will not be binding for this problem. A linear technology characterizes a competitive industry producing good 2 using good 1 as an input. Let c be the amount of good 1 required to produce one unit of good 2 ($c < \alpha + \frac{3}{2} - 3k$).

1. Determine the interior Pareto optima and the personalized taxes on good 2 that support the competitive equilibrium as a Pareto optimum when the government knows the characteristics θ.

2. In the case of incomplete information (the government does not know the individual θ, but only that characteristics are distributed uniformly), characterize the feasible revelation mechanisms $x_1(\theta)$ and $x_2(\theta)$ that induce consumers to reveal their true characteristics.

3. Determine the revelation mechanism that maximizes social welfare subject to the incentive constraints for a utilitarian government. Distinguish two cases, the one in which k is less than or equal to 2/3 and the one in which k is greater than 2/3. Determine the nonlinear tax schedule for good 2 ($t^*(x_2)$) that decentralizes the optimum. When can such taxes be interpreted as quotas?

Solution

1. The interior Pareto optima are obtained from solving the problem:

$$\max_{x_1(\cdot),\,x_2(\cdot)} \int_1^2 \left[x_1(\theta) + (\alpha + \theta)x_2(\theta) - \frac{x_2^2(\theta)}{2} - k\theta \int_1^2 sx_2(s)\,ds \right] d\theta$$

$$\text{subject to} \quad \int_1^2 [x_1(\theta) + cx_2(\theta)]\,d\theta = w_1 \tag{1}$$

However,

$$\int_1^2 \theta \int_1^2 sx_2(s)ds \, d\theta = \frac{3}{2} \int_1^2 \theta x_2(\theta) \, d\theta. \tag{2}$$

By substituting (1) and (2) into the integral, we obtain

$$\text{Max}_{x_2(\cdot)} \int_1^2 \left[w_1 + \left[\alpha + \theta \left(1 - \frac{3k}{2} \right) - c \right] x_2(\theta) - \frac{x_2^2(\theta)}{2} \right] d\theta,$$

which yields

$$x_2^*(\theta) = \alpha + \theta \left(1 - \frac{3k}{2} \right) - c$$

for any allocation $x_1(.)$ that satisfies (1).

The production price for good 2 is c. Let $t(\theta)$ be the function of personalized taxes on good 2. The tax schedule $t^*(\theta)$ that makes the competitive equilibrium Pareto optimal is derived from the problem

$$\text{Max} \left[x_1(\theta) + (\alpha + \theta)x_2(\theta) - \frac{x_2^2(\theta)}{2} - k\theta \int_1^2 sx_2(s) \, ds \right]$$

subject to $x_1(\theta) + [c + t^*(\theta)]x_2(\theta) = w_1.$

Solving for the tax schedule to support $x_2^*(\theta)$, we have $t^*(\theta) = 3k\theta/2$. This optimal personalized tax structure requires knowledge of θ, which is private information.

2. We look for the mechanisms $x_1(\theta)$ and $x_2(\theta)$ that lead the consumers to reveal their true characteristics. Agent θ maximizes the following with respect to θ':

$$x_1(\theta') + (\alpha + \theta)x_2(\theta') - \frac{x_2^2(\theta')}{2} - k\theta \int_1^2 sx_2(s) \, ds,$$

the first-order condition for which is

$$\frac{dx_1}{d\theta} + (\alpha + \theta)\frac{dx_2}{d\theta} - x_2(\theta)\frac{dx_2}{d\theta} = 0, \tag{3}$$

and the second-order condition is

$$\frac{dx_2}{d\theta} \geqslant 0. \tag{4}$$

Given that the objective function is linear in θ (see chapter 5), these conditions are sufficient. Since the government is not concerned with the distribution of good 1 among the consumers, condition (3) always holds. The only constraint imposed by the decentralization of information is (4). The feasibility constraint is (1).

3. The optimum subject to the constraint of decentralization of information is obtained by solving the problem

$$\underset{x_2(.)}{\text{Max}} \int_1^2 \left[w_1 + \left[\alpha + \theta \left(1 - \frac{3k}{2} \right) - c \right] x_2(\theta) - \frac{x_2^2(\theta)}{2} \right] d\theta$$

subject to $\dfrac{dx_2}{d\theta} \geqslant 0.$ (5)

The optimum of this problem without the constraint is the complete information optimum $x_2^*(\theta)$.

If $k \leqslant 2/3$, x_2^* is increasing in θ; constraint (5) is satisfied and therefore the complete information optimum is implemented by the mechanism

$$x_2^*(\theta) = \alpha + \theta \left(1 - \frac{3k}{2} \right) - c,$$

with $x_1^*(\theta)$ solving (3), positive for all θ and satisfying (1). Then we have

$$\frac{dx_1^*}{d\theta} = (x_2^*(\theta) - (\alpha + \theta)) \frac{dx_2^*}{d\theta} = - \left(1 - \frac{3k}{2} \right) \left(\frac{3k}{2} \theta + c \right)$$

$$x_1^*(\theta) = - \left(1 - \frac{3k}{2} \right) \frac{3k}{4} \theta^2 - \left(1 - \frac{3k}{2} \right) c\theta + h$$

$$\int_1^2 x_1^*(\theta)\, d\theta = - \left(1 - \frac{3k}{2} \right) \frac{7k}{4} - \left(1 - \frac{3k}{2} \right) \frac{3}{2} c + h$$

$$= w_1 - c \left[\left(1 - \frac{3k}{2} \right) \frac{3}{2} - c + \alpha \right],$$

which yields

$$h = w_1 + c^2 + \left(1 - \frac{3k}{2} \right) \frac{7k}{4} - \alpha c$$

$$x_1^*(\theta) = w_1 + c^2 + \left(1 - \frac{3k}{2}\right)\frac{7k}{4} - \left(1 - \frac{3k}{2}\right)c\theta - \left(1 - \frac{3k}{2}\right)\frac{3k}{4}\theta^2 - \alpha c,$$

which is positive for all θ if w_1 is large enough.

To decentralize this allocation with a nonlinear tax schedule, $t^*(x_2)$, it must be the case that

$$c + t(x_2) + t'(x_2)x_2 = \alpha + \theta - x_2 = \frac{3kx_2}{2 - 3k} + \frac{2c - 3\alpha k}{2 - 3k}.$$

Denote $t(x_2)x_2 = T(x_2)$. The differential equation can then be written as

$$T'(x_2) - \frac{3k}{2 - 3k}x_2 = \frac{-3k(\alpha - c)}{2 - 3k}.$$

Imposing $T(0) = 0$, we get the solution

$$T(x_2) = \frac{3kx_2^2}{2(2 - 3k)} - \frac{3k(\alpha - c)}{2 - 3k}x_2,$$

or

$$t^*(x_2) = \frac{3k}{2(2 - 3k)}x_2 + \frac{3k(c - \alpha)}{2 - 3k}.$$

If $k > 2/3$, constraint (5) is not satisfied by $x_2^*(.)$. The optimal solution is a constant $\bar{x}_2$ that maximizes

$$\int_1^2 \left[w_1 + \left[\alpha + \theta\left(1 - \frac{3k}{2}\right) - c\right]\bar{x}_2 - \frac{\bar{x}_2^2}{2}\right]d\theta.$$

Therefore

$$\bar{x}_2^* = \frac{3}{2}\left(1 - \frac{3k}{2}\right) + \alpha - c > 0,$$

since

$$c < \alpha + \frac{3}{2} - 3k.$$

The optimum with incomplete information corresponds to a constant quantity of good 2 consumed. It could be decentralized by a tax schedule of the type

$$t^*(x_2) = 0 \qquad \text{if} \quad x_2 = \bar{x}_2^*$$

$$\qquad = +\infty \quad \text{otherwise.}$$

If the price is c, this mechanism cannot be quite interpreted as a quota because the agents with $\theta \in]\frac{3}{2}, 2]$ do not wish to consume an amount as high as $\bar{x}_2^*$. If we decrease the price enough, all consumers will be constrained, but it will not quite be the optimal mechanism.

Supplementary Reading   Guesnerie, R., and J.-J. Laffont 1984, "A complete solution to a class of principal agent problems with an application to the control of a self-managed firm," *Journal of Public Economics*, 25, 329–369.

EXERCISES

Exercise 1
Efficient Allocation of Resources: Decreasing or Increasing Returns

Consider an economy with two goods, labor (good 1) and a heating fuel (good 2). Good 2 is obtained either from a constant-returns technology (coal mine) given by

$$y_2^1 = y_1^1 \qquad y_1^1 \geqslant 0 \qquad y_2^1 \geqslant 0,$$

or from a decreasing-returns technology (chopping down trees) given by

$$y_2^2 = 2\sqrt{y_1^2} \qquad y_1^2 \geqslant 0 \qquad y_2^2 \geqslant 0.$$

The economy consists of two consumers whose consumption sets are given by

$$X^i = \{(x_1^i, x_2^i)/x_2^i \geqslant 0, 0 \leqslant x_1^i \leqslant 3\}$$

where x_1^i indicates the supply of labor from consumer i, $i = 1, 2$. The preferences of consumer i are defined by

$$U^i(x_1^i, x_2^i) = \tfrac{1}{2} \operatorname{Log}(3 - x_1^i) + \tfrac{1}{2} \operatorname{Log} x_2^i \qquad i = 1, 2.$$

1. What are the feasible outcomes in this economy? Define the interior Pareto optima for this economy. In order to determine the set of Pareto optima, consider first of all the set of efficient production plans, that is, derive the aggregate production function for the economy (which makes up the boundary of the aggregate production set). Then show that all the interior Pareto optima are achieved from the same production plan. Characterize the projection into the utility space of the interior Pareto optima.

2. Now suppose that the production sector is nationalized. The planner decides to leave intact the characteristics of the two firms but to impose on them average cost pricing (in other words, a balanced budget). Therefore, each firm must set its price equal to average cost and satisfy all the demand forthcoming at this price. Each consumer is free to sell his labor on the labor market (at a wage rate p_1) and buy good 2 on its market (at a price p_2) with his wage income. Show that this institutional framework (average cost pricing and market clearing) makes impossible the attainment of certain points in the aggregate production set determined in the preceding

question. Determine the institutionally feasible production set. Calculate the characteristics of the equilibrium.

3. Taking account of the insufficiencies discovered in the first policy in question 2, the planner decides to create a conglomerate called "the Company of Fuels," which integrates the two firms. The conglomerate must choose its production plan to minimize the total cost of producing any level of output and it must price at average cost. Calculate the characteristics of the resulting equilibrium. Is this solution optimal?

4. Now the planner requires the conglomerate to price at marginal cost and transfer the fraction $\alpha(\alpha \in [0, 1])$ of the resulting profits to consumer 1 and the fraction $(1 - \alpha)$ to consumer 2. Calculate the characteristics of the equilibrium and show that, when α varies, the corresponding equilibria make up a strict subset of the set of Pareto optima determined in the first question. In what sense can we talk about a competitive equilibrium and decentralization with prices in this problem?

5. The results of the foregoing questions have justified a marginal cost pricing rule in the case where production sets are convex (nonincreasing returns to scale). Then the rule is compatible with decentralization with prices, since each firm maximizes its profit taking prices as given. To what degree is this rule still justifiable if some production sets are nonconvex? To shed some light on this question, we will assume that the extraction of coal occurs in two places under increasing returns in both. There are two mines A and B each having the same production set. The production set of mine A is characterized, with obvious notation, by

$x_2^{1a} = 0$ if $0 \leqslant x_1^{1a} \leqslant K$,

$x_2^{1a} = x_1^{1a} - K$ if $x_1^{1a} \geqslant K$,

where K is a real positive number.

How should we interpret K? For any efficient production plan, show that only one of the mines will be operating. Characterize the aggregate production set of the economy when K is equal to $1/4$. For any efficient production plan, show that marginal costs must be the same in the operating mine as in firm 2 (where trees are chopped down). What have we learned about regulating a public firm operating subject to increasing returns?

Exercise 2
The Principle of "He Who Pollutes Must Pay"

Consider the same economy as in exercise 1. Now suppose that firm 2 creates an amount of pollution (emissions) z given by

$$z = y_2^2.$$

This pollution negatively affects the welfare of the consumers, so that we write the utility function as

$$U^i(x_1^i, x_2^i, z) = (3 - x_1^i)^{1/2} \cdot (x_2^i)^{1/2} - \frac{z}{8} \qquad i = 1, 2.$$

Moreover assume that consumer 1 (resp. 2) owns firm 1 (resp. 2). Finally, we consider interior allocations only, that is, nonzero output for each firm and quantities consumed of good 2 and quantities of labor supplied by the consumers that are strictly positive.

1. Derive the competitive equilibrium with an externality for this economy. Show that the equilibrium level of pollution is $z^e = 2$.

2. Assume that the government can limit by regulation the pollution emitted to a level $\bar{z}$. Determine the resulting competitive equilibrium as a function of the ceiling level $\bar{z}$. At what level does each consumer want this ceiling fixed? At what level will it be fixed if the decision is taken by unanimous consent?

3. Assume that the government can achieve any redistribution of income through lump-sum transfers. Show that the achievable utility levels can thus be written as

$$U^1 + U^2 = \phi(\bar{z}).$$

Derive from this the existence of an optimal value $\hat{z} = 1$.

4. Let t be the rate of tax imposed on the emission of the polluter. The tax revenue, tz, is distributed to the consumers with the share λ_1 (resp. $1 - \lambda_1$) going to consumer 1 (resp. 2). What is the tax level that supports the optimal level of pollution $\hat{z}$ in a competitive equilibrium? Compare this with the results in questions 1 and 2.

5. The government creates an agency whose responsibility is to tax emissions at the rate t (generating tax revenue tz) and to subsidize at a rate s emission reduction with respect to the laissez-faire equilibrium of the first question (the amount of the subsidy equals $s(z^e - z)$). Show that we can set s and t both to balance the agency's budget and to obtain an optimal level of pollution $\hat{z}$. Compare this with the above results.

Supplementary Reading   Kolm, S., 1975, "Rendement qualitatif et financement optimal des politiques d'environnement," *Econometrica*, 43, 93–114.

Exercise 3
A Public Good with Possible Usage Exclusion

Consider an economy with a private good and a public good. The economy consists of two consumers whose utility functions are given by

$U^1(x_1, y) = \frac{1}{2} \text{Log } x_1 + \frac{1}{2} \text{Log } y$

$U^2(x_2, y) = \frac{1}{3} \text{Log } x_2 + \frac{2}{3} \text{Log } y.$

Consumer 1 (resp. 2) is endowed with the private good in amount $w^1 = 4$ (resp. $w^2 = 2$). Consumption of the public good is not required. If a quantity y is produced, each consumer may consume any nonnegative amount less than or equal to y. (take, for example, television programming). The production of the public good uses the private good as an input ($z \geqslant 0$) according to the linear technology

$y = z.$

1. Determine the set of Pareto optima. Show that the Pareto optima can be parametrized by the level of the public good y ($y \in [3, 4]$) so that

$U^1 = 3y(4 - y) \qquad U^2 = 2y^2(y - 3).$

Show that to every Pareto optimum we can associate personalized prices (p_1, p_2) for the public good and a transfer T from consumer 2 to consumer 1 so that the Lindahl equilibrium with transfers coincides with the Pareto optimum. Show that the Lindahl equilibrium without transfers corresponds to

$y = \frac{10}{3}; \quad p_1 = \frac{3}{5}, \quad p_2 = \frac{2}{5}, \quad x_1 = 2, \quad x_2 = \frac{2}{3}.$

2. Show that the voluntary-contribution equilibrium corresponds to an output level of the public good equal to $12/5$. What do you conclude from this?

3. Assume that there are institutional and technological ways of excluding people from using the public good (for example, by installing a coin box on each television set). Now we denote by p the price paid by a consumer for a unit of the public good. Let $\bar{y}$ be the aggregate quantity of the public good produced. Derive the constrained demand functions $y^1(p, \bar{y})$ and $y^2(p, \bar{y})$ for the two consumers. As a function of y, determine the characteristics of the allocation that assures a balanced budget for the firm producing the public good taking $\bar{y}$ as fixed. Compare these results with those in questions 1 and 2. In particular, show that the case in which $p = 1/2$ and consumer 1 is constrained is preferred in the Paretian sense to the case in which $p = 3/5$ and no consumer is constrained.

Supplementary Reading Drèze, J., 1980, "Public goods with exclusion," *Journal of Public Economics*, 13, 5–24.

Exercise 4
Procedures for Aggregating Preferences

Assume that there are three social states a_1, a_2, and a_3 and three agents. A total binary preference relation R can be represented by a matrix MR, the representative element of which, r_{ij}, is defined as

$r_{ij} = +1$ if $a_i R a_j$ and not $a_j R a_i$

    $= -1$ if $a_j R a_i$ and not $a_i R a_j$

    $= 0$ if $a_i R a_j$ and $a_j R a_i$.

1. Characterize the implications of the reflexivity property for the matrix MR. Show that there are 27 possible matrices. Show that there are only 13 if we impose the transitivity property as well.

2. We will represent a matrix MR by

$$\begin{matrix} 0 & a & -c \\ -a & 0 & b \\ c & -b & 0 \end{matrix}$$

where a, b, and c are elements of the set $\{-1, 0, +1\}$ (with 13 possible triplets). The distance between two preorderings R and $\tilde{R}$ is defined by

$$d(R, \tilde{R}) = \frac{1}{2} \sum_{i=1}^{3} \sum_{j=1}^{3} [r_{ij} - \tilde{r}_{ij}].$$

Show that d is indeed a distance measure.

3. Let R_1, R_2, and R_3 be the preorderings representing the preferences of the three agents. Define the median preordering R^m by minimizing over R on the set of preorderings the sum

$$\sum_{k=1}^{3} d(R_k, R).$$

Define the mean preordering R^M by minimizing over R in the set of preorderings the sum

$$\sum_{k=1}^{3} [d(R_k, R)]^2.$$

Show that

$$\sum_{k=1}^{3} d(R_k, R) = 9 - (a + b + c)$$

and

$$\sum_{k=1}^{3} [d(R_k, R)]^2 = (3 - a - b + c)^2 + (3 + a - b - c)^2 + (3 - a + b - c)^2.$$

Consider the profile $a_1 R^1 a_2 R^1 a_3; a_3 R^2 a_1 R^2 a_2; a_2 R^3 a_3 R^3 a_1$, that is, the preferences that give rise to the paradox of Condorcet. Show that there are three median preorderings and a unique mean preordering. Discuss this result. Show that these aggregation procedures satisfy the Pareto principle. Now alter the preferences of agent 2 so that they become $a_2 R'^2 a_1 R'^2 a_3$. By considering states a_1 and a_2, show that neither procedure satisfies the assumption of the irrelevance of independent alternatives.

Exercise 5
Local Public Goods and the Simple Majority Voting Procedure

Consider a community of I agents in which each agent's utility function is given by

$$\alpha \, \text{Log} \, x^i + \beta \, \text{Log} \, s^i + \gamma^i \, \text{Log} \, z \qquad i = 1, \ldots, I \qquad \beta > \gamma^i \text{ for all } i,$$

where

x^i is the quantity consumed of the numéraire,
s^i is the consumption of living space, and
z is the quantity of the public good supplied by the community.

The agents' utility functions are equivalent except for the coefficient γ^i which depends on income R^i (expressed in terms of the numéraire) in the following way:

$$\gamma^i = e^{aR^i} \qquad a < 0.$$

Then let the price of good x be normalized to equal 1 and let r be the price per unit of living space. A tax (property tax) is levied to finance the public good. Let h be the tax rate. The sum collected from the community is given by

$$T = \sum_{i=1}^{I} hrs^i.$$

Assume that the cost of the public good (expressed in terms of the numéraire) is 1, so that $z = T$.

1. Write the optimization problem for a typical agent given a level of tax h. For simplification, assume that the agent neglects the effect of his choice of living space on T and solve this problem.

2. Show that the indirect utility function of a typical agent (that is, the utility function expressed as a function of h) is a single-peaked (unimodal) function of h. Determine the level of h determined by a simple majority voting procedure. Show that the agent who desires the median level of the tax is the agent who has median income. Let $g(R^i)$ such that $\sum_{i=1}^{I} g(R^i) = 1$ be the proportion of agents with income R^i. Write the equation that determines the level of tax chosen by majority rule (neglecting the fact that we have a finite number of agents). How would you estimate such an equation?

3. Now suppose that there is a subset of the population in the community with the same characteristics (J agents) who, in addition to paying the property tax, also pay an income tax of δh ($(1 - \delta h) > 0$) (therefore, disposable income is $R^j(1 - \delta h)$ for agent j $j = 1, \ldots, J$). Generalize the

analysis in questions 1 and 2 for the case of a population made up of the two subsets described above ($I + J$ agents).

Exercise 6
Revelation of Preferences for Public Goods

Consider an economy with I agents and two goods, one private and one public. Agent i, $i = 1, \ldots, I$ has w^i units of the private good. Consider the determination of the appropriate output y of the public good. The government responsible for deciding this level wishes to share equally among agents the cost of the project given by $C(y) = (Iy^2)/2$, that is, each agent will be expected to pay $[C(y)]/I$. To make the correct choice, the government must know the preferences of the economic agents—but this is decentralized private information.

Let x^i be the quantity of the private good consumed by agent i. Assume that the preferences of agent i are represented by the utility function

$$U^i(y, x^i) = v(y, \hat{\theta}^i) + x^i \qquad i = 1, \ldots, I$$

with $\quad v(y, \hat{\theta}^i) = \hat{\theta}^i y.$

The government knows the functional form $v(.\,,.)$ but it does not know the true values of the parameters $\hat{\theta}^1, \ldots, \hat{\theta}^I$ characterizing individual preferences. A correct decision would be a level of the public good that achieves an interior Pareto optimum, that is, one that maximizes $\sum_{i=1}^I \hat{\theta}^i y - C(y)$.

1. A tentative first solution consists of the state simply asking each agent the true value of his parameter and claiming to choose the level of the public good that maximizes $\sum_{i=1}^I v(y, \theta^{*i}) - C(y)$, where θ^{*i} is the response of agent i, $i = 1, \ldots, I$.

Let $y^*(\theta^{*1}, \ldots, \theta^{*I})$ be the decision function obtained in this way. Show that the optimal response of agent i depends on the responses of the other agents. Show that, in general, a Nash equilibrium does not exist for this game.

2. The first question indicates the need for greater cooperation among the agents, that is, the need for an agreement about the decision mechanism supporting a correct choice. We look for compensatory transfers $t^i(\theta)$,

where $\theta = (\theta^1, \ldots, \theta^I)$ is the vector of responses, that lead the agents to tell the truth, that is, $\theta^i = \hat{\theta}^i$, $i = 1, \ldots, I$, when the government chooses y to maximize $\sum_{i=1}^I v(y, \theta^i) - C(y)$.

Characterize the continuously differentiable transfer functions $t^i(.)$ for which telling the truth is a dominant strategy. (Hint: write the first-order conditions of optimization for question 1 and try to integrate them). A mechanism will be given by an I-tuple of transfer functions $t^1(.), \ldots, t^I(.)$ and the decision function $y^*(.)$.

3. Show that the government budget required to make these mechanisms work is not always balanced, that is, we do not always have

$$\sum_{i=1}^I t^i(\theta) = 0 \qquad \forall \theta.$$

For $I > 2$, find a mechanism that balances the budget.

4. By assuming that for $i = 1, \ldots, I$, $\hat{\theta}^i \in (0, a^i)$, an open interval in R, find mechanisms which are individually rational, that is, ones for which each agent is certain that his utility will not be lower than it was in the initial situation.

5. Show that there is no mechanism that both balances the budget and is individually rational. Discuss this result.

Supplementary Reading Laffont, J.-J., and E. Maskin 1980, "A differentiable approach to dominant strategy mechanisms," *Econometrica*, 48, 1507–1520.

Exercise 7
Nonconvexities, the Second-Best Optimum, and Production Efficiency

Consider an economy with two goods and a consumer whose utility function is written as

$$U(x_1, x_2) = \text{Log}(3 - x_1) + \text{Log } x_2 \qquad x_1 \geqslant 0, \quad x_2 \geqslant 0,$$

where x_1 can be interpreted as an amount of labor that he can supply which is bounded above by 3. There is only one firm that produces good 2 using good 1 as an input according to the technology

$$y_2 = \sqrt{y_1 - 1} \quad \text{if} \quad y_1 \geqslant 1$$

$$= 0 \qquad \qquad \text{otherwise;}$$

that is, there is a fixed cost of 1 and decreasing returns thereafter.

1. Determine the Pareto optimum for this economy. Show that we can decentralize this optimum by using a price vector (1/2, 2/3) and granting a subsidy $S = 1/3$ to the firm as long as it produces a strictly positive amount. Interpret this as decentralization by a two-part tariff.

2. Now suppose that it is not possible to use a two-part tariff and that the firm must balance its budget. Show that the second-best optimum subject to the balanced budget constraint corresponds to a vector of prices $(1, 3\sqrt{2}/2)$, which are called Ramsey-Boiteux prices. Give a graphical interpretation.

3. As you will observe, production in the second-best optimum is efficient. Show that this result will hold so long as the preferences of the consumers are monotonic.

Supplementary Reading Diamond, P., and J. Mirrlees 1971, "Optimal production and public production I: Production efficiency," *American Economic Review*, 61, 8–27.

Exercise 8
Income Taxation and Financing a Public Good

Consider an economy with three goods, labor (good 2), a consumption good (good 1) and a public good (good 3) and with I consumers. The utility function of consumer i is written as

$$U^i(x_1^i, x_2^i, x_3) = \text{Log } x_1^i + \text{Log}(\alpha^i - x_2^i) + \log x_3$$

$$\alpha^i > 2; \quad \sum_{i=1}^{I} \alpha^i = 3I \qquad i = 1, \ldots, I$$

where x_2^i is the supply of labor (less than α^i), x_1^i is the quantity consumed of good 1, and x_3 is the quantity consumed of the public good.

The production of good 1 uses labor as an input according to the technology

$$y_1^1 = y_2^1 \qquad y_1^1 \geqslant 0 \qquad y_2^1 \geqslant 0.$$

The production of the public good uses labor as an input according to the technology

$$y_3^2 = y_2^2 \qquad y_3^2 \geqslant 0 \qquad y_2^2 \geqslant 0.$$

1. Determine the Pareto optimum corresponding to maximizing the utilitarian criterion.

2. Normalize the price of good 1 to 1, and let s be the wage rate, that is to say, the price of good 2. Determine the personalized lump-sum charges required from each consumer to finance the amount of the public good corresponding to this optimum in an otherwise competitive economy. Compare this to the Lindahl equilibrium.

3. Suppose that we cannot observe the α^i and we decide to finance the public good by a tax on labor income at the rate β. What is the optimal value of β when the government uses the utilitarian criterion? Discuss this result. What would be the result of a majority vote on β? Why?

4. Compare the above results with the case in which the public good is financed by a uniform lump-sum tax (in particular, analyze the case in which $I = 2$).

Exercise 9
Control of a Self-Managed Firm

Consider a firm that has a production function given by

$$y = \theta l^{1/2} \qquad \theta > 0,$$

where l is the number of workers (considered to be a continuous variable) and θ is a parameter known to the firm. Impose on this firm a fixed cost A expressed in units of the numéraire. Let p be the price per unit of the good produced competitively by the firm (good 1).

1. Assume that the firm is managed by the workers and that its objective function is

$$\frac{y - A}{l} = \frac{p\theta l^{1/2} - A}{l}.$$

Determine the optimal size (for the workers) of the self-managed firm.

Let w be the wage rate in the rest of the economy which is assumed to be competitive so that w represents the opportunity cost of labor in this economy. Why is the allocation of labor not optimal in general? What happens if w is too large?

2.[1] Consider the case in which w is small enough to justify the presence of a self-managed firm. Compute the tax per unit τ on good 1 that restores an optimal allocation of labor. Show that we could also use a lump-sum tax T on the revenue of the self-managed firm to achieve the same objective. (Assume that the self-managed firm is of negligible size with respect to the rest of the economy).

3. Now assume that the self-managed firm is a monopoly and that $p = a - by$ is the inverse market demand function for good 1. Show that optimality can be restored by using one of the two instruments introduced in question 2.

4. If the government does not know θ, describe the regulatory mechanisms $(l(\theta), t(\theta))$ that would allow the government to discover the value of θ in the case of a competitive self-managed firm (where $l(\theta)$ is the amount of labor that the firm must use and $t(\theta)$ is the monetary transfer that it receives if it announces θ). What would the optimal mechanism be if the government maximized the sum of the surplus of the consumers' purchase of the output of the self-managed firm plus the income of the workers of the self-managed firm?

5. Consider the questions in 4 above for the self-managed monopolist.

---

1. In questions 2 and 3, we assume that the government knows θ.

Index